AUGUSTUS
CAESAR

AUGUSTUS CAESAR

E. S. SHUCKBURGH

Barnes
&Noble
Books
NEW YORK

This edition published by Barnes & Noble, Inc.

1995 Barnes & Noble Books

ISBN 1-56619-667-1

Printed and bound in the United States of America

M 9 8 7 6 5 4 3 2 1

Preface

AUGUSTUS has been much less attractive to biographers than Iulius; perhaps because the soldier is more interesting than the statesman ; perhaps because the note of genius conspicuous in the Uncle was wanting in the Nephew. Yet Augustus was the most successful ruler known to us. He found his world, as it seemed, on the verge of complete collapse. He evoked order out of chaos; got rid one after the other of every element of opposition ; established what was practically a new form of government without too violent a breach with the past ; breathed fresh meaning into old names and institutions, and could stand forth as a reformer rather than an innovator, while even those who lost most by the change were soothed into submission without glaring loss of self-respect. He worked ceaselessly to maintain the order thus established, and nearly every part of his great empire had reason to be grateful for increased security, expanding prosperity, and added amenity of life. Nor can it be said that he reaped the credit due in truth to ministers. He had excellent ministers and agents, with abilities in this or that direction superior to his own ; but none who could take his place as a whole. He was the centre from which their activities radiated : he was the inspirer, the careful organiser, the unwearied manipulator of details, to whom all looked, and seldom in vain, for support and guidance. We may add this to a dignity never forgotten,

*

enhanced by a physical beauty and grace which helped to secure reverence for his person and office, and established a sentiment which the unworthiness of some of his successors could not wholly destroy. He and not Iulius was the founder of the Empire, and it was to him that succeeding emperors looked back as the origin of their power.

Yet his achievements have interested men less than the conquest of Gaul and the victories in the civil war won by the marvellous rapidity and splendid boldness of Iulius. Consequently modern estimates of the character and aims of Augustus have been comparatively few. An exhaustive treatise is now appearing in Germany by V. Gardthausen, which will be a most complete storehouse of facts. Without any pretence to such elaboration of detail, I have tried in these pages to do something to correct the balance, and to give a picture of the man as I have formed it in my own mind. The only modest merit which I would claim for my book is that it is founded on a study as complete as I could make it of the ancient authorities and sources of information without conscious imitation of any modern writer. These authorities are better for the earlier period to about B.C. 24, while they had the Emperor's own Memoirs on which to rely. The multiform activities of his later life are chiefly to be gathered from inscriptions and monuments, which record the care which neglected no part however remote of the Empire. In these later years such histories as we have are more concerned with wars and military movements than with administration. Suetonius is full of good things, but is without chronological or systematic order, and is wanting in the critical spirit to discriminate between irresponsible rumours and historical facts. Dio Cassius, plain and honest always, grows less and less full as the reign goes on. Velleius, who might at least have given us full details of the later German wars, is seldom definite or precise, and is tiresome from devotion to a single hero in Tiberius, and by an irritating style.

It has been my object to illustrate the policy of Augustus by constant reference to the Court view as represented by the poets. But in his later years Ovid is a poor substitute for Horace in this point of view. The Emperor's own catalogue of his achievements, preserved on the walls of the temple at Ancyra, is the best possible summary ; but a summary it is after all, and requires to be made to live by careful study and comparison.

The constitutional history of the reign is that which has generally engaged most attention. I have striven to state the facts clearly. Of their exact significance opinions will differ. I have given my own for what it is worth, and can only say that it has been formed independently by study of our authorities.

I have not tried to represent my hero as faultless or to make black white. Nothing can clear Augustus of the charge of cruelty up to B.C. 31. But in judging him regard must be had to his age and circumstances. We must not, at any rate, allow our judgment of his later statesmanship to be controlled by the memory of his conduct in a time of civil war and confusion. He succeeded in re-constituting a society shaken to its centre. We must acknowledge that and accept the bad with the good. But it is false criticism to deny or blink the one from admiration of the other.

I have to thank the authorities of the British Museum for casts of coins reproduced in this book : also the Syndics of the Pitt Press, Cambridge, for the loan of certain other casts.

Contents

CONTENTS

CHAPTER I

CHILDHOOD AND YOUTH, B.C. 63–44

Iam nova progenies
cælo demittitur alto.

In a house at the eastern corner of the Palatine, called "At the Oxheads,"[1] on the 23rd of September, B.C. 63—some nine weeks before the execution of the Catilinarian conspirators by Cicero's order—a child was born destined to close the era of civil wars thus inaugurated, to organise the Roman Empire, and to be its master for forty-four years.

Birth of Augustus, Sept. 23, B.C. 63.

The father of the child was Gaius Octavius, of the plebeian *gens Octavia*, and of a family that had long occupied a high position in the old Volscian town of Velitræ. Two branches of the Octavii were descended from C. Octavius Rufus, quæstor in B.C. 230. The elder branch had produced five consuls and other Roman magistrates, but of the younger branch Gaius Octavius, the father of Augustus, was the first to hold curule office. According to the inscription, after-

---

[1] *Ad capita bubula.* Lanciani (*Remains of Ancient Rome*, p. 139) says that this was the name of a lane at the eastern corner of the Palatine. Others have thought it to be the name of the house, as the *ad malum Punicum* in which Domitian was born (Suet., *Dom.* 1). So later we hear of a house at Rome *quæ est ad Palmam* (*Codex Theod.*, p. 3). The house may have had its name from a frieze with ox-heads on it, like the tomb of Metella, which came to be called *Capo-di-bove.* It seems less easy to account for a lane being so called. See also p. 205.

wards placed by his son in the *sacrarium* of the palace,[1] he had twice served as military tribune, had been quæstor, plebeian ædile, iudex quæstionum, and prætor. After the prætorship (B.C. 61) he governed Macedonia with conspicuous ability and justice. He is quoted by Cicero as a model administrator of a province; and he was sufficiently successful against the Bessi and other Thracian tribes—constant scourges of Macedonia—to be hailed as "imperator" by his soldiers. He returned to Italy late in B.C. 59, intending next year to be a candidate for the consulship, but early in B.C. 58 he died suddenly in his villa at Nola, in the same chamber as that in which his son, seventy-two years later, breathed his last.[2]

The mother of the young Gaius Octavius was Atia, daughter of M. Atius Balbus,[3] of Velitræ, and Iulia, sister of Gaius Iulius Cæsar. This connection with Cæsar—

The mother of Augustus.

already rising in political importance—may have made his birth of some social interest, but the ominous circumstances said to have accompanied it are doubtless due to the curiosity or credulity of the next generation. The people of Velitræ, it is reported, had been told by an oracle that a master of the Empire was to be born there. Rumours, it is said, were current in Rome shortly before his birth that a "king of the Roman people" was about to be born. His mother dreamed strange dreams, and the learned Publius Nigidius prophesied the birth of a lord of the world; while Catulus and Cicero had visions.[4] But there was, in fact, nothing mysterious or unusual in his infancy, which was passed with his foster-nurse at Velitræ. When he was two years

---

[1] C. I. L., vol. i. p. 279.

[2] Cicero, *ad Q. Fr.* I, I, 21; I, 2, 7. Velleius Pat., 2, 59; Sueton., *Aug.* 3.

[3] The plebeian Atii Balbi do not seem to have been important. M. Atius Balbus was prætor in B.C. 62 (with Cæsar), governor of Sardinia B.C. 61–60, and in B.C. 59 was one of the xx viri under the Julian land law (Cic., *ad Att.* ii. 4).

[4] These and other stories will be found in Sueton., *Aug.* 94, and Dio, 45, 2. Vergil makes skilful use of them in *Æn.*, vi. 797, *sqq.*

old his father, on his way to his province, carried out successfully an order of the Senate to destroy a band of brigands near
Thurii, survivors, it is said, of the followers of Spartacus and
Catiline. In memory of this success his parents gave the boy
the cognomen Thurinus. He never seems to have used the
name, though Suetonius says that he once possessed a bust of
the child with this name inscribed on it in letters that had
become almost illegible. He presented it to Hadrian, who
placed it in his private *sacrarium.*[1]

About B.C. 57 or 56[2] his mother Atia re-married. Her
husband was L. Marcius Philippus (prætor B.C. 60, governor
of Syria B.C. 59–7, Consul B.C. 56); and when
The stepfather
of Augustus. in his ninth year Octavius lost his foster-mother
he became a regular member of his stepfather's
household. Philippus was not a man of much force, but he
belonged to the highest society, and though opposed to Cæsar
in politics, appears to have managed to keep on good terms
with him.[3] But during his great-nephew's boy-
The great-uncle
of Augustus. hood Cæsar was little at Rome. Prætor in B.C.
62, he had gone the following year to Spain. He
returned in B.C. 60 to stand for the consulship, and soon

---

[1] Antony, when he wished to depreciate Augustus, asserted that his
great-grandfather had a rope-walk at Thurii ; and some such connection of
his ancestors with that place may account for the cognomen, which would
naturally be dropped afterwards (Suet., *Aug.* 7).

[2] The marriage could not have taken place earlier than the middle of
B.C. 57, for when Atia's first husband died Philippus was in Syria. He
was succeeded by Gabinius in B.C. 57, and reached Italy in time to stand
for the consulship, the elections that year being at the ordinary time, *i.e.,*
July (Cic., *ad Att.* 4, 2).

[3] L. Marcius Philippus was the son of the famous orator, and was a warm
supporter of Cicero. With his colleague as consul-designate he proposed
he prosecution of Clodius (Cic., *ad Q. Fr.* ii. 1). When the civil war was
beginning he was allowed by Cæsar to remain neutral (Cic., *ad Att.* ix. 15 ;
x. 4). But Cicero found him tiresome company, for he was garrulous and
prosy (*ad Att.* xii. 9, 16, 18) ; and in the troublous times following the
assassination of Cæsar he set little store by his opinion (*ad Att.* xvi. 14 ;
ad Brut. i. 17).

after the consulship, early in B.C. 58, he started for Gaul, from which he did not return to Rome till he came in arms in B.C. 49. But though occupied during the summers in his famous campaigns beyond the Alps, he spent most of his winters in Northern Italy—at Ravenna or Lucca—where he received his partisans and was kept in touch with home politics, and was probably visited by his relatives. Just before entering on his consulship he had formed with Pompey and Crassus the agreement for mutual support known as the First Triumvirate. The series of events which broke up this combination and made civil war inevitable must have been well known to the boy. He must have been aware that the laurelled despatches of his great-uncle announcing victory after victory were viewed with secret alarm by many of the nobles who visited Philippus ; and that these men were seeking to secure in Pompey a leader capable of outshining Cæsar in the popular imagination by victories and triumphs of his own. He was old enough to understand the meaning of the riots of the rival law-breakers, Milo and Clodius, which drenched Rome in blood. Election after election was interrupted, and, finally, after the murder of Clodius (January, B.C. 52), all eyes were fixed on Pompey as the sole hope of peace and order. There was much talk of naming him dictator, but finally he was created sole consul (apparently by a decree of the Senate) and remained sole consul till August, when he held an election and returned his father-in-law, Metellus Scipio, as his colleague.

The upshot of these disorders, therefore, was to give Pompey a very strong position. He was, in fact, dictator (*seditionis sedandæ causa*) under another name ; and the Optimates hastened to secure him as their champion. A law had been passed in B.C. 56, by agreement with Cæsar, giving Pompey the whole of Spain as a province for five years after his consulship of B.C. 55. As Cæsar's government of Gaul terminated at the end of B.C. 49,

The first Triumvirate and its results.

Pompey's position after B.C. 52.

Pompey would have imperium and an army when Cæsar left his province. He would naturally indeed be in Spain ; but the Senate now passed a resolution that it was for the good of the State that Pompey should remain near Rome. He accordingly governed Spain by three legati, and remained outside the walls of the city with imperium. The great object of the Optimates was that Cæsar should return to Rome a *privatus* while Pompey was still there in this unprecedented position. Cæsar wished to be consul for B.C. 48. The Optimates did not openly oppose that wish, but contended that he should lay down his provincial government and military command first, and come to Rome to make his *professio*, or formal announcement of his being a candidate, in the usual way.[1]

But Cæsar declined to walk into this trap. He knew that if he came home as a *privatus* there were many ready to prosecute him for his actions in Gaul, and with Pompey there in command of legions he felt certain that a verdict inflicting political ruin on him could be obtained. He therefore stood by the right—secured by a law of B.C. 55, and reinforced by Pompey's own law in B.C. 52—of standing for the consulship without coming to Rome, and without giving up his province and army before the time originally fixed by the law. He would thus not be without imperium for a single day, but would come to Rome as consul.

Here was a direct issue. Pompey professed to believe that it could be settled by a decree of the Senate, either forbidding the holder of the election to receive votes for Cæsar in his absence, or appointing a successor in his province. Cæsar, he

---

[1] The law of B.C. 52 allowed Cæsar to be "elected in his absence" (*absentis rationem haberi*), but said nothing of his being in possession of a province. By long prescription the Senate had the right of deciding when a provincial governor should be "succeeded." But then Cæsar's term of provincial government had been fixed by a *lex*, which was superior to a *Senatus-consultum* ; and he might also argue that if it was unconstitutional for a man to be elected consul while holding a province, the Senate had violated the constitution in allowing Pompey to be consul in B.C. 52.

argued, would of course obey a *Senatus-consultum*. But Cæsar was on firm ground in refusing to admit a successor till the term fixed by the law had expired, and also in claiming that his candidature should be admitted in his absence—for that too had been granted by a law. If neither side would yield the only possible solution was war.[1]

Cæsar hesitated for some time. He saw no hope of mollifying his enemies or separating Pompey from them. His daughter Iulia's death in B.C. 54 after a few years'

Provocation to Cæsar.

marriage to Pompey had severed a strong tie between them. The death of Crassus in B.C 53 had removed, not indeed a man of much strength of character, but one whose enormous wealth had given him such a hold on the senators that any strong act on their part, against his wishes, was difficult. After his death the actual provocations to Cæsar had certainly increased. The depriving him, under the pretext of an impending Parthian war, of two legions which were being kept under arms in Italy ; the insult inflicted upon him by Marcellus (Consul B.C. 51) in flogging a magistrate of his new colony at Comum, who if the colony were regarded as legally established would be exempt from such punishment ; —these and similar things shewed Cæsar what he had to expect if he gave up office and army. He elected therefore to stand on his legal rights.

Legality was on his side, but long prescription was in favour of the Senate's claim to the obedience of a magistrate,

Civil war.

especially of the governor of a province. There was therefore a deadlock. Cæsar made one attempt—not perhaps a very sincere one—to remove it. He had won over Gaius Curio, tribune in B.C. 50, by helping him

[1] The Senate did not insist on the *professio*, from which Cæsar had been exempted by name in Pompey's law. But its contention was that it still retained the right of naming the date at which a man was to leave his province, and of deciding in regard to an election whether a man was a legal candidate, which might depend on other things besides the making or not making a *professio*.

to discharge his immense debts. Curio therefore, instead of opposing Cæsar, as had been expected, vetoed every proposal for his recall. His tribuneship ended on the 9th of December, B.C. 50, and he immediately started to visit Cæsar at Ravenna. He told him of the inveteracy of his opponents, and urged him to march at once upon Rome. But Cæsar determined to justify himself by offering a peaceful solution—"he was willing to hand over his province and army to a successor, if Pompey would also give up Spain and dismiss his armies." Curio returned to Rome in time for the meeting of the Senate on the 1st of January, B.C. 49, bringing this despatch from Cæsar.

The majority of the Senate affected to regard it as an act of rebellion. After a debate, lasting five days, a decree was passed on January the 7th, ordering Cæsar to give up his province and army on a fixed day, on pain of being declared guilty of treason. This was vetoed by two tribunes, M. Antonius and Q. Cassius. Refusing, after the usual "remonstrance," to withdraw their veto, they were finally expelled and fled to Ariminum, on their way to join Cæsar at Ravenna. The Senate then passed the *Senatus-consultum ultimum*, ordering the magistrates and pro-magistrates " to see that the state took no harm," and a levy of soldiers—already begun by Pompey— was ordered to be held in all parts of Italy.

Cæsar, informed of this, addressed the single legion which was with him at Ravenna, urging it to support the violated tribunes. Satisfied with the response to his appeal, Cæsar crosses the Rubicon. he took the final step of passing the Rubicon and marching to Ariminum, outside his province. Both sides were now in the wrong, the Senate by forcibly interfering with the action of the tribunes, Cæsar by entering Italy. An attempt, therefore, was made to effect a compromise. Lucius Cæsar—a distant connection of Iulius—visited him at Ariminum, bringing some general professions of moderation from Pompey, though it seems without any definite suggestion.

Cæsar, however, so far modified his former offer as to propose a conference, with the understanding that the levy of troops in Italy was to be stopped and Pompey was to go to his Spanish province. On receiving this communication at Capua Pompey and the consuls declined all terms until Cæsar had withdrawn from Ariminum into Gaul; though they intimated, without mentioning any date, that Pompey would in that case go to Spain. But the levy of troops was not interrupted; and Cæsar's answer to this was the triumphant march through Picenum and to Brundisium. Town after town surrendered, and the garrisons placed in them by Pompey generally joined the advancing army, till finally a large force, embracing many men of high rank, surrendered at Corfinium. Cæsar had entered Italy with only one legion, but others were summoned from winter quarters in Cisalpine Gaul, and by the time he reached Brundisium Pompey had given up all idea of resisting him in Italy, and within the walls of that town was preparing to cross to Epirus, whither the consuls with the main body of his troops had already gone. Cæsar had no ships with which to follow him. He was content to hasten his flight by threatening to block up the harbour. Pompey safely out of Italy, he went to Rome to arrange for his regular election into the consulship. Meeting with opposition there [1]—one of the tribunes, L. Cæcilius Metellus, vetoing all proposals in the Senate—he hastened to Spain to attack the legates of Pompey, stopping on his way to arrange the siege of Marseilles (which had admitted Ahenobarbus, named successor of Cæsar in Gaul),

---

[1] The difficulty was that both consuls were absent. There was no one therefore capable of holding a consular election. But as the other curule magistrates still existed, " the *auspicia* had not returned to the Fathers," who could not therefore name an interrex. The Prætor Lepidus—though willing—could not " create" a *maius imperium*. The only way out of it was to name a Dictator (*com. hab. causa*); but one of the consuls, according to tradition, could alone do that. Eventually Lepidus, by a special vote of the people was authorised to name Cæsar as Dictator—which had precedents in the cases of Fabius Maximus and Sulla—and Cæsar, as Dictator, held the consular elections. Cæs., b. c. ii, 21 ; Dio, 41, 36.

and sending legati to secure Sicily, Sardinia, and Africa. Of these the only failure was in Africa, where Curio was defeated and killed. This province therefore remained in the hands of the Pompeians; but Cæsar's own successes in Spain, the fall of Marseilles, and the hold gained upon the corn supplies of Sicily and Sardinia placed him in a strong position. The constitutional difficulty was surmounted; he was named Dictator to hold the elections, returned himself as consul, and, after eleven days in Rome for the Latin games, embarked at Brundisium on January 3, B.C. 48, to attack Pompey in Epirus.

It is not necessary to follow the events of the next six months. Cæsar had to struggle with great difficulties, for
Iulius Cæsar
master of the
Roman world,
B.C. 47. Pompey as master of the sea had a secure base of supplies; and therefore, though Cæsar drew vast lines round his camp, he could not starve him out. Pompey, in fact, actually pierced Cæsar's lines and defeated him in more than one engagement. Eventually, however, Cæsar drew him into Thessaly; and the great victory of Pharsalia (August 9th) made up for everything. Pompey fled to Egypt, to meet his death on the beach by order of the treacherous young king; and though Cæsar still had weary work to do before Egypt was reduced to obedience, and then had to traverse Asia Minor to crush Pharnaces of Pontus at Zela, when he set foot once more in Italy in September, B.C. 47, he had already been created Dictator, and was practically master of the Roman world.

In these momentous events the young Octavius had taken no part. At the beginning of B.C. 49 he had been
Octavius takes
the *toga virilis*
and is made a
pontifex,
B.C. 48. sent away to one of his ancestral estates in the country. But we cannot suppose him incapable of understanding their importance or being an uninterested spectator. His stepfather Philippus was Pompeian in sympathy, but his close connection with Cæsar kept him from taking an active part in the war, and he was allowed to remain in Italy, probably for the most part

in his Campanian villa. From time to time, however, he came to Rome ; and Octavius, who now lived entirely with him, began to be treated with a distinction natural to the near relative of the victorious dictator. Soon after the news of Pharsalia he took the *toga virilis*, and about the same time was elected into the college of pontifices in the place of L. Domitius Ahenobarbus, who had fallen in the battle. This was an office desired by the highest in the land, and the election of so young a boy, just entering upon his sixteenth year, put him in a position something like that of a prince of the blood ; just as afterwards Augustus caused his two grandsons to be designated to the consulship, and declared capable of official employment as soon as they had taken the *toga virilis*.[1]

The boy, who three years before had made a great impression by his delivery of the *laudatio* at his grandmother Iulia's

Octavius's relations with his parents and his great-uncle. funeral, again attracted much attention by his good looks and modesty. He became the fashion ; and when (as was customary for the pontifices) he presided in a prætorian court during the *feriæ Latinæ*, it was observed to be more crowded by suitors and their friends than any of the others. It seems that the rarity of his appearance at Rome added to the interest roused by his great-uncle's successes. For his mother did not relax her watchfulness. Though legally a man he was still carefully guarded. He was required to sleep in the same simple chamber, to visit the same houses, and to follow the same way of life as before. Even his religious duties were performed before daylight, to escape the languishing looks of intriguing beauties. These precautions were seconded by his own cool and cautious temperament, and the result seems to have been that he passed through the dangerous stage of adolescence—doubly

---

[1] Nicolas (ch. 4) says that he took the *toga virilis* about fourteen (περὶ ἔτη μάλιστα γεγονὼς τεσσαρακαίδεκα). But Suetonius (*Aug.* 8) says that he spoke the *laudatio* of his grandmother in his twelfth year, and "four years afterwards" took the *toga virilis*.

dangerous to one now practically a prince—uncontaminated by the grosser vices of Rome. Stories to the contrary, afterwards spread abroad by his enemies, are of the most unsubstantial and untrustworthy kind.

But though he seems to have quietly submitted to this tutelage, he soon conceived an ardent desire to share in the activities of his great-uncle. Caesar had been very little at Rome since the beginning of the civil war. A few days in March, B.C. 49, thirteen days in December of the same year, were all that he had spent in the city. He was absent during the whole of his consulship (B.C. 48) till September, B.C. 47. On his return from Alexandria in that month, he stayed barely three months at Rome. On the 19th of December he was at Lilybæum, on his way to Africa to attack the surviving Pompeians. Octavius longed to go with him, and Caesar was willing to take him. But his health was not good, and his mother set herself against it. The Dictator might no doubt have insisted, but he saw that the boy was not fit to face the fatigues of a campaign. Octavius submitted, quietly biding his time. He was rewarded by finding himself high in his great-uncle's favour when he returned in B.C. 46 after the victory of Thapsus. He was admitted to share his triple triumph, riding in a chariot immediately behind that of the imperator, dressed in military uniform as though he had actually been engaged. He found, moreover, that he had sufficient interest with Caesar to obtain pardon for the brother of his friend Agrippa, taken prisoner in the Pompeian army in Africa. This first use of his influence made a good impression, without weakening his great-uncle's affection for him. Though Caesar did not formally adopt him,[1] he treated him openly as

Wishes to go to Africa with Caesar.

---

[1] Octavius was *sui iuris*, his father being dead ; his adoption therefore required the formal passing of a *lex curiata*. Now the opposition, supported by Antony, against this formality being carried out was one of the grounds of Octavian's quarrel with him in B.C. 44–3, and the completion of it was one of the first things secured by Octavian on his entrance into Rome in August, B.C. 43 [Appian, b. c. iii. 94 ; Dio, 45, 5]. This seems

his nearest relation and heir. Octavius rode near him in his triumph, stood by his side at the sacrifice, took precedence of all the staff or court that surrounded him, and accompanied him to theatres and banquets. He was soon besieged by petitions to be laid before Cæsar, and shewed both tact and good nature in dealing with them. This close connection with the wise and magnanimous Dictator, inspired him with warm admiration and affection, which help to explain and excuse the severity with which he afterwards pursued his murderers.

In order to give him experience of civic duties, one of the theatres was now put under his charge. But his assiduous attention to this duty in the hot season brought on a dangerous illness, one of the many which he encountered during his long life. There was a general feeling of regret at the prospect of a career of such promise being cut short. Cæsar visited him daily or sent friends to him, insisted on the physicians remaining constantly at his side, and being informed while at dinner that the boy had fainted and was in imminent danger, he sprang up from his couch, and without waiting to change his dining slippers, hurried to his chamber, besought the physicians in moving terms to do their utmost, and sitting down by the bed shewed the liveliest joy when the patient recovered from his swoon.

Octavius employed in civil duties, B.C. 46.

Octavius was too weak to accompany the Dictator when starting for Spain against Pompey's sons in December B.C. 46. But as soon as he was sufficiently recovered he determined to follow him. He refused all company except that of a few select friends and the

Octavius follows Cæsar to Spain, B.C. 45.

conclusive against the theory that Iulius adopted him in his lifetime. Moreover all authorities speak of the adoption as made by *Will.* Livy, *Ep.* 116, *testamento in nomen adoptatus est*; Velleius, ii. 59, *testamentum apertum est, quo C. Octavium nepotem sororis suæ Iuliæ adoptabat.* See also Appian, b. c. iii. 11; Dio, 45, 3; Plutarch, *Brut.* 22. It is true that Nicolas —speaking of the triumph of B.C. 46—(§ 8) says υἱὸν ἤδη πεποιημένος. But if he means anything more than "regarding him as a son," he twice afterwards contradicts himself : See § 17 ἀπήγγελλον τά τε ἄλλα καὶ ὡς ἐν ταῖς διαθήκαις ὡς υἱὸς εἴη Καίσαρι ἐγγεγραμμένος. *Cf.* § 13.

most active of his slaves. He would not admit his mother's wish to go with him. He had yielded to her before, but he was now resolved to take part in a man's work alone. His voyage, early in B.C. 45, proved long and dangerous; and when at length he landed at Tarraco he found his uncle already at the extreme south of Spain, somewhere between Cadiz and Gibraltar. The roads were rendered dangerous by scattered parties of hostile natives, or outposts of the enemy, and his escort was small. Still, he pushed on with energy and reached Cæsar's quarters near Calpe, to which he had advanced after the victory at Munda (March 17th). Gnæus Pompeius had fled on board a ship, but was killed when landing for water on the 11th of April, and it was apparently just about that time that Octavius reached the camp. Warmly received and highly praised for his energy by the Dictator, he was at once admitted to his table and close intimacy, during which Cæsar learned still more to appreciate the quickness of his intelligence and the careful control which he kept over his tongue.

Affairs in Southern Spain having been apparently settled (though as it proved the danger was by no means over), Octavius accompanied Cæsar to Carthage, to settle questions which had arisen as to the assignment of land in his new colony. The Dictator was visited there by deputations from various Greek states, alleging grievances or asking favours. Octavius was applied to by more than one of them to plead their cause, and had therefore again an opportunity of acquiring practical experience in the business of imperial government, and in the very best school.

Octavius accompanies his great-uncle to Carthage.

He preceded Cæsar on his return to Rome, and on his arrival had once more occasion to shew his caution and prudence. Among those who met him in the usual complimentary procession was a young man who had somehow managed to make himself a popular hero by pretending to be a grandson of the great Marius. His real name was Amatius or Herophilus, a veterinary surgeon according to some, but certainly of humble origin. As Marius had married Cæsar's aunt Iulia, this man was anxious to be recognised as a cousin by the Dictator. He had in vain applied to Cicero to undertake his cause, and to Atia and her half-sister to recognise him. The difficulty for Octavius was that the man was a favourite of the populace, of whose cause Cæsar was the professed champion; yet his recognition would be offensive to the nobles and a mere concession to clamour. Octavius avoided the snare by referring the case to Cæsar as head of the state and family, and refusing to receive the would-be Marius till he had decided.[1]

He did not remain long at Rome however. Cæsar returned in September, and was assassinated in the following March.

Octavius at
Apollonia,
B.C. 45-44. And during that interval, though he found time for many schemes of legislation, and of restoration or improvement in the city, he was much employed in preparing for two expeditions—calculated to last three years —first against the Daci or Getæ on the Danube, and secondly against the Parthians in Mesopotamia. These were the two points of active danger in the Empire, and Cæsar desired to crown his public services by securing their peace and safety. For this purpose six legions were quartered in Macedonia for the winter, in readiness to march along the Via Egnatia to the eastern coast of Greece. Returning from Spain Dictator for life, Cæsar was to have two "Masters of the Horse." One was to be Octavius, who had meanwhile been created a patrician by the Senate.[2] But for the present he was sent to pass the

---

[1] Cicero, *ad Att.* xii. 48, 49; Nicholas, § 14; Valer. Max., I, 15, 2. For the subsequent fate of the man see Cicero, *ad Att.* xiv. 6, 7, 8; App., b. c. iii. 2-3.

[2] The patrician *gentes* were dying out, and it was thought good to replenish their numbers, thus gradually forming a class of nobles distinct from these ennobled by office. In making the Octavii patricians, the initiative was taken by the Senate; in later times, however, the power of creating *patricii* was conferred on the imperator. Iulius seems also to have done it on his own authority. (Dio, 43, 47; Suet., *Aug.* 2.)

winter at Apollonia, the Greek colony at the beginning of the Via Egnatia, where he might continue his studies in quiet with the rhetors and other teachers whom he took with him or found there,[1] and at the same time might get some military training with the legions that were not far off. He was accompanied by some of the young men with whom he habitually associated. Among them were Agrippa and Mæcenas, who remained his friends and ministers to the end of their lives, and Salvidienus Rufus, who almost alone of his early friends proved unfaithful.[2]

He seems to have led a quiet life at Apollonia, winning golden opinions in the town and from his teachers for his studious and regular habits. The admiration and loyalty of his friends were confirmed; and many of the officers of the legions seem to have made up their minds to regard him as the best possible successor to the Dictator.

In the sixth month of his residence at Apollonia, in the afternoon of a March day, a freedman of his mother arrived with every sign of rapid travel and agitation. He delivered a letter from Atia, dated the 15th of March. It briefly stated that the Dictator had just been assassinated in the Senate House. She added that she " did not know what would happen next ; but it was time now for him to play the man, and to think and act for the best at this terrible crisis." [3] The bearer of the letter could tell him nothing else, for he had been despatched

News of Cæsar's assassination brought to Apollonia.

---

[1] He took with him Apollodorus of Pergamus, a well-known author of a system of rhetoric (Suet., *Aug.* 89 ; Strabo, 13, 4, 3 ; Quinct., 3, 1, 17). Other teachers of his, whether at Apollonia or elsewhere, are Areius of Alexandria, Alexander of Pergamus, Athenodorus of Tarsus (Suet. *l.c.* ; Dio, 51, 4 ; Plutarch, *Ant.* 11 ; Nicol. Dam., § 17 ; Zonaras, 10, 38).

[2] Suet., *Aug.* 65 ; Vell. Paterc., 2, 59, 64 ; App., b. c. 5, 66 ; Dio, 48, 33. The other instance of a friend who fell into disfavour and ruin quoted by Suetonius is Cornelius Gallus. But he does not seem to have been at Apollonia. He was nearly three years older than Augustus, and in B.C. 44–3 was perhaps with Pollio in Bætica. See Cic., *ad Fam.* x. 32.

[3] Nicolas, § 16 ; App., b. c. iii. 9–10.

immediately after the murder, and had loitered nowhere on the way ; only he felt sure that as the conspirators were numerous and powerful, all the kinsfolk of the Dictator would be in danger.

This was the last day of Octavius's youth.   From that hour he had to play a dangerous game with desperate players.   He did not yet know that by the Dictator's will he had been adopted as his son, and was heir to the greater part of his vast wealth ; but a passionate desire to avenge him sprang up in his breast, a desire strengthened with increasing knowledge, and of which he never lost sight in all the political complications of the next ten years.

CHAPTER II

*Vicinæ ruptis inter se legibus
urbes Arma ferunt ; sævit toto
Mars impius orbe.*

AT the death of Cæsar the Roman Empire had been for the most part won. Egypt was indeed annexed by Augustus,

Natural boundaries of the Roman Empire.

though on a peculiar tenure, but subsequent additions were in a manner consequential, the inevitable rectifications of a long frontier. Such were the provinces of the Rhine, the Alps, and the Danube as far east as Moesia ; and to a certain extent the province of Galatia and Lycaonia (B.C. 25). The Rhine, the Danube, and the Euphrates seemed already the natural boundaries of the Empire on the north and east, the Atlantic Ocean on the west, and the African and Arabian deserts on the south. And these boundaries, with occasional modifications, and for the most part temporary extensions, continued to the end.

But though the greater part of this wide Empire was already won, it was not all equally well organised and secured. Thus,

Its dangers.

in Northern Gaul, there were still Germans and other enemies to be conquered or repelled ; in Southern Spain a son of the great Pompey was in arms ; Macedonia was continually subject to invasion by Getæ, Bessi, and other barbarians ; the Dalmatians and neighbouring tribes made Illyricum an uncertain member of the Empire ;

in Syria, Cæcilius Bassus—an old officer of Pompey's—was defying Roman armies, and inviting the aid of the Parthians always ready to cross the Euphrates into the Roman province.

To confront two of these dangers Cæsar had collected a large army in Macedonia in the autumn of B.C. 45 to crush the Getæ, and then crossing to Syria to force the Parthian to respect the frontier of the Euphrates, or even to attack them in Mesopotamia. The former of these projects was no doubt important for the safety of the Empire, and was in after years successfully secured by Augustus and his legates. The latter was more visionary and theatrical, meant perhaps to strike the imagination of the Romans rather than to secure great practical advantage. After Cæsar's death Antony lost more than he gained by similar enterprises, and Augustus always avoided coming into actual contact with the Parthians, or attempting to extend his rule beyond the Euphrates. But there were dangers within the Empire no less formidable than from without. Its integrity had rested, and generally securely rested, on the loyalty of its provincial governors to the central authority as represented by the Senate, or, in the last resort, by the order of the people expressed in a *lex* or *plebiscitum*. It was the beginning of the end when these governors used the forces under their command, or the wealth and influence secured abroad, to defy or coerce the authorities at home. Sertorius, Sulla, and Cæsar himself, had shewn that this was not an impossible contingency. It was against this danger that, among other reforms in the government of the Provinces, Cæsar's own law had provided that the tenure of a proprætor should be confined to one, and of a proconsul to two, years. But now that he was going on a distant expedition, calculated as likely to occupy three years, he took other precautions. Having provided for the chief offices at home,[1] he was careful to see that the pro-

Cæsar's precautions and preparations.

---

[1] Dolabella consul for the last half of B.C. 44 with Antony ; Pansa and Hirtius, B.C. 43 ; Plancus and Dec. Brutus B.C. 42. Probably M. Brutus

vinces should be held by men whom he believed to be loyal to himself, and likely from their character and ability to maintain their peace and security. Being Consul and Dictator, and his *acta* being confirmed beforehand by Senate and people, he could make what nominations he pleased. A decree of the Senate was still taken as a matter of form, but the old practice (often a farce) of drawing lots for the provinces was abandoned; Pompey's law ordaining a five years' interval between curule office and a province was neglected, and Cæsar practically nominated the governors. But it raises a doubt as to the unfettered power or the insight of the Dictator that five of those thus nominated were among the assassins on the Ides of March.[2] Nor in other respects did his choice prove happy. The state of open war or dangerous unrest which shewed itself in almost all parts of the Empire after his death must be learnt by a review of the provinces, if we are to understand the problem presented to Augustus and his colleagues in the triumvirate, and the relief felt by the Roman world when Augustus finally took the administration into his own hands, and shewed himself capable of restoring law and order.

The GAULS now included three districts, the status of which was somewhat unsettled. (1) *Cisalpine Gaul*, that is, Italy
(1) THE GAULS. between Etruria and the Alps, was still nominally a province, though Cæsar's law of B.C. 48 had granted full *civitas* to the transpadane, as that of B.C. 89 had to the cispadane, towns. It had formed part of Cæsar's province from B.C. 58 to B.C. 48, and he seems to have retained it until after the battle of Pharsalia, when he appointed first Marcus Brutus and then C. Vibius Pansa to it. Though part of Italy, and generally peaceful, it had great military importance

---

and C. Cassius (or certainly the former) B.C. 41 [Plut., *Cæs.* 62 ; Cic., *ad Fam.* xii. 2]. For B.C. 43 prætors and other magistrates were named, but for the next years only consuls and tribunes.

[1] Dio, 43, 47, καὶ ἔς γε τὰ ἔθνη ἀκληρωτὶ ἐξεπέμφθησαν.

[2] M. Brutus, C. Cassius, Dec. Brutus, L. Cimber, C. Trebonius.

in case of an invasion from the north. After March B.C. 44 it was to be in the hands of Decimus Brutus, who had long served under Cæsar, and was regarded by him with special confidence and affection. Antony's attempt to wrest it from Decimus Brutus brought on the first civil war after Cæsar's death.

(2) *Transalpine Gaul* technically consisted of "the Province," that is, South-eastern France, from the Cevennes on the west to Italy, and from the Lake of Geneva on the north to the sea. But since Cæsar's conquests there had to be added to this the rest of France, Belgium, and Holland as far as the Rhine. No formal division into distinct provinces had yet been made. In B.C. 49 Decimus Brutus, after driving out Ahenobarbus, the governor named by the Senate, remained in command of the whole till B.C. 45, when he returned in Cæsar's train to Italy. But in the course of these four years, or on his return, (3) Belgica was separated from the rest and assigned to Hirtius, who, however, governed it by a legate named Aurelius, without going there himself.[1] In the course of the next year a farther division was made: Aurelius retained Belgica; Lepidus, with four legions, was appointed to "the Province" (afterwards called Gallia Narbonensis) together with Hispania Citerior; while L. Munatius Plancus governed the rest, consisting of what was afterwards two provinces—Aquitania and Lugdunensis. Plancus and Decimus Brutus were named consuls for B.C. 42, and therefore their governorships necessarily terminated at the end of B.C. 43, and might do so earlier. In the course of B.C. 43 Plancus founded Lugdunum [2] (Lyon), which was afterwards the capital of the central province of the four organised by Augustus. But though the organisation of this country was not complete, Cæsar's conquest had been so decisive that no advantage was taken of the civil war by the natives to attempt a rising.[3]

---

[1] Cic., *ad Att.* xiv. 9; Cæs., b. c. ii. 22; Plut., *Ant.* xi.   [2] Dio, 46, 60.

[3] Cæsar had auxiliaries in Spain from Aquitania B.C. 49; Cæs., b. c. i. 39.

There seem to have been some insignificant movements in B.C. 42, but it was not for some years later that any danger of importance arose there. The Belgæ had been expected to rise on Cæsar's assassination, but their chiefs hastened to assure Hirtius's legate of their adhesion to the Roman government.[1]

The province of ILLYRICUM had been formed about the same time as that of Macedonia (B.C. 146), but its limits had fluctuated, and it had not received much continuous attention. It included places, such as Dyrrachium, Corcyra, Issa, Pharus, which had been declared free after the contest with Queen Teuta in B.C. 228, but were practically under Roman control. Yet some of the most powerful tribes not only did not acknowledge Roman authority, but made frequent incursions upon Roman Illyricum. The most dangerous of these were the Dalmatians, with whom several wars are recorded. In B.C. 117 L. Cælius Metellus occupied Salonæ ; [2] in B.C. 87–5 Sulla won a victory over them ; [3] in B.C. 78–77 C. Cosconius, after a two years' campaign, took Salonæ by storm.[4] But little was really effected in securing the province against its enemies. It was let much alone so long as its tribute was paid, and was put under the governor sometimes of Macedonia, sometimes of Cisalpine Gaul. In Cæsar's case (B.C. 58) it was specially assigned, like the rest of his province, and he seems at first to have intended to go there in force and subdue the hostile barbarians. But the Gallic campaigns drew him away, and he only once actually entered Illyricum (B.C. 54) to overawe the invading Pirustæ. In the last year of his proconsulship (B.C. 50) some troops which he sent against the Dalmatians were cut to pieces. The result of this was that the barbarians, fearing his vengeance, adhered to Pompey in

(3) ILLYRICUM.

---

[1] Cicero, *ad Att.* xiv. 5, 8, 9.

[2] Livy, *Ep.* 62. Appian says that Metellus did not fight, but was received as a friend, wintered at Salonæ, and then went home and claimed a triumph (*Illyr.* xi.).

[3] Eutrop., v. 4.

[4] *Id.* vi. 4 ; Oros., v. 23.

the civil war, whose legate, M. Octavius, with a considerable fleet, maintained himself there,[1] and in B.C. 49 defeated and captured Gaius Antonius, whom Cæsar sent against him.[2] At the beginning of the next year Aulus Gabinius, while trying to lead a force round the head of the Adriatic to join Cæsar, lost nearly all his men in a battle with the Dalmatians.[3] After Pharsalia Gabinius was sent back to assist Cornificius, who had been despatched to Illyricum as pro-prætor after the mishap of Gaius Antonius ; but he was again defeated and shut up in Salonæ, where he died suddenly.[4] In B.C. 47, however, P. Vatinius, having joined Cornificius, defeated and drove Octavius out of the country.[5] After serving also in the African campaign of B.C. 46, Vatinius was sent back to Illyricum with three legions (B.C. 45) expressly to reduce the still independent tribes. At first he gained sufficient success to be honoured by a *supplicatio*,[6] but after Cæsar's death he was defeated by the Dalmatians with the loss of five cohorts, and was driven to take refuge in Dyrrachium.[7] Early in B.C. 43 he was forced to surrender his legions to M. Brutus, who, however, in the year and a half which preceded his death at Philippi, was too busy elsewhere to attend to Illyricum.[8] Hence the expeditions of Pollio in B.C. 39,[9] and of Augustus in B.C. 35 were rendered necessary, and they for a time secured the pacification of the country and the extension of Roman provinces to the Danube.

At the death of Iulius SPAIN was also a source of great danger and difficulty. Since B.C. 197 it had been divided into
(4) SPAIN. two provinces—Citerior and Ulterior—separated by the Saltus Castulonensis (*Sierra Morena*), each governed by a prætor or pro-prætor. In B.C. 54 Pompey

[1] Cæs., b. c. iii. 5, 9.   [2] Livy, *Ep.* 110 ; App., b. c. ii. 47.
[3] *Id.*, b. c. ii. 59.   [4] Cæs., *b. Alex.* 42–3.   [5] *Id.*, 34–6.
[6] Cic., *ad Fam.* v. 10 (*a*), 10, 11.   [7] App., *Illyr.* 13.
[8] App., b. c. iv. 75 ; Dio, 47, 21. Vatinius was ill, and his late reverses had lost him the confidence of his men, who insisted on being transferred to Brutus.   [9] Dio, 43, 42 ; Horace, *Odes*, iii. 1, 13.

introduced a triple division. Of his three legates Afranius held Hispania Citerior ; but the farther province was divided between Petreius, who held the district as far west as the Anas (*Guadiana*), afterwards called Bætica, while Terentius Varro governed the country west of that river with Lusitania. Having forced Pompey's legates to surrender the country (B.C.49), Cæsar seems not to have continued the triple division. Q. Cassius was sent to Hispania Ulterior, M. Lepidus to Hispania Citerior. But Cassius offended his own soldiers as well as the natives, and had to escape by sea, being drowned on his way home. Nor did his successor Trebonius do much better in B.C. 47 ; for many of his soldiers deserted to Gnæus Pompeius when he came to Spain after the defeat at Thapsus in the spring of B.C. 46.[1] And though Gnæus Pompeius perished soon after the battle of Munda (B.C. 45) his younger brother Sextus survived. At Cæsar's death he was already at the head of a considerable fleet which enabled him to control Sicily and re-occupy Bætica, when its last Cæsarean governor—the famous C. Asinius Pollio—left it to join Antony in Gallia Narbonensis in the summer of B.C. 43. The upper province had meanwhile been governed by the legates of Metellus, who was about to return to it and Gallia Narbonensis with four legions when Cæsar's death introduced new complications.[2]

SICILY for eight years after Cæsar's death was practically separated from the Empire. In B.C. 49 it had been easily won over to Cæsar's authority by C. Curio, and after his success in Spain against Pompey's legates Cæsar had nominated Aulus Allienus [3] as its proprætor. In B.C. 46 Allienus was succeeded by M. Acilius [4] (afterwards sent to Achaia), who in his turn was succeeded by T. Furfanius Postumus (B.C. 45). Finally, among Cæsar's arrangements for

(5) SICILY.

---

[1] Cæs., *b. Alex.* 48–64 ; *Hisp.* 7, 12.   [2] App., b. c. ii. 107.
[3] Wrongly called Aulus Albinus by Appian, b. c. ii. 48 ; see Klein, *die Verwaltungsbeamten der Provinzen*, p. 83.
[4] Cic., *ad Fam.* xiii. 30, 36, 50, 78, 79 ; Cæs., *b. Afr.* 2, 26, 34.

B.C. 44 was the appointment of Pompeius Bithynicus to Sicily. His father had served under Pompey and had perished with him in Egypt; and Bithynicus seems to have feared retaliation from the Pompeians if they returned to power; for on the death of Cæsar we find him writing to Cicero in evident anxiety as to his position.[1] He failed to hold the island against Sext. Pompeius, who landed in B.C. 43, and after sustaining a slight reverse at Messene forced Bithynicus to yield him a share in the government, and shortly afterwards put him to death because he believed him to be plotting against him.[2] Sicily therefore had to be restored to the Empire by the triumvirs, a task which fell chiefly to Augustus.

SARDINIA was important for its supply of corn. In B.C. 49 Cæsar's legate Q. Valerius Orca occupied it without difficulty, its governor, M. Aurelius Cotta, escaping to Africa. In B.C. 48 Orca was succeeded by Sext. Peducæus.[3]

(6) SARDINIA.

But the arrangements made between that date and B.C. 44 are not known, for Peducæus appears to have been in Rome from the end of B.C. 45.[4] In the first division of the provinces by the triumvirs (November, B.C. 43) it fell to Octavian's share,[5] though Suetonius remarks that Africa and Sardinia were the only two provinces never visited by him.[6] Meanwhile Sext. Pompeius occupied it,[7] and it was not recovered till B.C. 38.

---

[1] Cic., *ad Fam.* vi. 16, 17.

[2] Dio, 48, 17, 19; Livy, *Ep.* 123; Appian, b. c. iv. 84. A certain M. Casinius was nominated to Sicily for B.C. 43, but did not go there, perhaps owing to the order of the Senate (meant to support Dec. Brutus) made on the 20th of December, B.C. 44, that all governors should retain their provinces till farther orders (Cic., *ad Fam.* xii. 22, 25).

[3] App., b. c. ii. 48.   [4] Cic., *ad Att.* xv. 7; xvi. 3.

[5] App., b. c. iv. 2; Dio, 46, 55.

[6] Sueton., *Aug.* 47. This probably means after his accession to sole power. According to Nicolas, § 11–12, he visited Africa with Cæsar in B.C. 45. See p. 13. There is no record, however, of his ever having been to Sardinia.

[7] App., b. c. v. 67. The hold of Sext. Pompeius on Sardinia was recognised in the "treaty" of Misenum made in B.C. 39 (Dio, 48, 36; App., b. c. v. 72).

The province of AFRICA—the ancient territory of Carthage —may be taken with this western part of the Empire. It had long been a peaceful province, but in B.C. 46 it was the scene of the great rally of the Pompeians after the disaster at Pharsalia. Since their final defeat at Thapsus it had been farther secured by Cæsar's colony at Carthage (B.C. 46–5), and had been governed by a fervent Cæsarean, C. Calvisius Sabinus. At the end of B.C. 45 Sabinus returned to Rome, and Q. Cornificius (once Cæsar's quæstor) was named to succeed him. But affairs in Africa had been complicated by the formation of a new province from the dominions of Iuba, called sometimes New Africa, sometimes Numidia (B.C. 46). Of this new province the first proprætor was the historian Sallust, succeeded in B.C. 45 by T. Sextius with three legions. On Cæsar's death, therefore, there were two men in Africa who might possibly take different views of the situation. Cornificius indeed—friend and correspondent of Cicero—shewed at once that he meant to stand by the Senate. A few months later he was confirmed in this resolution by the fact of his continuance in office depending on the senatorial decree of the 20th of December,[1] whereas Antony had commissioned Calvisius Sabinus (who had never withdrawn his legates from Africa) to go back to the province.[2] Accordingly, after Antony's defeat at Mutina (April, B.C. 43), the Senate felt strong enough to order Sextius to transfer his three legions to Cornificius, who was himself under orders to send two of them to Rome.[3] This was done, and with the remaining legion Cornificius maintained his position in Old Africa, when the Triumvirate was formed in November, and was able to offer protection to many of the proscribed. But Sextius now claimed both provinces, as having fallen to Octavian's share. He enrolled troops in his own province and obtained the help of Arabion, of the royal family of Numidia and chief of the

(7) AFRICA. NUMIDIA.

---

[1] See Note [2] p. 24.   [2] Cicero, 3 *Phil.* § 26 ; *ad Fam.* xii. 22, 23, 30.
[3] Appian, b. c. iii. 85, 91.

robber tribe of Sittians ; and though Cornificius had the stronger force, he was presently defeated and killed. Octavian, however, looked upon Sextius as a partisan of Antony rather than of himself, and presently sent C. Fuficius Fango to supersede him. Sextius seems to have foreseen that differences would occur between Antony and Octavian likely to give him a chance of recovering his province. Therefore under pretence of wishing to winter in a genial climate he stayed on in Africa. His opportunity came with the new distribution of provinces after Philippi (October–November, B.C. 42). Old or " Prætorian " Africa fell to Antony, New Africa or Numidia to Octavian. But upon the quarrel between Octavian and Fulvia (supported by Lucius Antonius) in B.C. 41, Sextius was urged by Fulvia to demand the prætorian province from Fango as properly belonging to Antony. After several battles, in which he met with various fortunes, Fango was at last driven to take refuge in the mountains, and there killed himself. Sextius then held both provinces till, in B.C. 40, the triumvir Lepidus took possession of them as his share of the Empire.[1]

Thus the Western Provinces, in spite of Cæsar's precautions, were all in a condition to cause difficulty to his successors in the government. The Eastern Provinces were for the most part in a state of similar disorder. Illyricum has already been discussed, as most conveniently taken with the Gauls. For those farther east Cæsar's arrangements were no more successful in securing peace than in the West.

The victory at Pharsalia put MACEDONIA under Cæsar's control, and he apparently continued to govern it till B.C. 45 by his legates. While in Egypt (B.C. 48–7), (8) MACEDONIA. fearing, it seems, that it might be made a centre of resistance,[2] he directed Gabinius to go there with his legions, if the state of Illyricum allowed of it.[3] We

---

[1] Appian, b. c. iv. 36, 53–56 ; v. 26 ; Dio, 48, 21–23. It seems impossible to reconcile Appian and Dio. The course of events here indicated agrees chiefly with Dio, whose account appears on the whole the more reasonable.

[2] Cæs., b. c. iii. 102.   [3] *Id.*, b. *Alex.* 42.

have no farther information as to its government till the autumn of B.C. 45, when a large military force was stationed there; and in that, or the following year, Q. Hortensius—son of the famous orator—was made governor. Marcus Brutus was named by Cæsar to succeed him in B.C. 43, and Hortensius did, in fact, hand over the province to him at Thessalonica at the beginning of that year. But meanwhile Antony had induced the Senate to nominate himself (June, B.C. 44). He withdrew five of the legions and then managed to get the province transferred to his brother Gaius. When Antony was declared a *hostis*, the Senate revoked the nomination of Gaius and restored the province, along with Illyricum, to M. Brutus, who was in fact already in possession, having defeated and captured Gaius Antonius.

Closely connected with Macedonia was GREECE, which had been left, since B.C. 146, in a somewhat anomalous position. Thessaly indeed, was, to a great extent, incorporated with Macedonia; but the towns in Bœotia, as well as Athens and Sparta, were nominally free, though connected with Rome in such a way as to be sometimes spoken of separately as "provinces." So with the towns in the Peloponnese once forming the Achæan League. The League was dissolved and each town had a separate *fœdus* or charter.[1] But with all this local autonomy Greece was practically governed by Rome, and in certain cases the proprætor of Macedonia exercised jurisdiction in it. But as yet there was no "province" of Greece or even of Achaia, with a separate proconsul or proprætor. Cæsar, as in other cases, made temporary arrangements which afterwards became permanent under Augustus. In B.C. 48, Q. Fufius Calenus, one of his legates, was sent to take possession of Greek cities in Cæsar's interest, and remained at Patræ with troops till B.C. 47, exercising authority over the whole of the Peloponnese.[2] In

(9) GREECE.

---

[1] Drawn up by the commissioners after the fall of Corinth, B.C. 146.
[2] Cicero, *ad Att.* xi. 15 ; Cæsar, b. c. ii. 56, 106 ; Dio, 42, 14.

the autumn he went home and was rewarded by the consulship for the rest of the year. But in B.C. 46, Cæsar appointed Serv. Sulpicius Rufus governor of Greece, and his authority seems to have extended throughout the Peloponnese and as far north as Thessaly.[1] Sulpicius returned to Rome at the end of B.C. 45, or beginning of B.C. 44, and does not seem to have had a successor. Greece appears to have been tacitly allowed to revert to its old position of nominal freedom and real attachment to Macedonia. M. Brutus at any rate, as governor of Macedonia, assumed that he had authority in Greece. After the re-arrangement at Philippi (B.C. 42), it fell to Antony's share, who, for a time at least, yielded Achaia to Sext. Pompeius.[2]

As Cæsar was meditating a settlement of Syria, it was important that the Asiatic provinces should be in safe hands.

The Asiatic Provinces.

(10) BITHYNIA AND PONTUS.

To BITHYNIA and PONTUS—among the newest of Roman provinces—L. Tillius Cimber had been nominated. We know nothing of his antecedents except that we find him among the influential friends of Cæsar in B.C. 46 ; but his provincial appointment was readily confirmed by the Senate after his share in Cæsar's death.[3] He devoted himself to the collection of a fleet, with which he aided the pursuit of Dolabella, and afterwards assisted Brutus and Cassius.

The province of ASIA was quiet and wealthy. For financial and strategic reasons it was specially necessary at this time to have it in safe hands. Cæsar had nominated C.

(11) ASIA.

Trebonius, who had been his legate in Gaul and Britain, and had often been intrusted with important commands. He had stuck to his old general in the civil war and had been rewarded by the prætorship of B.C. 48, and the province of

---

[1] Servius had fought against Cæsar at Pharsalia, though his son was with Cæsar. After the battle he retired to Samos and refused to continue the war. See Cicero, *ad Fam.* iv. 3, 4, 11, 12 ; vi. 6 ; xiii. 17, 19, 23, 25, 28.
[2] App., b. c. v. 72.   [3] Cicero, *ad Fam.* vi. 12 ; App., b. c. iii. 2.

Farther Spain in the next year. Though he was not successful in Spain Cæsar continued to trust him sufficiently to send him to Asia. He did not actually strike a blow in the assassination, but he aided it by withdrawing Antony from the Senate on a treacherous pretence of business. His appointment was readily confirmed by the Senate, and he went to Asia purposing to fortify towns and collect troops to aid the party of the assassins. It was this—not alone his participation in the murder—which caused Dolabella, probably at the instigation and certainly with the approval of Antony,[1] to put him to death when refused admittance by him into Smyrna or Pergamus. At the end of the year the Senate had arranged that he was to be succeeded by one of the Consuls, Hirtius or Pansa. But after his murder the province remained in the hands of his quæstor,[2] and on the death of Hirtius and Pansa at Mutina it was transferred by the Senate to M. Brutus (to be held with Macedonia), who in the course of B.C. 42 made a progress through it to hold the *conventus*, to collect men and money, and to meet Cassius. It was, no doubt, heavily taxed; and after the battle of Philippi Antony took possession of it and again unmercifully drained its resources.

On quitting the province of CILICIA in July, B.C. 50, Cicero left it in charge of his quæstor, C. Cælius Caldus. Whether, in the confusion of the first years of civil war, any successor was appointed we do not know.
(12) CILICIA.
The province needed some re-settlement, for in B.C. 47 Cæsar stopped at Tarsus, on his way to Pontus, for some days, to meet the chief men and make certain regulations, of which he does not tell us the nature.[3] But it seems that then, or shortly afterwards, it was considerably reduced in extent. The

---

[1] See Cicero, 13 *Phil.* 23 (Antony's letter).

[2] P. Cornelius Lentulus Spinther. See his letter to Cicero, *ad Fam.* xii. 14, 15.

[3] Cæs., *b. Alex.* 66 : *rebus omnibus provinciæ et finitimarum civitatum constitutis* is all that we are told.

Phrygian "dioceses"—Laodicea, Apamea, and Synnada—were assigned to Asia, as well as most of Pisidia and Pamphylia. The remainder—Cilicia Aspera, and Campestris, with Cyprus —seem to have been held somewhat irregularly by Cæsar's own legates. It was afterwards treated by Antony as though at his own disposal, Cyprus and Cilicia Aspera being presented to Cleopatra, part of Phrygia with Lycaonia, Isaurica, and Pisidia to Amyntas, king of Galatia. The province, in fact, as known to Cicero, was almost separated from the Empire until reorganised by Augustus.

The province of SYRIA was extremely important in view of the danger from the Parthians. Bounded on the north by Mount Amanus it included Phœnicia and Cœle-Syria as far south as the head of the Red Sea and the eastern mouth of the Nile. On the east it was bounded by the Euphrates and the deserts of Arabia. After the organisation of Pompey in B.C. 63 it had been administered by proconsuls and the usual staff. In B.C. 57–6 it was held by Gabinius, who employed his forces for the restoration of Ptolemy Auletes to the throne of Egypt. In B.C. 54–3 it was held by Crassus; and after his fall at Carrhæ it was successfully defended and administered by C. Cassius as *quæstor* and *proquæstor*. In B.C. 51–50, while Cicero was in Cilicia, it was ruled by Bibulus; and in B.C. 49 Pompey secured it for his father-in-law, Q. Cæcilius Metellus Scipio, who collected troops and went to the aid of Pompey in Thessaly, and after Pharsalia escaped to Africa. It was then put in the hands of the quæstor, Sextus Iulius, a connection of the Dictator, with some legions, one of which had been left there by Cæsar in anticipation of the coming Parthian war. But a new complication had been introduced by Q. Cæcilius Bassus. This man had been with Pompey at Pharsalia and had escaped to Syria, where for a time he lived obscurely. But after a while, by tampering with the soldiers of Sextus Iulius, who was both incompetent and vicious, he induced them to assassinate their

(13) SYRIA.

commander and transfer their allegiance to himself.[1] Professing
to be lawful proconsul of Syria he fortified himself in Apamea,
and there repulsed forces sent by Cæsar under Antistius Vetus
and L. Statius Murcus successively. He made some agreement
with the Parthians which secured their aid ;[2] and though
Murcus was reinforced by Crispus governor of Bithynia, Bassus
was still unsubdued at the time of Cæsar's death. There had
been, therefore, a double need for a strong man in Syria, and
Cæsar had nominated C. Cassius, the former defender of it
against the Parthians. After Cæsar's death, however, Dolabella secured the passing of a law transferring Syria to himself
with the command against the Parthians. But some irregularity
in the auguries taken at the comitia gave Cassius a plausible
excuse for ignoring this law. Consequently when Dolabella
entered the province from the north, Cassius did so from the
south. After some successful movements in Palestine, Cassius
induced Murcus and Crispus, and finally Bassus himself, to
hand over their legions to him, as well as Trebonius's legate,
Allienus, who was bringing some legions from Egypt.[3] Thus
reinforced he shut up Dolabella in Laodicea and frightened
him into committing suicide. Syria therefore remained in the
hands of Cassius ; and when he fell at Philippi it was vacant.
In accordance with the agreement made with Octavian after
that battle it fell to the lot of Antony, who retained it
personally, or by his legates, till his death.

EGYPT was still an independent kingdom, ruled since B.C. 47
by Cleopatra. Nevertheless, there was a considerable Roman
force stationed in it, partly left by Gabinius, when
(14) EGYPT. he restored Ptolemy Auletes in B.C. 57–6, partly
stationed there by Cæsar himself. They must have been

---

[1] Dio, 47, 26. Appian gives two accounts of Bassus. In the first
he represents him as the real commander of the legions, while Sext. Iulius
was the nominal chief. He, however, gives an alternative account more
in accordance with that of Dio. See App., b. c. iii. 77 ; iv. 58, *sq.*

[2] Cicero, *ad Att.* xiv. 9.

[3] *Id., ad Fam.* xii. 11 (Cassius to Cicero) ; xii. 12.

somewhat in the position of the English troops supporting the authority of the Khedive, but prepared to resist all outside interference. So in this case the Romans retained a preponderating influence, though with no legal authority or right of raising revenue. These troops appear to have been in a very disorderly state, and in B.C. 50 murdered two of the sons of Bibulus who were among their officers.[1]

The district between Egypt and Roman Africa, called CYRENE, was once joined to Egypt and then governed by a king of its own (B.C. 117). This king (Ptolemy Apion), dying in B.C. 96 without issue, left his dominions to the Romans. The Roman government took over the royal estates, and placed a tax on the principal product of the country—silphium (valuable for its medicinal qualities)—but did not organise it as a province. The five principal cities[2] were allowed to retain a pretty complete autonomy. But upon disagreements between these states breaking out, the whole country in B.C. 74 was reduced to the form of a province governed by a *quæstor pro prætore*.[3] Six years later (B.C. 68–7) complaints as to the harbouring of pirates caused Q. Cæcilius Metellus to reduce CRETE also.[4] When Pompey superseded Metellus in B.C. 67, he introduced certain changes in the administration of both provinces, though there is no proof that he combined them as was done at a later date. In B.C. 44 indeed, they were assigned separately—Crete to Brutus and Cyrene to Cassius[5]—while Antony produced a memorandum of Cæsar's directing that Crete should be restored to liberty,[6] that is, should cease to pay *tributum*. At the division of the provinces after Philippi both were assigned

(15) CYRENE AND CRETE.

---

[1] Cicero, *ad Att.* vi. 5 ; Valer. Max., vi. 1, 15.

[2] Cyrene with four other cities—Apollonia, Ptolemais, Arsinoe, Berenice —formed a Pentapolis. (Livy, *Epit.* 70.)

[3] App., b. c. I. iii. *sq.* ; Sall., *hist. fr.* ii. 39.

[4] Vell. Pat., ii. 34 ; Dio, 36, 2 ; Iust. 39, 5 ; Livy, *Epit.* 100. The laws of Crete were left in force (Cic., *Mur.* § 74 ; *pro Flacc.* § 30).

[5] App., b. c. iii. 12, 16, 36 ; iv. 57 ; Dio, 47, 21.   [6] Cicero, 2 *Phil.* § 97.

to Antony, and he assumed the right some years later of forming out of them a kingdom for his daughter by Cleopatra.

It will be seen therefore that at Cæsar's death there was hardly any part of the Empire in which there were not elements of mischief more or less active. The most peaceful district was perhaps Greece, though it managed to put itself under the frown of the triumvirs by sympathising with Brutus, and later on under that of Octavian by sympathising with Antony. The disturbances which most affected the actual residents in Rome and Italy were those in Sicily and Sardinia, Gaul and Illyricum. The man who should put an end to these would seem a saviour of society. The struggles in the far East, though from a financial point of view they were of considerable importance, would not loom so large in the eyes of the Italians. We have now to trace the steps by which Augustus was able to satisfy the needs of the state; to restore peace and plenty to Italy; to organise and safeguard the provinces; and thus to be almost worshipped as the visible guarantee of order and tranquillity.

The general disorders in the Empire.

CHAPTER III

THE INHERITANCE

*Cui dabit partes scelus
expiandi Iuppiter ?*

THE news of his great-uncle's death reached Octavius at
Apollonia in the afternoon, just as he and his suite were
going to dinner. A vague rumour of some great
misfortune quickly spread through the town, and
many of the leading inhabitants hastened to the
house with zealous friendliness to ascertain its
truth. After a hasty consultation with his friends, Octavius
decided to get rid of most of them while inviting a few of the
highest rank to discuss with him what should be done. This
being effected with some difficulty, an anxious debate was
carried on into the night. Opinions were divided. One
party urged Octavius to go to the army in Macedonia, appeal
to its attachment to Cæsar, and call on the legions to follow
him to Rome to avenge the murdered Dictator.[1] Those who
thus advised trusted to the impression likely to be made by
Octavius's personal charm and the pity which his position
would excite. Others thought this too great an undertaking
for so young a man. They argued that the many friends
whom Cæsar had raised to positions of honour and profit

*News of Cæsar's
murder brought
to Apollonia,
March, B.C. 44.*

---

[1] The possibility of these legions crossing to Italy had caused no little
anxiety at Rome ; Cicero, *ad Att.* xiv. 16.

might be trusted to avenge his murder. They did not yet know that theirs were the very hands which had struck him down. After listening to the various opinions Octavius resolved to take no decisive step until he had reached Italy, had consulted his friends there, and had seen the state of affairs with his own eyes.

Preparations for crossing were begun at once, and in the few days before the start farther details of the assassination reached Apollonia. The citizens begged Octavius

Octavius
prepares to go
to Italy, April,
B.C. 44.

to stay, putting all the resources of the town at his disposal; and a number of officers and soldiers came from the army with tenders of service, whether to guard his person or to avenge the Dictator. But for the present he declined all offers. He thanked the Apolloniates and promised the town immunities and privileges—a promise which in after years he did not forget. He told the officers and soldiers that he would claim their services at some future time. For the present he did not need them: "only let them be ready when the time came." The conduct of the Martia and Quarta a few months later shewed that these feelings were genuine and lasting.

Octavius had a poor vessel and a stormy crossing, but landed in safety, probably at Hydruntum (*Otranto*), the nearest point in Calabria, and in fair weather only a five hours' voyage.[1] That fact and the state of the wind may have influenced the choice of the port. But he was also too much in the dark as to affairs in Italy to venture upon such a frequented landing-place as Brundisium, where he might have found himself in the midst of political enemies or hostile troops. From Hydruntum he went by land to Lupiæ, rather more than half way to Brundisium. There he first met some who had witnessed Cæsar's funeral, had heard the recitation of his will, and could tell him that he was adopted as Cæsar's son, and (with a deduction of a liberal legacy to the citizens) was heir

[1] Cicero, *ad Att.* xv. 21.

to three-quarters of his property,[1] the remaining fourth being divided between Cæsar's two other grand-nephews Q. Pedius and Lucius Pinarius. He learnt also that the Dictator's funeral, which by his will was to be conducted by Atia, had been performed in the Forum amidst great popular excitement, caused partly by the sight of his wounded body,[2] partly by Antony's speech, and had been followed by attacks on the houses of the chief assassins, who, after barricading themselves for three days on the Capitol, had found it necessary to retire from Rome, first to the villa of Brutus at Lanuvium, and then to Antium,[3] in spite of the amnesty voted in the Senate on the 17th of March.

Though deeply moved by this story Octavian did not allow his feelings to betray him into taking any false or hasty step. *Satis celeriter quod satis bene* was his motto now as in after life.[4] He went on to Brundisium, having ascertained that it was not occupied by enemies, and there received letters from his mother and step-father confirming what he had already heard.

Octavian accepts the inheritance and name, May, B.C. 44.

His mother begged him to join her at once, to avoid the jealousies roused by his adoption. Philippus advised him to accept neither inheritance nor name, and to hold aloof from public business. The advice was, no doubt, prompted by affection, and was

---

[1] Suetonius (*Iul.* 83) says, "three-fourths"; so also does Nicolas Dam. 17 (τρία μέρη τῶν χρημάτων). But Livy (*Ep.* 116) says "one-half" (*ex semisse*). It is possible Livy may refer to the amount left when the legacy of 300 sesterces to each citizen was deducted. Nicolas seems to think, however, that this legacy was charged on the remaining fourth. Octavian certainly undertook to pay it, but then Pinarius and Pedius handed over their shares to him.

[2] Appian (b. c. ii. 147) says that the body itself was not seen during Antony's *laudatio*, but that a wax figure was displayed which by some mechanical contrivance was made to revolve and show all the wounds.

[3] Nicolas (§ 17) would seem to send them straight to Antium. But from Cicero's letters it is clear that Brutus at any rate went first to Lanuvium, *ad Att.* xiv. 10, 21; xv. 9. They seem to have gone to Antium towards the end of May or beginning of June.

[4] Suet., *Aug.* 25.

natural in the circumstances. But though Octavian never blustered, neither did he easily turn aside : he wrote back declaring his determination to accept. His own friends henceforth addressed him as " Cæsar," his full name now being Gaius Iulius Cæsar Octavianus.[1] The adoption indeed was not complete without the formal passing of a *lex curiata ;* but though that was delayed for more than a year, the new name was assumed at once. He complied with his mother's wish that he should visit her first, and he soon had the satisfaction of feeling that though Philippus was still opposed, her heart was with him in the manly resolve to sustain the great part which Cæsar's affection had assigned to him. Cicero mentions in a letter of April 11th that Octavius had arrived in Italy, and on the 18th that he had reached Naples. On the 19th Balbus—the Dictator's friend and agent—called on him and learned from his own lips his resolve to accept the inheritance. On the 22nd Cicero met him at his stepfather's villa near Puteoli, and anxiously watched for any indication of his political aims. He was only partly satisfied.

"Octavius here treats me with great respect and friendliness. His own people addressed him as ' Cæsar,' but as Philippus did not do so, I did not do it either. I declare it is impossible for him to be a good citizen ! He is surrounded by such a number of people who actually threaten our friends with death. He says the present state of things is intolerable."[2]

It was not Octavian's cue as yet to break openly with the aristocrats. The first struggles for his rights were likely to be with Antony, in which the aid of Cicero and his party would be useful. At the same time he was too cautious and selfcontrolled to commit himself or betray his real intentions, which remained an enigma to the emotional orator, who hardly ever spoke without doing so. Cicero consoled himself by the

[1] The last being the adjectival form of his original name, in accordance with the usual custom in cases of adoption.

[2] Cicero, *ad Att.* xiv. 5, 10, 11, 12.

reflection that at any rate Octavian's ·claims must cause a quarrel with Antony. Yet he was indignant that this stripling could go to Rome without risk, while Brutus and Cassius and the other " heroes " of the dagger could not. Octavian's journey to Rome was for the twofold purpose of giving formal notice to the prætor urbanus that he accepted the inheritance, and of making a statement of his intentions as administrator of the will at a public assembly. For the latter he needed to be introduced to the meeting by a tribune. For this service he relied on Lucius Antonius. All three brothers were in office this year—Marcus consul, Gaius prætor, Lucius tribune ; and as supporters of the late Cæsar they could not in decency refuse him this opportunity of declaring his sentiments.

Octavian reached Rome in the first week of May, duly accepted the inheritance, and was introduced to a *contio* by

Octavian and M. Antonius. Lucius Antonius about the 10th of that month.[1] The speech was not satisfactory to the Ciceronian party. He declared his intention to carry out his " father's " will as to the legacy to the people, and to celebrate the games at the dedication of the temple of Venus promised by Cæsar. Preparations for them were begun at once, two of the Dictator's friends, Matius and Postumius, being selected to superintend them.[2] But though confining himself to expressions of veneration for his " father's " memory, and uttering no threats against any one, Octavian had not given up for a moment his resolve to punish the murderers. The amnesty voted in the Senate he regarded as a temporary expedient. All that was needed was an accuser, and he did not mean that such a person should be long wanting. But meanwhile his first business was to secure his own position and the possession of Cæsar's

[1] Cicero, *ad Att.* xiv. 20, 21. Dio (45, 6) says that the introducing tribune was Tib. Canutius. But it seems probable that this refers to a second speech.

[2] Cic., *ad Att.* xv. 2. There is a singularly manly and frank letter from Matius to Cicero (*ad Fam.* xi. 28), defending his attachment to Cæsar and his services to Octavian.

property. This at once brought him into collision with Antony.

The financial arrangements of the late Dictator were to a great degree to blame for this. He seems to have introduced the system of the *fiscus*, though without the name known in later times : that is, large sums of money were deposited in the temple of Ops to his order, separate from the public *ærarium* of the temple of Saturnus, and not clearly distinguished from his own private property. It was as though a Chancellor of the Exchequer paid portions of the revenue to his private banking account, and were to die suddenly without leaving any means of distinguishing between public and private property.[1] Cicero says that this money (700,000,000 sesterces, or about five and a half millions sterling) was the proceeds of the sale of confiscated properties,[2] and there was, it seems, much other property in lands and houses from the same source. The claim by an heir of Cæsar would be met by a double opposition—from the government, which would regard the whole as public ; and from the owners or their representatives, who might have hopes of recovering parts of it. For at Rome confiscation did not bar claims under marriage settlements, or for debts secured on properties. The large sum at the temple of Ops had been taken over entirely by Antony the Consul, nominally as being public money, really —as Cicero affirms—to liquidate his own enormous debts. It is very likely that Antony shared the spoil with others, perhaps with his colleague Dolabella, and they may have satisfied their

The money at the temple of Ops.

---

[1] Appian, b. c. 3, 20, τῶν προσόδων ἐξ οὗ παρῆλθεν ἐπὶ τὴν ἀρχὴν ἐς αὐτὸν ἀντὶ τοῦ ταμιείου συμφερομένων. The sole management of the Treasury had been committed to Cæsar in B.C. 45 (Dio, 43, 44, τὰ δημόσια χρήματα μόνον διοικεῖν). He had taken it out of the hands of the *quæstors* and appointed two *præfecti* to manage it : but it does not seem that they had anything to do with the money in the temple of Ops, as to which there was some doubt as to its being "public money" in the ordinary sense.

[2] Cicero, 1 *Phil.* § 17 ; 2 *Phil.* § 93.

consciences with some partial use of it tor public purposes.[1] At any rate it was not forthcoming when Octavian put in his claim. Even in regard to such property as was handed over to him he was constantly harassed by lawsuits. Claimants were instigated, as he believed, by one or other of the Antonies; while Gaius Antonius, acting *prætor urbanus* for Brutus, would often preside in the court. He was resolved, however, to carry out Cæsar's will, even if he had to sell his own paternal estate and draw upon his mother's resources. But it seems, after all, that the property of Cæsar which he did manage to get, or his own wealth, was so ample, that he was able to do this without crippling himself. Pinarius and Pedius got their shares, but handed them over to him, perhaps as being too heavily weighted with legacies to be of much value to them, or thinking that his great future made it a good investment. At any rate the legacies were paid, the games given, and when some months later he proceeded to enroll two legions of veterans he was able to pay each man a bounty amounting to something like £20 of our money.[2] At no time in his career does he seem to have had serious money difficulties. No doubt his resources were always large, but he must also have had the valuable faculty of husbanding them in small matters, while always having enough for large outlays.

But it was not only in regard to money that Octavian

---

[1] Cicero, in 2 *Phil.* § 93, seems to assume that Antony had taken the money all at once. But from Cicero's own letters it would seem that the process of despoiling the temple of Ops was a gradual one, and that the use made of the money by Antony was more or less a matter of conjecture. On the 27th of April he writes: "You mention plundering going on at the temple of Ops I, too, was a witness to that at the time" (*ad Att.* xiv. 14). On the 7th of May he says that Dolabella had a great share of it (*ad Att.* xiv. 18). In November he says that his nephew Quintus knew all about it, and meant to reveal it to the public (*ad Att.* xvi. 14). Appian (b. c. iii. 20) makes Antony say to Octavian : "The money transferred to my house was not so large a sum as you conjecture, nor is any part of it in my custody now. The men in power—except Dolabella and my brothers—divided up the whole of it as the property of a tyrant."

[2] Cic., *ad Att.* xvi. 8.

found himself thwarted by Antony and his brothers. A

Difficulties about
Octavian's
adoption.

tribune, probably Lucius Antonius himself, prevented the formal passing of the *lex curiata* for his adoption, with a view of weakening his claims upon the inheritance. When he wished to be elected tribune in the place of Cinna, who had fallen a victim to the mob in mistake for L. Cinna, a prætor who had spoken against Cæsar, he was prevented by the partisans of Antony.[1] There was indeed a legal obstacle in the fact that he was now a patrician,[2] was under age, and had not held the quæstorship, though this last was a breach of custom rather than of law. Lastly, Antony treated him with studied disrespect, keeping him waiting in his ante-room ; while Lucius Antonius and the other tribunes forbade him to place Cæsar's gilded chair in the Circus at his games.[3]

It was clear that a breach between the two was imminent. The younger man was not abashed by the years or high office

Octavian and
the Optimates.
After the meeting of the Senate
in June.

of the other ; and though some formal reconciliation was brought about by common friends or by military officers, Octavian seems to have allowed the Ciceronians to believe that he intended to join them in opposing Antony. His attentions to them became more marked after the meeting of the Senate of the 1st of June. To this meeting the Constitutionalists had been looking forward as likely to bring the uncertainty to an end. At it the question of the provinces was to be settled ; the two consuls, with the aid of a committee, were to report on what were the genuine *acta* of Cæsar ; and some means were to be found to enable Brutus and Cassius to carry on their duties as prætors in Rome with safety.

---

[1] Dio, 45, 6 ; this seems a different case from that mentioned by App., b. c. iii. 47, and referred to by Cicero, *ad Att.* xvi. 15, as happening later in this same year.

[2] See *ante* p. 14 : Dio, 45, 2 ; Sueton., *Aug.* 2, 10 ; Tac., *Ann.* xi. 25.

[3] Dio, 45, 4 ; Cicero, *ad Att.* xv. 3.

Meanwhile Antony had been availing himself of the papers of Cæsar as though the committee had already reported. He had also been securing himself—as he thought—

Antony and Cæsar's *acta* and veterans.

by visiting the colonies of Cæsar's veterans in Campania [1] and by gradually collecting a bodyguard. This had now assumed sufficiently formidable proportions to overawe the Senate.[2] It is true that he had experienced difficulties at Capua, where the existing coloni resented his attempt to plant others in the same territory ; but, on the whole, he seems to have improved his position by his tour in April and May. Then again Lepidus had visited Sext. Pompeius in Spain, and was reported to have induced him, on condition of recovering his father's property, to return to Rome and place his naval and military forces (amounting to more than six legions) at the disposal of the consuls.[3] This, thinks Cicero, would make Antony irresistible ; and so no doubt thought Octavian also.

Nor did the meetings of the Senate in June effect anything to dissipate these fears. What was done for Brutus and Cassius satisfied neither party. They were offered

The position of Brutus and Cassius. The change of provinces.

the *cura annonæ*, superintendence of the corn supply—Cassius in Sicily, Brutus in Asia—which would give them a decent pretext for being absent from Rome for the rest of the year. They, however, regarded this offer as an insult.[4] So also in regard to the provinces :

[1] Cicero, 2 *Phil.* § 100 ; *ad Att.* xiv. 20, 21.

[2] *Id., ad Att.* xiv. 3 (9th April) ; xv. 4 (24th May) ; 2 *Phil.* § 108 ; Appian, b. c. iii. 5. The Senate had been induced to vote him a bodyguard. See the letter of Brutus and Cassius to Antony in Cicero, *ad Fam.* xi. 2.

[3] Dio, 45, 10 ; Cic., *ad Att.* xvi. 1. The negotiation after all fell through on the question of Sextus's recovering the actual house and property of his father, much of which was in Antony's hands (Cic., *ad Att.* xvi. 4 ; Dio, 45, 9). He refused to accept a mere money compensation. Eventually, when the Senate had broken with Antony, it made terms with Sextus, appointing him commander of the naval forces of the Republic. Consequently he was proscribed by the Triumvirs. App., b. c. iii. 4.

[4] Cic., *ad Att.* xv. 10, 11.

Brutus and Cassius were deprived of Macedonia and Syria, which Cæsar had assigned to them respectively, and were offered the unimportant governorships of Crete and Cyrene. But Antony in the same meetings secured still greater military strength for himself by an arrangement with Dolabella. The latter was appointed to Syria and the command against the Parthians by a *lex ;* and he then induced the Senate to give Macedonia to himself, with the command of the legions stationed there, one of which he had bargained with Dolabella to hand over to him. These decrees having been passed,[1] he sent his brother Gaius over at once to announce the fact to the legions in Macedonia and to give them notice that they might at any time be summoned to Italy. For Antony himself had no intention of going to Macedonia. His private resolve was to hold Gallia Cisalpina with the largest force possible, as giving him most hold on Italy. He had only accepted Macedonia in order to get these legions into his hands. At the same time he carried a repeal of Cæsar's law confining the tenure of a province for a proprætor to one, and for a proconsul to two, years.

Though this increasing power of Antony was naturally calculated to alarm Octavius, he was, on the other hand, opposed

Antony gets himself nominated to Cisalpina Gaul.

to Decimus Brutus—one of the assassins—retaining Gallia Cisalpina. He therefore supported Antony in carrying a law conferring that province on him at the end of his consulship.[2] The Senators now saw that they had been tricked. They had given Antony the Macedonian legions without conditions, and he would now use them in another province given him by a *lex*—over which they had no control. Suggestions were made to remove

---

[1] Cicero (2 *Phil.* § 109) declares that Antony's bodyguard was stationed round the Senate—some of them being foreign mercenaries—and that his opponents therefore did not venture to enter the house.

[2] Appian, b. c. iii. 29–30. But Appian in regard to the order of events here is very confused and often wrong.

Gallia Cisalpina from the list of provinces, and incorporate it (as was afterwards done by Augustus) in Italy, thus doing away with any pretext for a proconsul residing there with legions. But for the present the law stood which assigned it to Antony for B.C. 43. It appears to have been passed by the beginning of July, and he at once sent word to his brother to bring the legions over. They were expected in July,[1] but did not actually arrive till nearly three months later. Meanwhile a war of recriminations was maintained between Antony the consul and Brutus and Cassius the prætors by letters or edicts. Antony accused the prætors of collecting forces hostile to the government, the prætors accused Antony of making it impossible for them to come to Rome by denouncing them in speeches and edicts, in breach of his promise. On the 1st of August L. Calpurnius Piso—father-in-law of the late Cæsar— inveighed against Antony in the Senate, ending with a hostile motion, of the exact nature of which we are not informed. But he could get no one to speak or vote with him, so completely cowed were the Senators by Antony's military forces.[2] On the other hand, Antony was uneasy at the growing popularity of Octavian, especially among the veterans. He had himself made a bid for their favour by two commissions for assigning land to them both in Italy and the provinces. But the veterans were suspicious; they had expected some signal act of vengeance for the murder of Cæsar; and at the same time Antony's lavish grants of public land to unworthy favourites impoverished the exchequer and diminished the amount available for distribution. They lowered his popularity with the veterans as much as they annoyed the Senators, who yet did not venture to oppose him.

The friction between the two men—varied by occasional reconciliations—became more and more acute, until about the end of September it was rumoured that Octavian had suborned

[1] Cicero, *ad Att.* xvi. 4, 5.
[2] *Id.,* 1 *Phil.* § 14 ; *ad Att.* xvi. 7 ; *ad Fam.* xii. 2.

men to assassinate Antony. Of course Octavian disclaimed it, and upon Antony giving out that certain men had been found in his house with daggers, he went openly with an offer to serve along with his friends among his bodyguards. The popular belief was that Antony had invented the whole story to discredit him ; but Cicero and others of his party both believed and approved, and subsequent writers are divided in opinion. Nicolas of Damascus probably gives Octavian's own version, according to which Antony was unable to produce the pretended assassins to a council of his friends, or to induce them to advise active retaliation upon Octavian. Appian points out that it was not to Octavian's interest just then that Antony should disappear, for it would have been a great encouragement to the party of the Assassins, of whose real sentiments towards himself he was no doubt aware.[1]

Attempted assassination of Antony.

For with this party his alliance was a matter of great doubt. In June Cicero had said of him :

Octavian and the Optimates.

"In Octavian, as I have perceived, there is no little ability and spirit ; and he seems likely to be as well disposed to our heroes as I could wish. But what confidence one can feel in a man of his age, name, inheritance, and upbringing may well give us pause. His stepfather, whom I saw at Antium, thinks none at all. However, we must foster him, and, if nothing else, keep him estranged from Antony. Marcellus will be doing admirable service if he gives him good advice. Octavian seems devoted to him, but has no great confidence in Pansa and Hirtius."[2]

Philippus was not a man for whom Cicero had a great respect.[3] But Marcellus, the husband of Octavia (Cos. B.C. 50),

---

[1] Nicolas (§ 30), Appian (b. c. iii. 39), Plutarch (*Ant.* 16), acquit Augustus. The two writers who adopt Cicero's view of the truth of the accusation are Seneca (*de Clement.* 1, 9, 1) and Suetonius (*Aug.* 10). See Cicero, *ad Fam.* xii. 23.

[2] *ad Att.* xv. 12 [3] See *ante*, p. 3.

was a sound aristocrat and a trustworthy man. Still Octavian had done nothing since to identify himself with the conservative party, in spite of his differences with Antony. With Cicero himself he kept up friendly communications; yet at the final breach between Cicero and Antony in September, it does not seem to have occurred to Cicero to put forward Octavian as Antony's opponent; nor does he mention him in the first two Philippics. It was Octavian's own independent action which first shewed that he was ready and able to assume that position, and Cicero viewed this at first with anxiety and almost dismay.

Antony left Rome on the 9th of October to meet the Macedonian legions at Brundisium. Octavian no longer hesitated. Sending agents to tamper with the loyalty of the newly arrived legions, he himself went a round of the veterans in Campania, offering them a bounty of 500 denarii (about £20), if they would enlist again. In doing this he acted wholly on his own initiative and without authority from Senate or people, and without holding any office giving him military command.[1] In after years Augustus regarded this as the first step in his public career, the first service rendered to the State : "When nineteen years old I raised an army on my own initiative and at my own expense, with which I restored to liberty the republic which had been crushed under the tyranny of a faction." And not only did he reckon this his first public service; the wording of this statement is a declaration that he thereby adopted the policy and was continuing the work of his "father," for he uses the very phrase which Cæsar had used in justifying himself.[2]

Octavian enrolls veterans.

[1] He had the title *Imperator* inherited from Cæsar (Dio, 43, 44) ; but this was a mere honorary title, and could not be held to give *imperium*. He was careful to use it however, as in the inscription recording the formation of the triumvirate. . . . EMILIVS M. ANTONIVS. IMP. CÆSAR. III VIR R.P.C. A.D. IV KAL. DEC. AD. PRID. KAL. IAN. SEXT. . . .

[2] *Monum. Ancyr.* I, annos undeviginti natus exercitum privato consilio et privata impensa comparavi : per quem rem publicam *dominatione factionis*

This phrase illustrates another point also. Ostensibly the enrolment of veterans was to protect himself against Antony. Perhaps he did not yet see how it was to be done, but at the bottom of his heart was the purpose of checkmating, if not destroying, the clique which had caused Cæsar's murder, though for the moment he was with them in opposition to Antony, and was eager to have Cicero's support and approval. Yet how doubtful and uneasy the orator felt is shewn by two letters in which he tells what Octavian was doing.

"Puteoli, 2 November. On the evening of the 1st I got a letter from Octavian. He is entering upon a serious undertaking. He has won over to his views all the veterans at Casilinum and Calatia. And no wonder : he gives a bounty of 500 denarii apiece. Clearly his view is a war with Antony under his own leadership. So I perceive that before many days are over we shall be in arms. But whom are we to follow ? Consider his name, consider his age ! Again, he demands to begin with a secret interview with me at Capua of all places ! It is really quite childish to suppose that it can be kept quiet. I have written to explain to him that it is neither necessary nor practicable. He sent a certain Cæcina of Volaterræ to me, an intimate friend of his own, who brought me news that Antony was on his way to the city with the *Alaudæ*, was imposing money contribution on the municipal towns, and was marching at the head of the legion with colours flying. He wanted my opinion, whether he should start for Rome with his legion of 3,000 veterans, or should hold Capua, and so intercept Antony's advance, or should join the three Macedonian legions now sailing by the Mare Superum, which he hopes are devoted to himself. They refused to accept a bounty offered them by Antony, as my informant at least asserts. They even used grossly insulting language to him and moved off when he attempted to address them. In short, Octavian offers himself as our military leader, and thinks that our right policy is to stand by him. On my part I advised his making for Rome. For I think he will have, not only the city mob, but, if he can impress them with confidence, the loyalists also on his side. Oh, Brutus ! Where are you ! What an opportunity you are losing ! I did not actually foresee this, but I thought that something of the sort would happen."

----

oppressam in libertatem vindicavi. Compare Cæsar, *b. civ.* 1, 22, ut se et Populum Romanum *factione paucorum oppressum in libertatem vindicaret,*

"Puteoli [3] November. Two letters on the same day from Octavian! His present view is that I should come to Rome at once, and that he wishes to act through the Senate. I told him that a meeting of the Senate was impossible before the 1st of January, and I believe it is so. But he adds also, 'and by your advice.' In short he insists, while I suspend judgment. I don't trust his youth, I am in the dark as to his disposition. I am not able to do anything without your friend Pansa. I am afraid of Antony succeeding, and I don't like moving far from the sea. At the same time I fear some great *coup* being struck without my being there. Varro for his part dislikes the youth's plan. I don't agree with him. He has forces on which he can depend. He can count on Decimus Brutus, and is making no secret of his intentions. He is organising his men in companies at Capua, he is paying them their bounty money. War seems to be ever coming nearer and nearer."

In spite of these half-hearted and doubtful expressions of Cicero, the Senate at his own suggestion was presently glad to approve Octavian's action, and to accept his aid.

Antony's breach
with the Senate,
November—De-
cember, B.C. 44. For events now followed quickly. When Antony met the legions at Brundisium, sent over by his brother Gaius,[2] he seems at first to have found them ready to obey him. But difficulties were presently promoted by the agents of Octavian, who offered the men liberal bounties, or scattered *libelli* among them denouncing Antony's tyranny and neglect of Cæsar's memory, and urging Octavian's claim on their allegiance. Signs of mutiny soon shewed themselves, and after a stormy meeting at which some officers and men used insubordinate language, Antony arrested and put to death several of the officers as ringleaders, and about 300 men.[3] These severities, followed by more liberal offers and some conciliatory language, seemed for the time to put an end to the mutiny. Selecting therefore a "prætorian cohort" from the legions, Antony started for Rome, ordering the rest to march in detachments up the coast road to Ariminum, where the *via Æmilia* through the valley of the Po begins. In Cicero's letters

---

[1] Cicero, *ad Att.* xvi. 8 and 9   [2] *Id.*, *ad Fam.* xii. 23.
[3] App., b. c. iii. 43-45 ; Cic., 3 *Phil.* § 10 ; Dio, 45, 13.

of the 8th, 11th, and 12th of November are recorded the various
rumours of his approach, and the anxieties as to what he intended
to do at Rome.[1] He arrived about the 20th in full military
array, and entered the city with a strong bodyguard, the rest
of his men being encamped outside the walls. He did not stay
long however. Having summoned the Senate for the 25th, in
an edict, in which he denounced the character and aims of
Octavian,[2] he went to Tibur, where he had ordered his new
levies to muster. Here he delivered a speech, which Cicero
afterwards described as " pestilent." [3] On the 25th, however, he
did not appear in the Senate. A second edict postponed the
meeting to the 29th. Cicero insinuates that his non-appearance
on the 25th was caused by some extra debauch. But, in fact,
the reason may have been the news about the *legio Martia*,
which, instead of going to Ariminum, had turned off from the
coast road and reached Alba Fucensis. It might be of course
that the legion was on its way to join Antony at Tibur, to
which there was a good road from Alba Fucensis (*via Valeria*).
Antony therefore went to Alba, but found the gates closed,
and was greeted by a shower of arrows from the walls. It was
clear that this legion at least did not mean to serve him. He
came to Rome for the meeting of the Senate on the 29th, but
was informed just before it that the Quarta had followed the
example of the Martia, and was at Alba Fucensis. He understood that these legions meant to join Octavian, and he no
longer thought it possible to get Octavian declared a *hostis*,
though one of his partisans was ready to propose it. Having
therefore transacted some formal business—chiefly the allotment
of provinces, in which his brother Gaius obtained Macedonia,
and a supplicatio in honour of Lepidus, he hurriedly returned to Tibur. His friends and supporters visited him in
great numbers ; but within a few days he was on his march to

[1] Cic., *ad Att.* xvi. 10, 13 a, 13 b, 14.
[2] *Id.*, 3 *Phil.* § 19.
[3] *pestifera*, 13 *Phil.* § 19.

Ariminum to join what remained of the five Macedonian legions.[1]

Antony's object was to attack Decimus Brutus, whose forces were concentrated at Mutina. But at any rate, he was gone from Rome, and Octavian had won the first trick in the game. Cicero attributes Antony's lowered tone in the Senate, and his hurried departure, to Octavian's promptness and success in raising the veterans, and inducing the Martia and Quarta to desert him. At first, however, he had not felt easy as to the young man's intentions. Writing from Puteoli on the 5th of November he tells Atticus that he gets a letter from Octavian every day, begging him to come to Capua and once more to save the republic, or, if not, at least to go to Rome. Cicero is "shamed to refuse and yet afraid to take"; but owns that Octavian is acting with vigour, and will probably enter Rome in great force. But he doubts whether the young man understands the situation, or the terrorism established by Antony in the Senate. He had better wait, he thinks, till the new consulate begins on January 1st.[2] About the 12th of November, he tells Atticus that if Octavian wins now, the fear is that he will confirm Cæsar's *acta* more completely than ever, which will be against the interests of Brutus, while, if he is beaten, Antony will become more despotic still.[3] Early in December (or the end of November), he mentions with alarm the possibility of Octavian being elected for a chance vacancy in the Tribunate[4]; and assents to a remark made by Atticus, that though Octavian had given

Cicero's doubts as to Octavian's intentions.

---

[1] Cicero, 3 *Phil.* §§ 19–27 ; 5 *Phil.* § 23 ; 13 *Phil.* § 19 ; App., b. c. iii. 45.
[2] Cic., *ad Att.* xvi. 11.   [3] *Id.* xvi. 14.
[4] *Id.* xvi. 15. It seems from Appian (b. c. iii. 31) that Octavian was not a candidate, but he was generally supposed to wish it, and that therefore many were going to vote for him. He ostensibly supported another candidate—Flaminius. Antony stopped the election on the ground that there was no need to fill up a vacancy so late in the year. This settled the question. But it is doubtful whether this does not refer to an earlier occasion.

Antony a notable check, "they must wait to see the end."
Again he says to Oppius, " I cannot be warmly on his side
without having some security that he will cordially embrace
the friendship of Brutus and Cassius and the other tyran-
nicides." [1]

On the 9th of December, however, when he came to Rome
after Antony's departure, Cicero made up his mind that for the
present all distrust was to be dismissed or at
least concealed. Octavian had mustered his forces
at Alba Fucensis, and after some communications
with the Senate—which warmly welcomed his offer of aid—had
started with his legions on the track of Antony ; who before
the end of the year began the investment of Mutina, upon
the refusal of Decimus Brutus to quit the province.

*Octavian begins
his march.*

Accordingly, on the 20th of December, Cicero himself proposed a resolution in the Senate authorising the Consuls-desig-
nate to provide for the safe meeting of the Senate on the 1st of
January ; approving of an edict of Decimus Brutus, just
arrived, in which he forbade any one with imperium entering
his province to succeed him ; directing all provincial governors
to retain their provinces till successors were named by the
Senate ; and, lastly, approving the action of " Gaius Cæsar "
in enrolling the veterans, and of the Martia and Quarta in
having joined him. These resolutions were to be formally put
to the Senate on the 1st of January by the new consuls. [2]
Accordingly on that and the following days, after somewhat
stormy debates, these decrees were passed, as well as one which
acknowledged the services of Octavian, and gave
him the rank of proprætor with imperium. It
was also enacted that in regard to elections to
office he should be considered to have held the
quæstorship. He thus became a member of the Senate, with
a right of speaking among the *prætorii*, and consequently with
a plausible claim to stand for the consulship, in spite of his

*Octavian is
recognised by
the Senate, and
obtains impe-
rium, Jan.
B.C. 43.*

[1] Cicero, *ad Att.* xvi. 15, 3.   [2] *Id., ad Fam.* xi. 6 ; 3 *Phil.* §§ 37–39.

youth. A second decree—after the battles at Mutina—gave him *consularia ornamenta.*[1]

Octavian was now fully launched on his public career. He had shown both Antony and the Senate that he was no negligible quantity. Though the Senate neither liked nor trusted him, he had played his cards with such skill that it was forced to treat him as its champion ; while Antony had contrived to put himself in such clear opposition to the constitutional claims of the Senate, that Octavian could attack him without thereby committing himself to the support of the Assassins, and had made himself so strong that (if he proved successful against Antony) he would hereafter be able to dictate his own terms. Cicero saw this clearly enough, but he hoped that the defeat of Antony would secure to the side of the Senate the governors of Gaul and Spain with their legions,[2] and that thus supported they would be able to discard their youthful champion. " He was," he said later on, " to be complimented, distinguished, and —extinguished." [3] We shall now see how the hopes of the sanguine orator were once more blasted, and how all these intrigues were baffled by the wary policy and cool persistence of " the boy."

---

[1] The passages are Cicero, 5 *Phil.* §§ 45–47 ; 11 *Phil.* § 20 ; 13 *Phil.* § 39 ; *Monum. Ancyr.* § 3 ; Livy, *Ep.* 118 ; C. I. L. x. 8375 ; Suet., *Aug.* 10, 26. Dio (40, 29) says that he was in the Senate ἐν τοῖς τεταμιευκόσι---*inter quæstorios.* This may be a misunderstanding of Cicero's proposal that for *purposes of election* he was to count as having been quæstor. The rank of proprætor was necessary for his command in the army, not for his entrance into the Senate.

[2] Pollio in Bætica, Lepidus in Gallia Narbonensis and Hispania Citerior, and Plancus in Northern Gaul.

[3] *Laudandum, ornandum, tollendum* (Cic., *ad Fam.* xi. 20, 21). This epigram seems to have been inspired by the exultant hopes roused by the news of the battle of Forum Gallorum.

CHAPTER IV

THE CONSULSHIP AND TRIUMVIRATE

Gravesque
principum amicitias.

THE campaign of Mutina, in which Octavian had now embarked, was ended by two battles—one at Forum Gallorum on

Octavian's position at the beginning of B.C. 43.

the 15th, and another at Antony's camp on the 21st of April. After the latter date there were military movements of some interest and importance, but no actual conflict. Before these battles Octavian's position had been difficult and delicate ; and though it was much improved after them, it was not in the way expected by the Senate. The change was due to his own prudence and energy. Since his start from Alba to follow Antony the aspect of affairs at Rome had been much modified, and he had had good reason to doubt the favour of the party over whom Cicero was now exercising a predominant influence. Cicero appears indeed to have kept up a constant correspondence with Octavian, in which he did his best by flattery and argument to retain his aid and lull his suspicions. But there were facts which it must have been difficult for him to explain to Octavian's satisfaction. It is true that besides the honours voted to him in the Senate in the first week of B.C. 43, he had been joined with the other magistrate in the *Senatus-consultum ultimum*, empowering them to "see that the state took no harm."[1] But though the decrees also gave him a constitutional right to command soldiers,[2] yet the despatch of the two consuls to the seat of war deprived him of the chief command; while the more moderate party had carried over Cicero's head a resolution to send three commissioners to negotiate with Antony. Cicero asserts that they were only authorised to convey to Antony the Senate's order that he was to quit the Gallic province. That was not, however, the view of the commissioners themselves. One of them—Serv. Sulpicius Rufus—died on the journey; but the other two—L. Calpurnius Piso and L. Marcius Philippus —brought back some proposals from Antony in February, which, had they been accepted, might perhaps have secured the safety of Brutus and Cassius, but would certainly have left Octavian out in the cold, without any pretext for keeping up his military force.

Antony proposed to give up the Cisalpine province, on condition of receiving Transalpine Gaul—exclusive of Narbonensis—with the six legions already under him, supplemented by those at present commanded by Dec. Brutus, for five years, or for such time as Brutus and Cassius should be consuls or proconsuls. Secondly, on condition that the *acta* of his consulship—including the use of the money from the temple of Ops and his grants of lands—should be left intact ; and that those serving with him should have complete indemnity.[3] The envoys were against the extreme measure of declaring a state of war (rather than a *tumultus*) and proclaiming Antony a *hostis*, and the majority of the Senate agreed with them and voted for further negotiations. It was a strange position. Octavian

Antony's proposals.

----

[1] *Monum. Ancyr.* § 1, respublica ne quid detrimenti caperet me pro prætore cum consulibus providere iussit. This was a general order, neither Antony nor any particular *hostis* being named.

[2] Octavian first assumed the *fasces* (symbol of imperium) on the 7th of January (C. I. L. x. 8375.)   [3] Cicero, 8 *Phil.* §§ 25–28.

had been authorised by the Senate to drive Antony from Cisalpine Gaul. One of the consuls—Aulus Hirtius—had left Rome with two legions, and had, in fact, come into contact with the enemy in a cavalry skirmish at Claterna ; the other consul, Pansa, was also preparing to follow. Yet the Senate was negotiating with Antony as though he were not a *hostis*, but a citizen with a grievance. The time was soon to come when Octavian, too, would find it convenient to make terms with Antony ; but nothing could have been more against his interests than the present action of the Senate. It would seem to him a cynical disregard of their mutual obligations. Nor was this the worst. Antony's offer as to Brutus and Cassius was only an offer to recognise an accomplished fact. These two leaders in the assassination had been already nominated by the Senate to Macedonia and Syria. Cicero was in constant correspondence with them, addressing them as the chief hope of the constitution, and suggesting that their armies might be used to maintain the hold of the party on Italy. Trebonius, moreover, had been sent to Asia with the express understanding that he was to fortify that province and collect money to support Brutus and Cassius. When news came that Trebonius had been put to death by Dolabella, the latter was declared a *hostis* by the Senate, and his punishment entrusted to Cassius.

These facts must have gradually made it quite clear to Octavian that the complete triumph of the Ciceronian party

Antony's letter to Octavian. would be no less damaging to him than that of Antony. But though skilful use was made of them by Antony himself in a letter addressed to Hirtius and Octavian,[1] the young Cæsar was not to be induced to take

---

[1] The letter is preserved in the 13th Philippic, with Cicero's bitter comments. It dwells on the favours and honours voted to the chief assassins, as well as the abolition of many of Cæsar's *acta*. Antony also asserts that Lepidus and Plancus are on his side and warns Octavian that Cicero is playing him false.

any premature step. The Senate might be dealt with here-after : for the present the first necessity was to prevent Antony from becoming strong enough to dictate terms to himself as well as to the Senate. He therefore quietly continued to take his part in the campaign.

The Senatorial armies commanded the district round Mutina, except Bononia, Regium Lepidi, and Parma. Of these towns, The military situation in the spring of B.C. 43. the first was twenty-three miles east of Mutina along the Æmilian road ; the other two about the same distance west of it. They were in the hands of Antony, affording him bases of operation on either side of Mutina. In the middle of February Cicero was daily expecting to hear of Dec. Brutus ending the war by a sally from Mutina. At that time Antony's headquarters were at Bononia, only a part of his troops actually investing Mutina. Hirtius was at Claterna, eleven miles east of Bononia ; Octavian at Forum Cornelii (Imola), nine miles farther east. Bad weather had prevented serious operations, but some time in March Antony evacuated Bononia to push on the siege of Mutina with his full force. Hirtius and Octavian at once occupied Bononia, and gradually pushed out fortified posts towards Mutina ;[1] for Dec. Brutus was hard pressed for food, and they feared that he would have to surrender. But not being on an equality with Antony, especially in cavalry, they were anxious to wait for the fresh legions from Rome under Pansa. Some minor skirmishes took place from time to time,[2] but as the days dragged on and Mutina was not relieved, the anxiety at Rome grew greater and greater. "I am restlessly waiting for news," writes Cicero on the 11th of April ; "the decisive hour is upon us ; for

[1] The country is very flat, but was intersected by drains and water-courses, making military evolutions difficult, if not impossible, in the rainy season. (App., b. c. 3, 65.)

[2] Such as the cavalry engagement between Pontius Aquila and Tib. Munatius Plancus at Pollentia (Dio, 46, 38). Octavian also suffered some loss by the desertion of some Gallic cavalry (*ib.* 37).

our whole hope depends on relieving Dec. Brutus."[1] On the 15th and 16th there was a panic in the city caused by the prætor Ventidius Bassus. He had enrolled two legions of veterans, and was believed to be about to enter Rome. He, however, marched off to Potentia to watch the result of the struggle in Gallia Cisalpina; and a few days later came the news of the victory of Forum Gallorum, which changed this unreasonable panic into an exultation almost as unreasonable.[2]

Pansa was expected to reach the seat of war about the 16th of April. A detachment, consisting of the Martia and two prætorian cohorts, was sent out to conduct him and his four new legions into camp. In order to intercept this force Antony concealed two legions in Forum Gallorum, only allowing his cavalry and light armed to be seen. On the 14th Pansa encamped near Bononia, and next morning started to join Hirtius in his camp near Mutina, along with the troops sent out to meet him. The main force marched over the open country; the two prætorian cohorts kept to the *via Æmilia*. Near Forum Gallorum there was some marshy and difficult ground. The Martia got through this first, and suddenly sighted Antony's cavalry. The men could not be held back: enraged at the recollection of their comrades executed at Brundisium, they broke into a charge. Pansa, unable to stop them, tried to bring up two new legions to their support. But Antony was too quick for him. He suddenly led out his legions from the village, and Pansa, in danger of being surrounded, had to retire upon his camp of the previous night, having himself

Battle of Forum Gallorum, April 15th, B.C. 43.

---

[1] Cic., *ad Brutum*, ii. 2.

[2] In enrolling legions Bassus was probably justified by the *SCtum ultimum*, which included the prætors. He was known to be a supporter of Antony, and might be thought capable of occupying Rome in his interest. We shall see afterwards that he joined him in Cisalpine Gaul. Some rumour of his being likely to act in this way had been rife before January 1st, when he was only prætor-designate. (See Cic., *ad Att.* xvi. 1; *ad Brut.* i. 3.)

received two wounds, while the prætorian cohorts on the Æmilian road were cut to pieces. Antony seemed to have won the day. But he attempted too much. He pushed on towards Bononia, hoping to storm the camp, but was beaten off and forced to retire to his own quarters near Mutina. He was, however, many hours' march from them. His men were tired, and when they reached Forum Gallorum again they were met by Hirtius, who, having heard of Pansa's disaster, had come out with twenty veteran cohorts. Antony's wearied men were utterly routed almost on the ground of their morning's victory, and he had to escape with his cavalry to his camp near Mutina, which he did not reach till long after sunset. Hirtius had no cavalry to pursue him, and accordingly went on to visit the wounded Pansa.

Though the prætorian cohorts which had suffered so severely on the road were Octavian's, he was not leading them, nor does he seem to have been engaged in either of the battles. But it appears that some of Antony's men had threatened the camp in charge of which he had been left, and that his success in repelling this attack was sufficiently marked for his soldiers to greet him with the title of Imperator as well as Hirtius and Pansa.[1]

The news of this victory reached Rome on the 20th, and the extravagant exultation of the Ciceronians may be gathered from the Fourteenth Philippic. But Antony was still investing Mutina, and though he had lost heavily, so also had his opponents, especially the Martia and Octavian's prætorian cohorts. Pansa, disabled by his wounds, had been carried to Bononia, and for some days nothing of importance was attempted. But on the 21st Hirtius and Octavian moved to the west of Mutina, where

Antony's second defeat at Mutina, 21 April.

---

[1] Cicero says of Octavian that he *secundum proelium fecit* because he *castra multarum legionum paucis cohortibus tutatus est* (14 *Phil.* § 28). The attack on the camp is not mentioned elsewhere (*ib.* § 37). For his being greeted as Imperator see C. I. L. ix. 8375.

the lines of investment were less complete, with the hope of relieving the town on that side. Antony sent out his cavalry to intercept them, and, after some skirmishing, two legions to support it. Octavian attacked and drove them back to their camp, into which Hirtius forced his way, but was killed within the vallum. Octavian got possession of the body, but had presently to evacuate the camp. Still Antony's losses in these two battles had been so severe that he feared being himself invested by Octavian, who would in that case, he felt sure, be joined by Lepidus and Plancus. Whatever might then be the fate of Decimus Brutus, he at any rate would be paralysed. He resolved to make a dash for the Transalpine province, hoping there to be joined not only by Pollio, Lepidus, and Plancus, but by Ventidius also. He accordingly raised the siege, and with a strong body of cavalry marched along the *via Æmilia*. At Dertona he left the road, and made the difficult pass of Aquæ Statiellæ, leading to the coast at Vada Sabatia. There he was joined by Ventidius, and proceeded along the Riviera into the province. Decimus Brutus did not start in pursuit till the third day, partly owing to the exhausted state of his men after their long investment, partly because he wished to induce Octavian to join him.

The news of Antony's retirement reached Rome on the 26th. The exultant Ciceronians regarded the war as at an end, and next day, under Cicero's influence, Antony and his adherents were declared *hostes* in the Senate.[1] He was believed to be utterly ruined, and the Senate was regarded as once more supreme. Decimus Brutus would of course cut to pieces the poor remains of Antony's troops ; Lepidus and Plancus would hold their provinces in obedience to the Senate. Octavian was no longer necessary, and was immediately made to feel it. Not only were scandalous rumours spread abroad, charging him with causing the death of Hirtius, and suborning his physician to

The exultant Ciceronians slight Octavian.

---

[1] Cic., *ad Brut.* I, 3, 5.

poison the wounds of Pansa,[1] but in the vote of thanks to the army no mention was made of him. The vote also was so framed as to introduce divisions in the army itself by naming certain cohorts for honour and passing over others; while the legates conveying these thanks and honours were instructed to communicate directly with the men, not through Octavian as their commander. The legions of Pansa were transferred to Decimus Brutus, even the Martia and Quarta, formerly commended for joining Octavian. At the same time, all those most likely to be hostile to him were promoted. Sext. Pompeius was declared head of the naval forces of the republic; Brutus and Cassius were confirmed in their provinces and given special powers in all other provinces east of the Adriatic; a commission of ten was appointed to revise the *acta* of Antony's consulship, in which Octavian had no place.[2] Lastly, his claim to a triumph and to be a candidate for one of the vacant consulships was rejected, though as a kind of sop he was granted *consularia ornamenta*,[3] and Cicero appears to have proposed his having an ovation.[4] But it was about the same time that Cicero's unlucky epigram as to "distinguishing and extinguishing" him was reported to Octavian.[5] If Cicero, who was in constant correspondence with him, and was even discussing the possibilities of their holding the consulship as colleagues,[6] could thus speak, what was he to think of the rest? No doubt all these circumstances contributed to fix Octavian's resolve. He at once declined to co-operate with Decimus Brutus, or to surrender his legions to him. Although those under Hirtius and Pansa had been assigned bodily by the Senate to Brutus, the Martia and Quarta refused to obey the

---

[1] Suet., *Aug.* 11 ; Cic., *ad Brut.* i. 6.   [2] Cic., *ad Fam.* xi. 21.
[3] Dio, 46, 41 ; Livy, *Ep.* 118.   [4] Cic., *ad Brut.* i. 15.
[5] *Id.*, *ad Fam.* xi. 20, 21, see *ante* p. 52.
[6] *Id.*, *ad Brut.* i. 4 ; App., b. c. iii. 82 ; Dio, 46, 42 ; Plut., *Cic.* 46. There was evidently some rumour of Cicero intending to be consul, though he speaks with rather affected indignation of Octavian wishing to be elected also (*ad Brut.* i. 10).

order, and declared their loyalty to Octavian. Their example was followed by the other veterans, who refused to serve under an assassin of their old imperator. Thus fortified, Octavian adopted a line of conduct which partly alarmed and partly puzzled the other commanders of troops. He established secret communications with Antony, releasing prisoners taken from his army, and allowing certain officers to rejoin him; while he himself, remaining inactive for some months, was privately preparing to enforce his claim on the consulship. The departure of Decimus Brutus left him in undisturbed command of the greater part of Cisalpine Gaul, and there were no military forces between him and Rome, now that Ventidius had accomplished his rapid march from Potentia to the western coast at Vada.

The gradual disillusionment of the Ciceronians as to the victory over Antony ; the perplexity caused by the inactivity of Octavian ; the delays and helplessness of Decimus Brutus—all these are faithfully reflected in the Cicero correspondence of this period. At first everything is *couleur-de-rose*. On the 21st of April, on the receipt of the news of the battle of Forum Gallorum, he writes :—

Revulsion of feeling at Rome.

"In the youthful Cæsar there is a wonderful natural strain of virtue. Pray heaven we may govern him in the flush of honours and popularity as easily as we have held him up to this time ! This is certainly a more difficult thing, but nevertheless I have no mistrust. For the young man has been convinced, and chiefly by my arguments, that our safety is his work, and that, at any rate, if he had not diverted Antony from the city, all would have been lost." [1]

On the 27th (after hearing of the fight at the camp) he thinks Octavian is with Decimus Brutus in pursuit of Antony or, as he says, "of the remnant of the enemy." [2]

[1] Cic., *ad Brut.* 1, 3   [2] *Id.* § 4

But presently he is informed that Octavian is not thus acting, or serving the interests of the Senate. Decimus Brutus writes from Dertona on the 5th of May:—

" If Cæsar had hearkened to me and crossed the Apennines, I should have reduced Antony to such straits that he would have been ruined by failure of provisions rather than the sword. But neither can any one control Cæsar, nor can Cæsar control his own army—both most disastrous facts." [1]

Decimus Brutus was inaccurately informed as to the relations between Octavian and his troops,[2] but was quite right in concluding that he had no help to expect from him. He wrote again on the 12th of May, attributing his delay in beginning the pursuit to the fact that "he could not put any confidence in Cæsar without visiting and conversing with him." [3] He had, however, gained nothing by the interview, and had been specially dismayed to find that the Martia and Quarta refused to join him.[4] On the 24th of May he writes again, warning Cicero that Octavian has heard of his epigram; that the veterans are indignant at the proceedings in Rome ; and that Octavian had secured all the troops lately commanded by Pansa.[5] Later in the same month he appears to have suggested the recall of M. Brutus, and that meanwhile the defence of Italy should be intrusted to Octavian.[6]

This last suggestion shows how far he had failed to penetrate the policy of Octavian. The mistake was shared by L. Munatius Plancus, governor of Celtic Gaul, who was moving down towards the province expecting to be joined by Octavian in opposing Antony, or, at any rate, supposing

---

[1] Cic., *ad Fam.* xi. 10.

[2] He was perhaps deceived by the report that Octavian's legions had taken an oath not to fight against any that had served under Iulius Cæsar. This applied to some men at present with Antony. But Dio implies that the oath was at the secret instigation of Octavian himself (Dio, 46, 42).

[3] Cic., *ad Fam.* xi. 13.   [4] *Id.* xi. 19.

[5] *Id.* xi. 20.   [6] *Id.* xi. 14.

that Octavian's army was at the disposal of the Senate. "Let Cæsar," he says, on the 6th of June, "come with the best troops he has, or, if anything prevents him from coming in person, let his army be sent."[1] Some weeks later he too had learnt that Cæsar's real purpose had been misunderstood. He writes on the 28th of July :—

"I have never ceased importuning him by letter, and he has uniformly replied that he is coming without delay, while all the time I perceive that he has given up that idea, and has taken up some other scheme. Nevertheless, I have sent our friend Furnius to him with a message and a letter, in case he may be able to do some good."[2]

While the generals in Gaul were thus being gradually brought to see that Octavian had an independent policy of his own, the hopes of support entertained by Cicero at home were one by one disappearing. By the middle of May he knew that Antony's retreat was not the disorganised flight supposed, nor the end of the war.

"The news which reached Rome," he says, about the 15th of May, "and what everybody believed, was that Antony had fled with a small body of men, who were without arms, panic stricken, and utterly demoralised. But if he is in such a position (as Græceius tells us) that he cannot be offered battle without risk, he appears to me not to have fled from Mutina, but merely to have changed the seat of war. Accordingly there is a general revulsion of feeling."[3]

In these circumstances Cicero could do nothing but try to keep Decimus Brutus, Lepidus, and Plancus loyal to the Senate, and urge them to act with vigour.

"Be your own Senate," he writes to Plancus about the 27th of May, "and follow wherever the interests of the public service shall lead you. Let it be your object that we hear of some brilliant operation

---

[1] Cic., *ad Fam.* x. 23.   [2] *Id.* x. 24.   [3] *Id.* xi. 12 and 14.

by you before we thought that it was going to happen. I pledge you my word that whatever you achieve the Senate will accept as having been done not only with loyal intention, but with wisdom also."[1]

But on the 29th of May Lepidus joined Antony.[2] On the 3rd of June Decimus Brutus writes for the last time in despairing tones to Cicero from near Grenoble,[3] and though a subsequent junction with Plancus kept him from destruction for a few weeks longer, he was never able to do anything of any account again. The only hope remaining to Cicero was to induce M. Brutus or C. Cassius, or both, to come to Italy with their armies. He had not, indeed, quite given up hope of Octavian's loyalty, but his old doubts were recurring, and though he still used flattering words to him, he must have been conscious that Octavian had gauged their value. Late in June, writing to urge M. Brutus to come to Italy, he says : " The protecting force of the young Cæsar I regard as trustworthy ; but so many are trying to sap his loyalty that at times I am mortally afraid of his giving in."[4]

It does not seem true that Octavian yielded to the influence of others in the steps which he now took. As at other times in his life he may have listened to advice, but the

Octavian, after some vain negotiations, at length moves on Rome. Aug., B.C. 43. final decision was always his own, adopted from no passing sentiment or passion, but with the cool determination of settled policy. He had decided that to be able to treat with Antony on equal terms he must obtain one of the vacant consulships. This would make him legally head of the State, and add to his military strength the prestige and authority of that position. If possible he would be elected without any show of force, and therefore began negotiations with the Senate soon after the battles of Mutina through Cicero. But the Senate suspected Cicero of wishing for the consulship himself, and would not

---

[1] Cic., *ad Fam.* x. 16.　　　[2] *Id.* x. 35 ; xii. 35.
[3] *Id.* xi. 26, *cp.* xi. 13.　　　[4] *Id., ad Brut.* i. 10.

listen to the suggestion. The constitutional difficulty about the election gave the Senate a decent excuse for postponement. Both consuls were dead, and the prætor was unable to "create" a higher imperium than his own. There was no one to name a dictator, and as magistrates with imperium still existed the *auspicia* had not reverted to the *patres*, therefore they could not name *interreges*. On the 1st of January, when the curule offices would all be vacant, the *auspicia* would revert to the Senate. Accordingly, after some discussion, Cicero tells a correspondent at the end of June, it had been held to be best, "in the interests of the constitution, to put off the elections till January."[1] But Octavian had no intention of being thwarted by this technical difficulty. He had no wish for the present to farther weaken Antony, and bring the whole weight of the Ciceronians upon himself, but he was resolved that the consulship was necessary in order to be on an equal footing with him.[2] He therefore allowed a deputation of four hundred of his soldiers to go to Rome to demand the payment of the bounties voted to them, with the understanding that they were also to ask for the consulship for Octavian. There would be some show of reason in combining these two demands, for they needed his protection against the decemvirs, who were likely to interfere in the allotment of lands made both by Iulius and Antony. But the deputation, though admitted to the curia, received an unfavourable answer. We are told that the Senate insisted on their appearing unarmed, but that one of them left the Senate house and returned with a sword and the remark, "If you do not give Cæsar the

[1] A similar technical difficulty had occurred in B.C. 49 (both consuls being absent, and unwilling, of course, to name a dictator), and had been got over by the nomination of a dictator by the prætor under a special law. See p. 8 ; Cic., *ad Fam.* x. 26 ; *ad M. Brut.* i. 5.

[2] Plancus (Cic., *ad Fam.* x. 29) expresses surprise that Cæsar wished to give up the glory of defeating Antony for the sake of "a two months' consulship." But this only shows that Plancus did not understand Octavian's object or policy.

consulship this will do so." Whereupon Cicero exclaimed, " If that is your way of pressing his suit, he will get it." The same story is told of Iulius, and one is always suspicious of such dramatic scenes.[1] At any rate, Octavian regarded the attitude of the Senate as hostile, and determined to march on Rome with his eight legions,[2] a corresponding force of cavalry, and some auxiliary troops.

He moved in two columns, the first consisting of his swiftest and most active men, led by himself ; for among other causes of anxiety was a fear that his mother and sister might meet with ill-treatment in Rome. The Senate had no troops to oppose to this formidable army, and in its terror sent legates with the money promised to the men, but lately refused to the deputation. Octavian however refused them entrance into the camp, and pushed on without stopping. The panic in the city grew daily more acute, and Cicero, who had pledged his credit for Octavian's loyalty,[3] found himself an object of suspicion and retired from Rome. Then every concession was made in the Senate : the bounty promised to some of the troops was doubled, and extended to all the troops alike, though the exchequer was exhausted by the payment of only two legions.[4] Octavian was to have the distribution of lands and rewards instead of the decemvirs, and was allowed to be a candidate for the consulship in his absence. Messengers were sent to announce these concessions to him ; but he had

Octavian enters Rome and obtains the consulship. August, B.C. 43.

---

[1] Suet., *Aug.* 26 ; Dio, 46, 43 ; Plut., *Pomp.* 58. Appian (b. c. 3, 82), without alluding to this scene, regards the application itself as the result of a secret intrigue with Cicero, and Cicero's exclamation, if made, may have been intended as encouraging and not sarcastic.

[2] The number given by Appian (b. c. iii. 88). Octavian had five legions when he went to Gaul : two raised in Campania of veterans, one of *tirones*, the Martia and Quarta (App., b. c. iii. 47). The other three must have been made up from the armies of Pansa and Hirtius. None of the veteran legions in these two armies would consent to follow Decimus Brutus (Cic., *ad Fam.* xi. 19).

[3] Cic., *ad Brut.* 1, 18.   [4] *Ib.* and App., b. c. iii. 90.

scarcely heard them when he was informed of a change of sentiment in Rome. The legions, summoned by the Senate from Africa, had arrived ; Cicero had reappeared ; the decrees were rescinded ; and measures were being taken to defend the city. The two legions from Africa were to be supported by a levy *en masse* and by a legion enrolled by Pansa but not taken with him. The city prætor M. Cornutus was to be commander-in-chief. At the same time boats and other means of transport were being prepared in the Tiber for the escape of the chief citizens, their families and property, in case of defeat ; while a vigorous search was being made for Octavian's mother and sister as hostages. Octavian felt that no time was to be lost. Sending forward messengers to assure the people that they would not be harmed,[1] he continued his advance on Rome. A day's march from the city he was met by a large number of real or pretended sympathisers ; and felt it safe to leave his troops and enter Rome with a strong body-guard. Enthusiastic crowds greeted his entrance, and as he approached the temple of Vesta he had the happiness of seeing his mother and sister, who had taken sanctuary with the Vestals, and now came out to embrace him. The three legions in Rome, in spite of some opposition from their officers, declared for him ; and the prætor Cornutus killed himself in despair. It was all over, and Octavian was master of the situation. For a moment indeed there seemed a gleam of hope. A rumour reached the city that the Martia and Quarta had refused to follow Octavian to Rome. Cicero hastily gathered some partisans into the Senate house in the evening to discuss the possibility of further resistance. But while they were in conference they learnt that the rumour was false. There was nothing for it but to disperse, and Cicero was fain to seek out Octavian and offer a tardy congratulation—received with ironical courtesy.

[1] The panic had been increased by some damage done by his soldier on the march to properties of known anti-Cæsareans.

The constitutional difficulty as to the election was at once surmounted by the investment of two men with pro-consular powers to hold it. The rest was a mere form, and on the 19th of August Octavian, with his cousin Q. Pedius, entered upon their consulship.

The consulship and other honours.

The now obsequious Senate proceeded to heap honours upon him. He was to have money to pay the promised bounties ; to enjoy an imperium, when with an army, superior to the consuls ; to do whatever he thought necessary for the protection of the city ; and to take over the army lately assigned to Decimus Brutus. The *lex curiata* for his adoption under Cæsar's will was at once passed, and he was now by right as well as by courtesy a Cæsar. His colleague, Q. Pedius, at the same time carried a law for the trial of all concerned in the murder of Iulius, and the *quæstio* seems at once to have been instituted. All were condemned in their absence and lost their citizenship and the protection of the laws.[1] Brutus and Cassius, with the rest of the assassins, were thus put at a great disadvantage. It was an act of war on their part, as condemned men, to hold their provinces or command troops. That the Senate, in which the majority were doubtless in favour of Brutus and Cassius, should have practically sanctioned these measures,[2] shews how completely it was cowed. Octavian's position was, in fact, a very strong one. It was not possible for M. Brutus to transport a sufficient force from Macedonia to crush him, much less for Cassius from Syria. The two combined would no doubt hope some day to be able to attack him ; but meanwhile he had time to fortify himself by new coalitions.

---

[1] Confiscation of property and the forbidding of "fire and water" followed as a matter of course. One of the assassins—P. Servilius Casca —was tribune, and as such could not legally be condemned, but he vacated his tribuneship by flying from Rome and was condemned with the rest.

[2] The Senate had nothing to do with this *quæstio*, which was established by a *lex*, but its attitude to Octavian amounted to a condonation if not an active approval.

Cæsar—as we should now call him—only stayed in Rome to see these measures secured. He then left the city under the care of Pedius, and marched once more into Cis-

Octavian goes to meet Antony. alpine Gaul. His nominal object was to destroy Decimus Brutus—now a condemned man—but his real purpose was to come to an understanding with Antony and Lepidus. Letters had already passed between them, and some plan of action had been agreed upon. Antony was to crush Decimus Brutus and Plancus, while the Senate was persuaded by Pedius to rescind the decrees declaring Antony and Lepidus *hostes*. This news was sent to Cæsar while on his leisurely march, and passed on by him to Antony; who thereupon proceeded to fulfil his part of the bargain. He was by this time, or shortly afterwards, reinforced by Asinius Pollio [1] with two legions from Spain, who at once succeeded in securing the cohesion of Plancus. The greater part of the troops under Decimus Brutus also insisted on following Plancus; and Brutus was obliged to fly with a small force.

This settled the fate of Decimus Brutus, and left Northern Italy open to Antony, unless Cæsar still chose to oppose him. After various fruitless attempts to escape,

Death of Decimus Brutus. Brutus was put to death by a Sequanian Gaul, under orders from Antony,[2] who then with Pollio and Lepidus [3] marched into Cispadane Gaul with a large part

---

[1] According to Appian (b. c. iii. 97), Pollio for some time declined to join Antony and Lepidus. He seems to have done so when their outlawry was removed.

[2] Decimus Brutus first tried to reach Ravenna, hoping to sail to Macedonia and join M. Brutus. Headed back by Cæsar's advance, he recrossed the Alps (being gradually deserted by his men) and trusted himself to a Gaul, who had received favours from him of old. But his host communicated with Antony, and by his orders put him to death. There were other versions of his death. Perhaps neither Antony nor Cæsar cared to ask questions so long as he was dead. (App., b. c. iii. 97–98 ; Dio, 46, 53 ; Velleius Pat., ii. 64 ; Livy, *Ep.* 120.)

[3] Plancus did not accompany Antony into Italy; he stayed in Gaul, busying himself with the foundation of Lugdunum, and apparently suppressing some movements in the Eastern Alps, for at the end of the year

of their forces, the rest being left to guard the province. The invading army marched along the Æmilian road as though to attack Cæsar. But the real intention on both sides was to come to terms. On an islet in a tributary of the Po, between Mutina and Bononia, the three leaders, Antony, Lepidus, and Cæsar met for conference, though not till elaborate precautions had been taken against treachery. For two days they sat from

The triumvirate arranged, Nov., B.C. 43. morning till night in earnest debate, in full view of their respective armies. On the third the soldiers of both sides were summoned to a *contio*,

and informed of the articles which had been agreed upon, though the last and most terrible of them—the proscription— was not communicated. The terms announced were: (1) Cæsar agreed to abdicate the consulship, which was to be held for the remainder of the year by Ventidius Bassus; (2) Lepidus and Plancus were to be consuls for B.C. 42; (3) Lepidus, Cæsar, and Antony were to be appointed by a *lex* for the remainder of the year, and for five years from the next 1st of January, *triumviri reipublicæ constituendæ*—a board of three for settling the constitution.

The Triumvirate was practically a dictatorship in commission. The word was avoided owing to its prohibition in Antony's

Powers of the Triumvirate. law. But the triumvirs were to exercise all the powers of a dictator; their *acta* were to be authoritative; they were to be independent of the

Senate; superior to all magistrates; to have the right of proposing laws to the *Comitia*; to regulate the appointment of magistrates and provincial governors. The colleagueship was an apparent concession to the fundamental principle of the constitution; but from the first it was practically a duum-

---

coming home to enter on his consulship, he celebrated a triumph *ex Rhætis* [Inscrip. Neap., 4089; Fast. Capitol. 29 Dec. A. V. 711.] Pollio, who had presently to assent to the proscription of his father-in-law, L. Quintius, was left in charge of Transpadane Gaul, to arrange for lands for the veterans. It was in this business that he came across Vergil and his farm.

virate rather than a triumvirate, Lepidus being treated almost at once as inferior. The Empire east of the Adriatic was for the moment separated from this home government, being held by Brutus and Cassius ; but the western part was to be divided among the three—Cæsar taking Africa, Sardinia, and Sicily ; Antony, Cisalpine Gaul and Transalpina, with the exception of Narbonensis ; Lepidus, Gallia Narbonensis and Upper Spain. In these districts each would be supreme and govern personally or by their legates. But the greater part of Cæsar's share was still in the hands of Sextus Pompeius, and would have to be won back. It was accordingly arranged that in the following year Lepidus, as consul, should be responsible for the order of Italy, while Cæsar undertook to put down Sextus, and Antony to confront M. Brutus and Cassius.

The soldiers of both armies, having no desire to fight each other, received the announcement with enthusiasm. Their devotion to Iulius Cæsar's memory was warmed by the belief that the anti-Cæsarean clique at Rome meant to deprive them of the money and lands assigned to them. The Triumvirs, on the other hand, promised them allotments in the choicest parts of Italy—Capua, Rhegium, Venusia, Vibo, Beneventum, Ariminum, Nuceria. There was land at most of these places which from one cause or another had become *ager publicus ;* and when that failed there would always be owners, whose part in the war just over, and that about to take place, would give opportunity for confiscation. This combination of military chiefs therefore suited the views and wishes of the soldiers, and some of them urged that the bond should be drawn still closer by Cæsar's marriage with Antony's step-daughter Clodia.[1] Cæsar assented to the betrothal, but as Clodia was still quite young, he prudently deferred the marriage. He doubtless foresaw possible inconveniences in being too closely allied with Antony.

The next step was for the three to enter Rome and obtain

[1] Daughter of Fulvia by her first husband, P. Clodius.

a legal confirmation of their appointment. But they did not

The
Proscription. wait till their arrival in the city to begin the vengeance. They had agreed to follow the precedent of Sulla by publishing lists of men declared to be out of the pale of the law. The larger list was reserved for farther consideration; but a preliminary list of seventeen names was drawn up at once, and soldiers were sent with orders to put the men to death wherever found. Among these were Cicero, his brother, and nephew. Plutarch tells us that Cicero's name was put upon the list as a compromise. Octavian bargained for Lucius Cæsar, Antony's uncle, and in return conceded to Antony the inclusion of Cicero, while Lepidus consented to his brother, L. Paulus, being entered.[1] Four of the seventeen were found at once and put to death. Cicero escaped till the arrival of the triumvirs in Rome, but was killed near Formiæ on the 7th of December, his brother and nephew having already been put to death in Rome. Cæsar was the first to arrive in the city, and was quickly followed by Antony and Lepidus, each with a strong prætorian guard. Their appointment was duly confirmed in the *Comitia* on the proposal of the tribune Titus Titius, and on the 27th of November they entered upon their office.[2]

Naturally the sudden execution of three of the seventeen who were found in Rome had created great alarm in the city, where no one knew whose turn was to come next. The panic was somewhat lessened by Pedius publishing the list of the seventeen, with the assurance that no more executions were intended. He appears to have honestly believed this, but the agitation of the night of horror was too much for him, and he died within the next twenty-four hours. On the day after the installation of the triumvirs (November 28th) the citizens were horrified to see an edict fixed up in the Forum, detailing the causes of the executions which were to follow, and offering

[1] Plut., *Ant.* 19 ; App., b. c. iv. 6 ; Dio, 46, 44.
[2] The usual interval (*tres nundinæ*) for *promulgatio* was dispensed with.

a reward for the head of any one of those named below—25,000 sesterces to a freeman, 10,000 and freedom to a slave. All who aided or concealed a proscribed man were to suffer death themselves. Below were two tablets, one for Senators and one for equites. They contained 130 names, besides the original seventeen, to which were shortly added 150 more. Additions were continually being made during the following days, either from private malice or covetousness. In some cases men were first killed and then their names inserted in the lists. The edict made it the interest of slaves to betray their masters, against whom perhaps in many cases these unfortunate men had a long list of injuries to avenge. They had now the fierce gratification of seeing their oppressors grovelling at their feet. But it also placed a severe strain on the affection of the nearest kinsmen whose lives were forfeited if they concealed or aided the proscribed. The sale of confiscated property at low rates gave opportunities for the covetous, and many a man perished because he possessed house or land desired by Fulvia or some friend of Antony. But though the terror revealed much meanness and treachery, it also brought to light many instances of courage and devotion. Wives and sons risked death for husbands and fathers; and there were slaves who assumed the dress of their masters and died for them.

The massacre began with Salvius, though holding the sacrosanct office of tribune. Two prætors—Minucius and L. Velleius—were cut down while engaged in their courts. To shew how no connections, however high, were to save any man, at the head of the list was a brother of Lepidus, an uncle of Antony, a brother of Plancus, and the father-in-law of Asinius Pollio. But as usual in times of such horror, many perished who from their humble position or their youth could have had no share in politics. The total number eventually proscribed, according to Appian, was "three hundred Senators and about two thousand equites." Livy says that there were

130 names of Senators on the lists, and a large number (*plurimi*) of equites. Livy is probably giving the number of Senators who actually perished.[1] In Rome itself the terror was probably brief. It would not take long to find those who stayed in the city ; the gates and roads were strictly guarded, and it was difficult to evade military vigilance. But many were hiding in the country, and the search for them went on into the first months of the next year, and all through Italy soldiers were scouring towns, villages, woods, and marshes in search of the proscribed. Probably the exact number of those executed was never known. But it seems likely that about half escaped, some of whom in happier times rose to high office. There were three possible places of refuge, the camp of M. Brutus in Macedonia, of Cassius in Syria, and the fleet of Sext. Pompeius in Sicily. Pompeius sent vessels to cruise round the southern coasts of Italy and pick up refugees ; and tried to counteract the edict by offering those who saved any one of them double the sum set upon their heads by the triumvirs. He was liberal in relieving their necessities, and found commands or other employments for those of high rank.[2] At length, early in B.C. 42 Lepidus informed the Senate that the proscriptions were at an end. He seems to have meant by this that no new list was to be issued, not that those already proscribed were to be pardoned ; and Cæsar, who was present, entered a protest against being bound even by this declaration.[3]

In fact another list was published, but this time it was of properties to be confiscated, not of lives to be taken. In spite of the already large confiscations the triumviral government was in financial difficulties. Confiscated properties were liable to reductions for the

Protest of Ladies.

---

[1] Appian, b. c. iv. 5 ; Livy, *Ep.* 120. Of the 69 names given by Appian he records the escape of 31. This tallies roughly with the discrepancy between his and Livy's reckoning.

[2] Appian, b. c. iv. 36. [3] Suet., *Aug.* 27.

dowries of widows, 10 per cent. to sons, and 5 per cent. to daughters.[1] These claims were not always paid perhaps, but they sometimes were. Again, besides the natural fall of prices caused by so much property coming into the market at once, much of it was sold to friends and partisans at great reductions, few venturing to bid against men in power or soldiers. The treasury, therefore, was not enriched as much as might have been expected ; and as the triumvirs had two wars in the immediate future to face, they were in great need of money. The tributum and tax on slaves were re-imposed, but failed to produce a surplus. A device therefore was hit upon something like the fines on ." Malignants " in England, under the Commonwealth. Lists of persons more or less suspect were put up, who were ordered to contribute a tenth of their property. Each man had to value his own estate, and this gave rise to frequent accusations of fraud, generally resulting in the confiscation of the whole. Others found it impossible to raise the money without selling property, which could only be done just then at a ruinous sacrifice. An alternative was offered to such men which proved equally ruinous. They might surrender their whole estate and apply for the restoration of a third. The treasury was not likely to be prompt in completing the transaction, for it had first to sell and satisfy charges on the estate, nor to take a liberal view of the amount due to the owner. It was an encumbered estates act, under which the margin of salvage was always small, and tended to disappear altogether.[2] Among those thus proscribed were about fourteen hundred ladies. They did not silently submit, but applied to Octavia, as well as to Antony's mother Iulia, and his wife Fulvia. By Octavia and Iulia they were kindly received, but were driven from Fulvia's door. Undismayed they appeared before the tribunal of the triumvirs, where Hortensia, daughter of the orator Hortensius, pleaded their cause with something of her father's eloquence. "If they were guilty," she argued, "they

[1] Dio, 47, 14.   [2] *Id.* 47, 16–17.

ought to have shared the fate of their relations. If not it was as unjust to injure their property as their persons. They had no share in political rights, and therefore were not liable to taxation. Women had of old voluntarily contributed their personal ornaments to the defences of the country ; but they had never contributed, and, she hoped, never would contribute to a civil war, or shew sympathy on either side." The triumvirs received the protest with anger, and ordered their lictors to drive the ladies away. But they were struck by marks of disapproval among the crowd ; and next day a new edict was substituted, which contained only four hundred names of women, and, instead of naming individual men, imposed on all properties above 100,000 sesterces (about £800) an immediate tax of 2 per cent. of the capital, and one year's income for the expenses of the war.[1]

For a just view of the character of Augustus, it is important to decide how far he acquiesced in the cruelties of the proscription. With the general policy he seems to have been in full accord ; and as far as a complete vengeance on those implicated in the murder of Iulius was concerned, he was no doubt inexorable. But his administration as sole head of the state was so equitable and clement, that many found it difficult to believe that he did more than tacitly acquiesce in the rest of the proscriptions. Augustus himself, in the memoir left to be engraved after his death, omits all mention of them, and conveniently passes from the legal condemnation of the assassins to the assertion that he spared the survivors of Philippi. Paterculus only alludes to them in a sentence, which contains a skilful insinuation that Augustus only joined in them under compulsion. Appian makes no distinction between the three. He tells us, indeed, some stories of mercy shown by Augustus, and of his expressing approbation of acts of fidelity on the part of friends or slaves. But he also credits Antony with at least one act of a similar

Responsibility of Augustus for the proscriptions.

[1] App., b. c. 4, 34.

kind. Plutarch says that most blame was thought to attach to Antony, as being older than Cæsar and more influential than Lepidus. Dio goes more fully into the question. He affirms that Antony and Lepidus were chiefly responsible for the proscriptions, pointing out that Octavian by his own nature, as well as his association with Iulius, was inclined to clemency ; and moreover, that he had not been long enough engaged in politics to have conceived many enmities, while his chief wish was to be esteemed and popular ; and lastly, that when he got rid of these associates, and was in sole power, he was never guilty of such crimes. The strongest of these arguments is that which claims for Cæsar's youth immunity from widespread animosities ; and it does seem probable that outside the actual assassins and their immediate supporters, Augustus would not personally have cared to extend the use of the executioner's sword. But he cannot be acquitted of a somewhat cynical indifference to the cruelties perpetrated under the joint name and authority of the triumvirs. None of them have been directly attributed to him, except perhaps in the case of his (apparently unfaithful) guardian Toranius ; but neither is there any record of his having interfered to prevent them. Suetonius seems to give the truer account, that he resisted the proscription at first, but, when it was once decided upon, insisted that it should be carried out relentlessly. The proscription was an odious crime ; but a proscription that did not fulfil its purpose would have been a monstrous blunder also. I do not, however, admit Seneca's criticism that his subsequent clemency was merely "cruelty worn out."[1] The change was one of time and circumstance. Youth is apt to be hard-hearted. With happier surroundings and lengthened experience his character and judgment ripened and mellowed.

While these horrors were just beginning Cæsar lost his

---

[1] *Lassam crudelitatem*, Sen. *de Clem.* I, 9, 2. The other opinions referred to are Velleius, ii. 66 ; App., b. c. iv. 42, 45 ; Plut., *Ant* 21 ; Dio, 47, 7 ; Sueton., *Aug.* 27. For Toranius, see Nic. Dam. 2.

mother Atia, the tender and careful guide of his childhood and
youth, the first of his near kin to recognise and
Death of Atia. approve his high destiny. She died while he was
still consul, that is, between the 19th of August
and the 27th of November, B.C. 43. Devoted to her in her
life Cæsar now obtained for her the honours of a public funeral.
During the campaign of Mutina she was, it seems, at Rome ;
and when his estrangement from the Senate made her position
unpleasant or dangerous, she had taken sanctuary with the
Vestal Virgins accompanied by Octavia, and was ready to greet
him when he returned to Rome. Nicolas of Damascus gives
an attractive picture of Octavian's relations with his mother ;
and even the uncomplimentary Suetonius owns that his dutiful
conduct to her had been exemplary. She had brought up her
son with strictness, and the author of the *de oratoribus* classes
her with the mother of the Gracchi. But her strictness had
not forfeited her son's affection, nor failed to impress upon him
a high sense of duty. Her second husband Philippus survived
her several years.[1]

[1] Sueton., *Aug.* 61 ; Dio, 47, 17 ; [Tacit.] *de orat.* 29.

CHAPTER V

Cum fracta virtus, et minaces
turpe solum tetigere mento.

THE first task of the Triumvirs, after securing their power at
Rome, was the restoration of unity and peace to the Empire,
which was threatened at two points : Brutus and
Cassius were in arms in the East, Sext. Pompeius
in the West. The opposition of Brutus and
Cassius seemed the more formidable of the two. Brutus,
indeed, after holding Macedonia throughout B.C. 43, after
capturing and eventually putting to death Gaius Antonius,
and after winning some laurels in contests with surrounding
barbarians, had towards the end of the year practically abandoned
the province and removed to Asia, in which a decree of the
Senate had given him proprætorial authority along with
Cassius. But at Cyzicus and on the coast of Bithynia he had
collected a considerable fleet, and having thus strengthened
himself and levied large sums of money, he sent urgent
messages to Cassius to join him in the defence of the
republic.

Meanwhile Cassius had done much towards securing the
rest of the East to their cause. At the end of B.C. 44 he had
entered Palestine, and been joined successively by the forces of
L. Statius Murcus, proconsul of Syria ; of M. Crispus, pro-

M. Brutus and C. Cassius in the East.

consul of Bithynia ; of Cæcilius Bassus, the old Pompeian officer who had seduced the troops of Sextius Iulius from their allegiance ; and by four legions from Egypt under Aulus Allienus, whom Dolabella had sent to bring them to himself. With twelve legions he had shut up Dolabella at Laodicea-ad-Mare, aided by a fleet raised in part by Lentulus, the pro-quæstor of Asia, and had eventually terrified him into suicide. He had himself also, or by his legates, collected a fleet strong enough to prevent Cleopatra sending aid to Antony and Octavian, while part of it, under Statius Murcus and Cn. Domitius Ahenobarbus, was to watch the harbour of Brundisium and prevent the despatch of troops from Italy.

In the spring of B.C. 42, therefore, when Brutus and Cassius met at Smyrna they were both in possession of formidable forces, naval and military, and Cassius at any rate was also well supplied with money. They did not, however, at once push on to Macedonia, for they believed that the danger threatened by Sext. Pompeius would delay the advance of the Triumvirs. They therefore spent some months in farther securing the East. Brutus proceeded to reduce the cities in Lycia, Cassius sailed against Rhodes, while one of his legates invaded Cappadocia, and defeated and killed King Ariobarzanes. Both encountered some resistance, but when they met again in the summer at Sardis they had successfully carried out their objects ; and Cassius had refilled his exchequer by the taxes of Asia, the towns in which had been compelled to pay nearly ten years' revenue in advance.

Having told off a portion of his fleet to keep up the watch over Cleopatra and at Brundisium, the two proconsuls set out together for Abydos, and thence crossed to Europe. They marched along the coast road, formerly traversed by Persian invaders, their fleet also, like that of the Persian king of old, coasting along parallel with their march, till they came to the part of the Pangæan range which covers the ten miles between Philippi and its harbour Neapolis (Datum). There they found the road blocked by Gaius Norbanus and Decidius Saxa, with eight legions, sent in advance by Antony. When they left the main road and attempted to pass nearer Philippi they found the heights immediately south of the town also guarded. They drove off the enemy and encamped on two hills which they connected by a trench and stockade ; and eventually farther secured their position by occupying a line of hills commanding the road to the sea. They thus kept up communication with the fleet at Thasos as a base of supplies. Norbanus and Saxa did not venture to attack them, but retired upon Amphipolis, and thence sent intelligence to Rome, meanwhile keeping the enemy in check by skirmishing parties of cavalry. Brutus and Cassius were in no hurry to advance, for they had an excellent position, and were sure of supplies while in touch with their fleet ; whereas their opponents depended on the country, which was neither rich nor well stocked. The fleet of Murcus and Domitius might also delay, and perhaps prevent Antony and Cæsar from bringing reinforcements, while the fleet at Thasos could stop supplies being conveyed by sea.

Nor were these the only difficulties in the way of the Triumvirs. Ever since the battle of Munda (B.C. 45) Sextus Pompeius had been leading a piratical life in the Western Mediterranean. His forces had been continually increased by fugitive Pompeians and by natives from Africa, until he had become possessed of a formidable power against which the successive governors of Southern Spain had been able to effect little. After the death of Iulius Cæsar an attempt was made through Lepidus to come to terms with him, and he had agreed to submit to the government on condition of a *restitutio in integrum,* including the restoration of his father's property. But though Antony obtained a confirmation from the Senate the arrangement was never carried out. Probably the immense sum named as the value of the property—about five millions sterling—made it impossible, especially when the money in the temple of Ops

The difficulties of Antony and Cæsar with Sextus Pompeius.

had been squandered. Moreover Pompeius seems to have demanded the actual house and estates of his father, and these were in Antony's hands, who would not easily surrender them. Sextus therefore stayed in Spain or with his fleet. When the Senate broke with Antony it renewed negotiations with Sextus, promised him the satisfaction of his claims, passed a vote of thanks to him for services, and confirmed him in his command of all Roman ships on active service.[1] The Triumvirs deposed him from this command, and put his name on the proscription list.   His answer was to sail to Sicily, force Pompeius Bithynicus to surrender Messana, and take possession of the island.   Here he was joined by numerous refugees of the proscribed and many skilful seamen from Africa and elsewhere. By thus holding Sicily and Sardinia he could do much towards starving out Italy, upon the southern shores of which he also made frequent descents. He acted as an independent ruler, and presently put Bithynicus to death on a charge of plotting against him.[2]

Cæsar and Antony suspected Lepidus of keeping up communication with Pompeius, and consequently he was practically shelved.   He was to remain at Rome to keep order and carry out formal duties, while Antony was to transport his legions from Brundisium to attack Brutus and Cassius, and Cæsar was to conduct the war against Sextus Pompeius.   But the strength of Pompeius seems not to have been fully realised. Cæsar despatched a fleet under Q. Salvidienus to Sicily, while he himself went by land to Rhegium.   But Salvidienus was badly defeated by Pompeius and had to retire to the Italian shore to refit,[3] and before Cæsar had time to do anything more he was called to the aid of Antony, who was in difficulties at Brundisium, the

The campaign of Philippi.

---

[1] Cicero, 13 *Phil.* §§ 8–12, 50 ; Velleius, ii. 73. The decree was passed on the 20th of March, B.C. 43.

[2] Dio, 48, 17 *sq.* ; Livy, *Ep.* 123.

[3] App., b. c. iv. 85 ; Dio, 47, 36 ; Livy, *Ep.* 123.

exit of the harbour being blocked by the ships of Statius Murcus, presently reinforced by those of Ahenobarbus. The arrival of Cæsar and his fleet enabled the transports to cross, and Antony marched along the Egnatian Way to join his advanced army at Amphipolis. Cæsar was once more attacked by illness and obliged to stay at Dyrrachium; but hearing that Antony, on his arrival, had suffered some reverses in cavalry skirmishes, he resolved to join him at all hazards. It was indeed a crisis of the utmost importance to him. He was leaving Italy exposed to a double danger, on the east from Murcus and Ahenobarbus, on the south from Sextus Pompeius. If Antony were defeated Cæsar would be in a most alarming position; if Antony won without him, his own prestige would be damaged and he might have to take a second place in the joint government. As before in the Spanish journey his resolution conquered physical weakness, and he reached the seat of war before any general engagement had taken place. He found the army somewhat discouraged. Antony had left his heavy baggage at Amphipolis, which had been secured by Decidius and Norbanus, and had advanced over the wide plain (about sixty miles) to within a mile of the high ground on which Brutus and Cassius were entrenched. But they were too strongly posted to be attacked, and he had suffered some losses in his attempts to draw them down. His men were getting demoralised by the evidently superior position of the enemy, who were protected on the right by mountains, and on their left by a marsh stretching between them and the sea, so that it was impossible to turn their position on either side. Delay was all in favour of Brutus and Cassius, whose fleet afforded abundant provisions, while Antony would have great difficulty in feeding his army during the winter, and the season was already advanced. In mere numbers there was not much difference. Both had nineteen legions; and, though those of Brutus were not at their full strength, he and Cassius had 20,000 cavalry, as against 13,000 of Antony and Cæsar.

The first battle (late in October) was brought on by an attempt of Antony's to get across the marsh by a causeway which he had himself constructed, and storm an earthwork which Cassius had thrown up to prevent him. Repulsing a flank attack made by the division of Brutus, he carried the earthwork and even took the camp of Cassius, who with his main body retired to the heights nearer Philippi with heavy loss. But Antony had also suffered severely, and the fate of the day could not be considered decided until it was known how Brutus had fared, who after the unsuccessful attack on Antony's flank, had attacked Cæsar's division which was opposite him. In this last movement he had been entirely successful. Cæsar's camp had been stormed and his men driven into flight, he himself being absent through illness. The result of this cross victory was that both armies returned to their original positions. Antony, finding that the left wing was defeated, did not venture to remain in the camp of Cassius. Cassius might have returned to it, but for a mistake which cost him his life. He was wrongly informed that Brutus had been defeated, and being short-sighted he mistook a squadron of cavalry that was riding up to announce Brutus's success for enemies, and anticipated what he supposed to be inevitable capture by suicide. Brutus, informed of this, withdrew his men from the attack on Cæsar's camp, and retired behind their lines, occupying again Cassius's abandoned quarters.

First battle at Philippi.

Nearly at the same time as this indecisive battle the cause of the triumvirs had suffered a disaster nearer home. A fleet of transports conveying the Martia, another legion, and some cavalry was destroyed by Murcus and Ahenobarbus, and the greater part of the men had been lost at sea or forced to surrender. Though Brutus did not yet know this he held his position for about a fortnight longer. But the tidings when they came made it more than ever necessary for Antony and Cæsar to strike a blow; for

Second battle at Philippi, November.

they were still more isolated than before and more entirely cut off from supplies. On the other hand, the officers and men in the army of Brutus were inspired by it with an eager desire to follow up the good news by fighting a decisive battle. Brutus yielded against his better judgment and drew out his men. Antony and Cæsar did the same. But it was not until the afternoon was well advanced that the real fighting began. After spending more time than usual in hurling volleys of pila and stones, they drew their swords and grappled in a furious struggle at close quarters. Both Antony and Cæsar were active in bringing up fresh companies to fill up gaps made by the fallen. At last the part of the line against which Cæsar was engaged began to give way, retiring step by step, and fighting desperately all the while. But the order grew looser and looser, until at length it broke into downright flight. The camp of Brutus was stormed and his whole army scattered. Cæsar was left to guard the captured camp, while Antony (as at Pharsalia) led the cavalry in pursuit. He ordered his men to single out officers for slaughter or capture, lest they should rally their men and make a farther stand. He was particularly anxious to capture Brutus, perhaps as hoping to avenge his brother. But in this his men were foiled by a certain Lucilius, who threw himself in their way professing to be Brutus, and the mistake was not discovered till he was brought to Antony. Brutus had, in fact, escaped to high ground with four legions. He hoped with this force to recapture his camp and continue the policy of wearing out the enemy by delay. But a good look-out was maintained by Antony during the night, and the next morning his officers told Brutus that they would fight no more, but were resolved to try to save their lives by making terms with the victors. Exclaiming that he was then of no farther use to his country, Brutus called on his freedman Strato to kill him, which he immediately did.

There is some conflict of testimony as to the severitie

inflicted after the victory. The bulk of the survivors with their officers submitted and were divided between the armies of the two triumvirs. A certain number who had been connected with the assassination and included in the proscription lists felt that they had no mercy to expect, and saved farther trouble by putting an end to their own lives. But some also, as Favonius the Stoic, imitator of Cato, were executed. Suetonius attributes to Cæsar not only special severity, but cruel and heartless insults to those whom he condemned. To one man begging for burial he answered that " that would be business of the birds." A father and son begging their lives he bade play at *morra* for the privilege of surviving. And he ordered the head of Brutus to be sent home that it might be placed at the foot of Iulius Cæsar's statue. As usual there remain some doubts as to these stories. That of the father and son, for instance, is related by Dio, but placed after Actium.[1] And the story as to the head of Brutus is somewhat inconsistent with the honourable treatment of the body attributed to Antony.[2] The refusal of funeral rites is contrary to his own assertion in his autobiography ; and, in the *Monumentum Ancyranum*, he declares that he "spared all citizens." [3] But it must be conceded that until the assassins and their supporters were finally disposed of he shewed himself relentless. The milder sentiments are those of a later time. The plea of a duty to avenge his "father's" murder may mitigate, but cannot annul, his condemnation.

Conduct of Cæsar after the victory.

The victory of Philippi reunited the eastern and western parts of the Empire, and therefore necessitated a fresh distribution of spheres of influence among the triumvirs. The new agreement was reduced to writing and properly attested, partly that Cæsar might silence opposition

Second division of the Empire, B.C. 42.

[1] Dio, 51, 2 ; Suet., *Aug.* 13.

[2] At any rate the head never reached Rome, but was lost at sea. App., b. c. iv. 135 ; Dio, 47, 49 ; Plut., *Ant.*, 22 ; *Brut.* 53 ; Sueton., *Aug.* 13.

[3] Ulpian (dig. 48, 24) quotes this lost autobiography ; see *Mon. Ancyr.* § 3.

at Rome, but partly also because the two men had already begun to feel some of their old distrust of each other. During the late campaign, when there seemed some chance of defeat, Antony had expressed regret at having embarrassed himself with Cæsar instead of making terms with Brutus and Cassius, and such words, however hasty or petulant, would be sure to reach Cæsar's ears. The respect also shewn by Antony to the remains of Brutus, and the evident tendency of the defeated party to prefer union with him rather than with Cæsar, as well as the more generous terms which he was willing to grant, must all have suggested to Cæsar the precarious nature of the tie between them. It was necessary therefore to put the arrangement now made beyond dispute.

The division did not, as two years later, distinguish between East and West. It was still only the western half of the Empire which was to be divided. Italy was to be treated as the centre of government, open to all the triumvirs alike for recruiting and other purposes. The provinces were to be administered in the usual way by governors approved of by them, except that Antony was to have Gaul and Africa, Cæsar Spain and Numidia, thus securing to each a government in the west and south roughly equal in extent and in importance, now that Sicily and Sardinia were in the hands of Sextus Pompeius and thus actually hostile to Italy. But the last article in the agreement, though intended to provide only for a passing state of affairs, did in fact foreshadow the division of the Empire into East and West. By it Antony undertook to go at once to Asia to crush the fragments of the republican party still in arms in the East, and to collect money sufficient for the payment of the promised rewards to the veterans. Cæsar, on the other hand, was to return to Italy to carry on the war against Sextus Pompeius and arrange the assignation of lands. Lepidus was still consul as well as triumvir, but if the suspicion of his being in correspondence with Pompeius was confirmed he was to have no province and was to be suppressed by Cæsar. If it did not turn out to be true Antony undertook to hand over Africa to him. He was throughout treated as subordinate—

> "a slight, unmeritable man,
> Meet to be sent on errands."

The real governors of the Empire were to be Antony and Cæsar. The force of circumstances ordained that for the next ten years Antony was to govern the East and Cæsar the West. And as yet the heart and life of the Empire was in the west. It was this, as much as the difference of his character, which eventually secured to Cæsar the advantage over his colleague and made him master of the whole.

CHAPTER VI

PERUSIA AND SICILY

*actus cum freto Neptunius
dux fugit ustis navibus.*

THE campaign which ended with the second battle at Philippi and the death of Brutus had been won at the cost of much physical suffering to Cæsar, who only completed his twenty-first year some days after it. He had been in bad health throughout, barely able to endure the journey across Macedonia, and only performing his military duties with the utmost difficulty and with frequent interruptions. On his return journey he had to halt so often from the same cause that reports of his death reached Rome. The slowness with which he travelled also gave time for all kinds of rumours to spread abroad as to farther severities to be exercised upon the republican party on his return, and many of those who felt that they were open to suspicion sought places of concealment for themselves or their property.

Augustus returns to Rome after Philippi, early in B.C. 41.

Cæsar sent reassuring messages to Rome, but he did not arrive in the city till the beginning of the next year (B.C. 41). He found Lucius Antonius consul, who had celebrated a triumph on the first day of the year for some trifling successes in Gaul. The real control of affairs, however, was being exercised by Fulvia, the masculine wife of Marcus Antonius, widow successively of Clodius and Curio, against whom

B.C. 41 Consuls
L. Antonius Pietas, Serv. Vatia Isauricus II. Allotting lands for the veterans.

Lepidus had been afraid or unable to act. Fulvia and Lucius professed to be safeguarding the interests of Marcus and fulfilling his wishes, and Lucius adopted the cognomen *Pietas* as a sign of his fraternal devotion. But the moving spirit throughout was Fulvia. Cæsar's first business in Rome was the allotment of land to the veterans. This had been begun a year before in Transpadane Gaul, on the establishment of the Triumvirate, by Asinius Pollio, left in command of that district ; and Vergil has given us some insight into the bitterness of feeling which it often roused :

> "Shall some rude soldier hold these new ploughed lands ?
> Some alien reap the labours of our hands ?
> Ah, civil strife, what fruit your jangling yields !
> Poor toilsome souls—for these we sowed our fields !"

When there was public land available for the purpose, the allotment could generally be made without much friction ; but as there was not enough of it, the old precedent of "colonisation" was followed. A number of Italian towns (nineteen in all) were selected, in the territories of which the veterans of a particular legion were to be settled as *coloni*, with a third of the land assigned for their support. No doubt in each case the lands held by men who had served in the opposite camp were first taken as being lawfully confiscated ; but it must often have happened that there was not enough of such lands, and that those of persons not implicated in the civil wars were seized wholly or in part. In such cases it was understood that the owners were to be compensated by money arising from the sale of other confiscations. But this money was either insufficient or long in coming. Petitions and deputations remonstrating against the injustice poured in upon Cæsar, who, on the other hand, had to listen to many complaints from the veterans of inadequate provision made for them and of promises still unfulfilled.

This was a sufficiently thorny task in itself. But it was

made still more irksome by L. Antonius and Fulvia. Their pretext was that the veterans in Antony's legions were less liberally treated than those in Cæsar's own ; and Lucius claimed, as consul and as repre-senting his brother, the right of settling the allot-ments of Antony's veterans. Cæsar retorted by complaining that the two legions to which he was entitled by his written agreement with Antony had not been handed over to him. Starting from these counter charges they were soon at open enmity, embittered by the frequent collision between the constitutional authority of the consul and the extra-constitu-tional *imperium* of the triumvir. Lucius and Fulvia made capital out of this, maintaining that Marcus was ready to lay down his extraordinary powers as triumvir, and to return to Rome as consul. Fulvia was credited with a more personal motive. Antony's infatuation for Cleopatra was becoming known in Rome, and it was believed that Fulvia designedly promoted civil troubles in the hope of inducing her husband to return.[1] At any rate she and Lucius took advantage of the ill-feeling against Cæsar caused by the confiscation of land. They feigned to plead for the dispossessed owners, maintaining that the confiscations had already produced enough for the payment of all claims, and that, if it were found that this was not so, Marcus would bring home from Asia what would cover the balance. They thus made Cæsar unpopular with both sides—with the veterans who thought that he might have satisfied their claims in full ; with the dispossessed owners, who, over and above the natural irritation at their loss, thought that his measure had not been even necessary, and that he might have paid the veterans without mulcting them, or might

[1] The first meeting of Antony and Cleopatra, when the queen was rowed up the Cydnus in her barge, dressed as Venus with attendant cupids, seems to have been in the autumn of B.C. 42 (Plut., *Anton.* 25–6.). He had seen her once before in B.C. 56 when he accompanied Gabinius to restore her father. But she must have been a mere child then.

Marginal note: L. Antonius and Fulvia take advantage of the discontent.

have waited for the money from Asia. Specially formidable was the anger of landowners who were in the Senate. The discontent was increased by the hardness of the times; for corn was at famine price owing to Sextus Pompeius and Domitius Ahenobarbus infesting the Sicilian and Ionian seas. Cæsar was therefore in a serious difficulty. Unable to satisfy veterans and Senators at the same time, he found how powerless is mere military force against widespread and just resentment. His one answer to senatorial remonstrance had been, "But how am I to pay the veterans ?" Now, however, he found it necessary to let alone the properties of Senators, the dowries of women, and all holdings less than the share of a single veteran. This again led to mutinies among the troops, who murdered some of their tribunes, and were within a little of assassinating Cæsar himself. They were only quieted by the promise that all their relations, and all fathers and sons of those who had fallen in the war, should retain lands assigned to them. This again enraged a number of the losers, and fatal encounters between owners and intruding "colonists" became frequent. The soldiers had the advantage of training, but the inhabitants were more numerous, and attacked them with stones and tiles from the housetops, both in Rome and the country towns. The burning of houses became so common that it was found necessary to remit a whole year's rent of houses let for 500 denarii (£20) and under in the city, and a fourth part in the rest of Italy.

Cæsar was also made to feel that attachment to Antony meant hostility to himself; for two legions de-

Other provocations offered to Augustus. He takes steps to protect himself.

spatched by him to Spain were refused passage through the province by Q. Fufius Calenus and Ventidius Bassus, Antony's legates in Gallia Transalpina.[1] Alarmed by the aspect of affairs, he tried to come to

---

[1] These legions had behaved badly at Placentia, demanding a sum of money from the inhabitants. Calenus and Ventidius may have justified their action on this score (Dio, 48, 10).

some understanding with Lucius and Fulvia, but found them resolutely hostile. The mediation of officers in the army, of private friends and Senators proved of no avail; though he produced the agreement drawn up between Marcus and himself, and offered to allow the Senate to arbitrate on their disputes. Satisfied that by the refusal of this offer Lucius and Fulvia had put themselves in the wrong, he determined to rely upon his army. For Lucius had been collecting men among those offended by Cæsar, and Fulvia, accompanied by many Senators and equites, had occupied Præneste with a body of troops, to which she regularly gave the watchword as their commander, appeared among them wearing a sword, and frequently harangued the men.

The men of Cæsar's army, no doubt acting on a hint from himself, now took the matter into their own hands. They suddenly entered Rome, affirming that they wished to consult the Senate and people. Assembling on the Capitol, with such citizens as ventured to come, they ordered the agreement between Cæsar and Antony to be read, voted its confirmation, constituted themselves judges between the disputants, and named a day on which Fulvia, Lucius, and Cæsar were to appear before them at Gabii. Having ordered these resolutions to be written out and deposited with the Vestals, they peaceably dispersed. Cæsar was present and of course consented to appear; but Lucius and Fulvia, though at first promising to attend at Gabii, did not do so. They scoffed at the idea of a mob of soldiers, a *senatus caligatus* [1] (a "Tommy-Atkins-parliament"), presuming to speak for Senate and people. They were therefore voted in their absence to be in the wrong, and Cæsar's *acta* were confirmed. The show of legality thus gained for him was used by his officers to justify the collection of money in all directions. Temples were stripped of silver ornaments to be coined into money, and troops were summoned from Cisalpine Gaul, which in

[1] From *caliga*, "a soldier's boot."

spite of the claims of Marcus Antonius, was now made a part of Italy without a provincial governor having a right to maintain troops.[1]   Lucius also, as consul, enrolled men wherever his authority was acknowledged, and once more there was civil war in Italy.   It was in many respects a recrudescence of the republican opposition lately headed by Brutus and Cassius.   For Sextus Pompeius had been joined by Murcus with vessels carrying two legions and 500 archers, and was reinforced with the remains of the armies of Brutus and Cassius, which had taken refuge in Cephallenia.   In Africa Antony's legate, Titus Sextius, though he had surrendered the province to Cæsar's legate Lurco, had resumed possession and put Lurco to death.   Lastly, Domitius Ahenobarbus was threatening Brundisium with seventy ships.   It was not clear how far these movements were known or approved by Antony; but the old republican party hoped that their upshot would be the dissolution of the triumvirate, the downfall of Cæsar, and the restoration of the old constitution.

For the present Cæsar left Sextus Pompeius alone.   But he sent a legion to Brundisium and summoned Salvidienus with

Open war between Augustus and L. Antonius B.C. 41-40.

his six legions from his march into Spain. Salvidienus had been opposed by Antony's legates Pollio and Ventidius, and was now harassed in his rear by them when he turned homeward along the *via Cassia.*   Open hostilities, however, began elsewhere.   Some legions at Alba Fucensis showed signs of mutiny, and both Cæsar and Antonius started for Alba, hoping to secure their adhesion.   But Antonius got there first, and by lavish promises won them to his side.   Cæsar only came in time to skirmish with Antonius's rearguard under C. Furnius, and then moved northward to renew his attack on Furnius, who had retreated to Sentinum in Umbria.   On his way he unsuccessfully attacked Nursia, where Antonius had a

[1] Dio, 48, 12.

garrison, and while he was thus engaged Antonius himself led his main army to Rome. Such troops as Cæsar had left in or near the city surrendered to him ; while Lepidus, without attempting resistance, fled to Cæsar,[1] and the other consul made no opposition. Lucius summoned a *contio*, declared that he meant to depose Cæsar and Lepidus from their unconstitutional office, and to re-establish the just authority of the consulship, with which his brother Marcus would be fully satisfied. His speech was received with applause; he was hailed *imperator ;* and the command in a war was voted to him, though without the enemy being named. Reinforced by veterans of his brother's army he started along the *via Cassia* to intercept the returning Salvidienus.

Informed of these transactions Cæsar hurried to Rome, leaving Sentinum still besieged. But it was Agrippa who struck the decisive blow. With such forces as he could collect he, too, marched on the heels of Antonius along the *via Cassia*, and occupied Sutrium, about thirty miles from the city. This cut off L. Antonius's communications with Rome, who, with Salvidienus in front of him and Agrippa in his rear, could neither advance or retire along the *Cassia* without fighting. With an enemy on both sides of him he did not venture to give battle, but turned off the road to Perusia. At first he encamped outside the town expecting to be soon relieved by Pollio and Ventidius. But finding that they were moving slowly, and that three hostile armies—under Cæsar, Agrippa, and Salvidienus—were threatening him, he retired within the walls; where he thought he might safely winter. Cæsar at once began throwing up lines of circumvallation, and cut him off from all chance of supply. Perusia is on a hill overlooking the Tiber and the Trasimene lake. But its position, almost impregnable to assault, made it also somewhat easy to blockade. Fulvia was active in urging the

---

[1] Appian, b. c. 4, 30 ; Dio, 48, 31. Livy, however (*Ep.* 121), says *M. Lepido fuso,* as though he had resisted and had been beaten.

legates of Antony in Gaul and North Italy to come to the relief of Lucius. But Pollio and Ventidius hesitated and doubted, not feeling certain of the wishes of Marcus; and though Plancus cut up one legion on its march to join Cæsar, neither he nor any of the others ventured to engage him when he and Agrippa threw themselves in their way. Pollio retired to Ravenna, Ventidius to Ariminum, Plancus to Spoletium, leaving Lucius to his fate ; while Fufius Calenus remained in the Alpine region without stirring. Meanwhile Salvidienus proceeded to Sentinum, which he took, and shortly afterwards received the surrender of Nursia.

Cæsar was thus able to use his whole force against Perusia. The blockade lasted till March, B.C. 40, when L. Antonius

B.C. 40 Cos. C.
Asinius Pollio,
Cn. Domitius
Calvinus.
Fall of Perusia.

was compelled to surrender by hunger. Cæsar had taken an active share in the siege throughout, and had run serious risks, at one time being nearly captured in a sally of gladiators while engaged in sacrifice ; at another being in danger from a mutiny in his own army. On the fall of Perusia the townsmen suffered severely from the victorious soldiery, apparently without the order, and perhaps against the wish, of Cæsar ; and in the course of the sack the town itself was accidentally set on fire and in great part destroyed. There is again a conflict of testimony as to Cæsar's severities. Suetonius says that he executed a great number, answering all appeals with a stern "Death !" (*moriendum est*) : and his enemies asserted that he deliberately enticed L. Antonius into the war to have an excuse for thus ridding himself of his opponents. Some also reported that he caused 300 to be put to death on the Ides of March, at an altar dedicated to Iulius. On the other hand, it is certain that L. Antonius was allowed to go away in safety ; and Livy says that Cæsar pardoned him and "all his soldiers." Appian attributes the death of such leading men as fell to the vindictiveness of the soldiers. Velleius, of course, takes the same view ; while Dio, equally of course, agrees rather with Suetonius. The first

writer to mention the *Perusinæ aræ* is Seneca; but as his
object was to contrast the clemency of Nero with the cruelty
of Augustus, it is fair to suspect that he was not very particular
as to the historical basis for his allegations. If there were some
executions and also some altar dedicated to Iulius—both of which
are more than probable—it would be easy for popular imagination to connect the two. No doubt all in Perusia who were
implicated in the assassination, or had been on the proscription
lists, would have short shrift.[1] The altar story is unlike the
usual good sense of Augustus; but it seems that in this siege
he desired to emphasise the fact that he was the avenger of
his "father," some at least of the leaden bullets used by the
slingers bearing the words *Divom Iulium*.[2] At any rate,
whether during the siege or by executions after it, there seems
no doubt that at Perusia a blow was struck at the old republican
party—already decimated by civil war and proscription—from
which it never recovered. The victory, moreover, left Cæsar
supreme in Italy. The legates of M. Antonius for the most
part abandoned their legions and went to join him, or to Sicily
to join Sextus Pompeius, who was already negotiating with
Antony. Fufius Calenus, indeed, refused to surrender his eleven
legions; but he died shortly afterwards, and his son handed
them over to Cæsar. Plancus, abandoned by his two legions,
escaped to Antony. Ventidius seems to have done the same;
while Pollio, though not leaving Italy, hung about the east
coast in expectation of Antony's arrival. Among others,
Tiberius Nero abandoned a garrison which he was commanding,
Livia. and, with his wife Livia (soon to be the wife of
Augustus) and his infant son (afterwards the
Emperor Tiberius), fled to Sextus Pompeius. Thither also went

---

[1] Livy, *Ep.* 126; Velleius, ii. 74; App., b. c. v. 48–49; Dio, 48, 14; Seneca,
de Clem. I, II, I. The uncertainty of historical testimony is illustrated by
the fact that both Dio and Appian name C. Canutius (Tr. Pl. B.C. 44) among
the victims at Perusia, while Velleius (ii. 64) says that he was the first to
suffer under the proscription in B.C. 43.   [2] C. I. L., i. 697.

Antony's mother Iulia, whom Pompeius received with respect and employed as envoy to her son ; while Fulvia embarked at Brundisium and sailed to Athens to meet her husband. In Italy there was no one to rival Cæsar, who by these surrenders and desertions had now a formidable army. What he had still to fear was a combination of Antony and Sextus Pompeius and an invasion of Italy by their joint forces.

Such an invasion was, in fact, contemplated. Antony was in Asia when he heard of the fall of Perusia. Crossing to Athens he met Fulvia and his mother Iulia, the latter bringing an offer from Sextus Pompeius of support against Cæsar. Antony was in no good humour with his wife or his agents, whom he must have regarded as having blundered. Nor was he prepared to begin hostilities at once. But he promised that if Sextus did so he would accept his aid ; and that, even if he did not, he would do his best to include him in any terms made with Cæsar. Meanwhile, though the veterans were shy of enlisting against Antony, Cæsar found himself at the head of more than forty legions, and with such an army had no fear of not holding his own on land. But his opponents were strong at sea, and, if they joined with Sextus Pompeius, would have the coasts of Italy at their mercy. He therefore tried on his own account to come to an understanding with Pompeius. With this view he caused Mæcenas to negotiate his marriage with Scribonia, sister of Scribonius Libo, and aunt to the wife or Pompeius. He had been betrothed in early life to a daughter of his great-uncle's colleague, P. Servilius Isauricus, and in B.C. 43 to Antony's stepdaughter, Clodia. But neither marriage had been completed, and at the beginning of Fulvia's opposition, in B.C. 41, he had repudiated Clodia. The present union was one of political convenience only. Scribonia had been twice married, and by her second husband had a son only a few years younger than Cæsar himself. She was therefore much the older, and seems also to have been of difficult temper.

Fresh terms with M. Antonius.

Marriage with Scribonia, B.C. 40.

That at least was the reason he gave for the divorce which followed a year later, on the day on which she gave birth to her daughter Iulia. But a truer reason (besides his passion for Livia) was the fact that by that time circumstances were changed, and it was not necessary, or even convenient, to have such a connection with Sextus Pompeius any longer.

Antony arrived off Brundisium in the summer of B.C. 40, and was joined by Sextus and Domitius Ahenobarbus. The three made some descents upon the coast and threatened Brundisium with a blockade. But before much damage had been done the interference of common friends brought about a reconciliation. Antony consented to order Sextus Pompeius to return to Sicily, and to send away Ahenobarbus as propraetor of Bithynia. A conference was held at Brundisium, at which Pollio represented Antony, Maecenas Caesar, while M. Cocceius Nerva (great-grandfather of the Emperor) attended as a common friend of both. The reconciliation here effected was to be confirmed by the marriage of Antony (whose wife Fulvia had just died at Sicyon) to Caesar's sister Octavia, widow of C. Claudius Marcellus, the consul of B.C. 50. The two triumvirs accordingly embraced, and agreed to a new division of the Empire. An imaginary line was to be drawn through Scodra (*Scutari*) on the Illyrian coast. All west of this line, up to the Ocean, was to be under the care of Caesar, except Africa, which was already in the hands of Lepidus ; all east of it, up to the Euphrates, was to go to Antony. The war against Sextus Pompeius (unless he came to terms) was to be the common care of both, in spite of Antony's recent negotiations with him. Caesar, on his part, agreed to amnesty all who had joined Antony from the armies of Brutus and Cassius, in some cases even though they had been among the assassins.[1]

First reconciliation of Brundisium, and new division of the Empire.

---

[1] This was to safeguard Cn. Domitius Ahenobarbus. There is some doubt, however, as to his having been an assassin. Cocceius denied it (App., b. c. v. 62). Suetonius (*Nero* 3) does the same. But Cicero (2 *Phil.*

Lastly, both were to have the right to enlist an equal number of soldiers in Italy. This agreement was followed by an interchange of hospitalities, in which Antony displayed the luxury and splendour learnt at the Egyptian court, while Cæsar affected the simplicity of a Roman and a soldier.[1]

But Sextus did not tamely submit to be thus thrown over. He resumed his old plan of starving out Italy. His freedman, Menodorus, wrested Sardinia from the governor sent by Cæsar, and his ships, cruising off Sicily, intercepted the corn-ships from Africa. The people of Rome were threatened with famine, and on the arrival of Cæsar and Antony to celebrate the marriage, though an ovation was decreed to both, there were serious riots in which Cæsar's life was in danger, and which had to be suppressed by Antony's soldiers. They were forced by the outcry to renew negotiations with Sextus, whose brother-in-law Libo—in spite of the advice of Menodorus—arranged a meeting between him and the triumvirs at Misenum, early in B.C. 39. Every precaution was taken against treachery at the hands of Pompeius. And not without reason. The execution of Bithynicus three years before had been followed and surpassed by the treacherous murder of Statius Murcus, followed by the cruel crucifixion of his slaves on the pretence that the crime had been theirs. The conference was therefore

A new agreement with Sext. Pompeius, B.C. 39.

§§ 27, 30) says that he was ; and Appian himself does the same (b. c. v. 59). Dio thrice speaks of him as a σφαγεύς (48, 7, 29, 54). At any rate he was condemned by the *lex Pedia*, as though he had been an assassin. He may have been one of those who joined the assassins on the Capitol *after* the murder.

[1] Appian, b. c. v. 65. It has been doubted whether this or the meeting of B.C. 37 was the one to which Horace accompanied his patron Mæcenas. In favour of this one is the mention of Cocceius Nerva by Horace (*Sat.* 1 v. 28, 50), against it is the way in which he is mentioned with Mæcenas as *aversos soliti* componere amicos, as if he had been so engaged before. But though in the second meeting he is not mentioned by Appian, he may have been there. Something has been made of the mention of the croaking frogs (l. 14), as this meeting could hardly have been earlier than July, when the Italian frogs are said to be silent. For the Ovations see C. I. L., i. p. 461.

held on temporary platforms erected at the end of the mole at Puteoli, with a space of water between them. But an agreement having been reached, Antony and Cæsar accepted a banquet on board his ship ; and when Menodorus suggested to Pompeius that he should cut the cables and sail away with them as prisoners, he answered that Menodorus should have done it without asking, but that he himself was bound by his oath. The terms made between them were that Sextus Pompeius was to remain governor of Sicily, Sardinia, and Corsica, with his fleet, as well as in Peloponnesus, but was to remove al garrisons from Italian towns and undertake not to hinder commerce or receive runaway slaves,[1] and should at once allow the corn which he had impounded to reach Italy. On the other hand, all men of rank who had taken refuge with him were to have restitution of civil rights and property. If they had been on the proscription lists, they were to recover only a fourth ; and if they had been condemned for the assassination, they were to be allowed a safe place of exile. Those—not coming under these three classes—who had served in his army or navy, were to have the same claim to pensions as those in the armies of the triumvirs.

Pompeius then returned to Sicily, the triumvirs to Rome. Thence they went different ways : Antony and Octavia to Athens ; Cæsar to Gaul, where the disturbed state of the country required his presence. Now, therefore, begins the separate administration of East and West, and the different principles on which it was carried on contributed largely to the final rupture between the two men. Antony's was the otiose policy of setting up client kings who would take the trouble of government off his hands and yet be ready to pay him court and do him service, because their dignity and power depended upon his supremacy. Thus Darius, grandson of Mithradates, was appointed to Pontus ; Herod to Idumæa and

---

[1] This was one of the chief grievances. Hor., *Ep.* ix. 9, *minatus urbi vincla, quæ detraxerat servis amicus perfidis.*

Samaria; Amyntas to Pisidia; Polemon to a part of Cilicia. To Cæsar, on the other hand, fell the task of preserving order and establishing Roman rule in countries nearer home, peace and good government in which were essential to the comfort of the city. Above all, he was bound to prevent Sextus Pompeius from again interrupting the commerce and corn supply of Italy. The only service of any of Antony's partisans near enough to be of active interest to Rome was the victory of Pollio over the Parthini, for which he was awarded a triumph.[1]

But the war with Sextus Pompeius soon became Cæsar's chief task, and its renewal was with some justice laid at Antony's door. For being as he thought unfairly treated by Antony as to the Peloponnese, which the latter had declined to hand over till he had collected the year's taxes, Pompeius once more began harassing the Italian shores and intercepting corn-ships. Cæsar answered this by bringing troops from Gaul and building ships. He established two depôts—at Brundisium and Puteoli—and invited Antony's presence at Brundisium to discuss the question of war. Antony doubtless found it inconvenient to be closely pressed on this matter, for he was greatly responsible for the difficulty. Though he came to Brundisium, therefore, he left again immediately, without waiting for Cæsar, who had been delayed. He gave out that he was opposed to any breach of the treaty with Pompeius, ignoring the fact that Pompeius had already broken it. He even threatened to reclaim Menodorus as his slave, on the ground that he had been the slave of Cn. Pompeius, and had therefore passed to him as the purchaser of Pompey's confiscated estate. Unable, therefore, to reckon on help from Antony, Cæsar undertook the business himself. He

B.C. 38, renewed war with Sextus Pompeius.

[1] Hor., *Od.* ii. 1, 15-16; Dio, 48, 41; C. I. L., i. p. 461. Pollio after this withdrew from active political life and devoted himself to literature. He seems to have taken no part in the subsequent quarrels between Antony and Augustus.

strengthened assailable points on the Italian coasts; collected ships at Rome and Ravenna; and took over Corsica and Sardinia from Menodorus, who deserted to him and was made joint admiral with Calvisius. He set sail himself from Tarentum, Calvisius from Cosa in Etruria; while a large army was stationed at Rhegium. Pompeius was almost taken by surprise, but yet managed to reach Cumæ and all but defeat his enemy's fleet. This was followed by a violent storm in which Cæsar's fleet suffered severely, off the Skyllæan promontory, and by a second battle in which it only escaped destruction by nightfall. A second terrible storm, which Pompeius's more experienced mariners managed to avoid, still further reduced Cæsar's sea forces. Pompeius, elated by these successes, assumed the title of son of Neptune, and wore sea-green robes as a sign of his origin.[1]

Cæsar did not give in, but he changed his generals. Agrippa was summoned from Gaul, where he had been very successful, and for the first time since the ex-pedition of Iulius Cæsar, had led an army across the Rhine. The construction and command of a new fleet were entrusted to him. With characteristic energy he not only built and manned a large number of ships, but began the formation of a new harbour (*portus Iulius*) for their safety and convenience, by piercing the causeway between the sea and the Lucrine Lake, deepening the lake itself, and connecting it with the lake Avernus. Here he practised his ships and men during the winter, and by the summer of B.C. 36 was ready for action. Meanwhile fresh negotiations with Antony were conducted by Mæcenas, and in the spring of B.C. 37 a reconciliation was arranged at Tarentum, with the help of Octavia. The two triumvirs met on the river Taras, and after an interchange of hospitalities they agreed: First, that the triumvirate should be renewed for a second period of five years, that is, to the last day of

Marginal note: Activity of Agrippa, B.C. 37–6. Second reconciliation with Antony.

[1] Dio, 48, 19, 48; Hor., *Epod*, 9, 17.

B.C. 33.[1] Secondly, that Antony should supply Cæsar with 120 ships for the war against Sextus, and Cæsar give Antony 20,000 men for the Parthian war, which was now becoming serious. Some farther mutual presents were made through Octavia, and Antony started for Syria leaving her and their child with her brother.

Cæsar's plan of campaign for B.C. 37 was that on the 1st of July a combined attack should be made on Sicily, from three points—from Africa by Lepidus, from Tarentum by Statilius Taurus, and from Puteoli by himself. Another violent storm baffled this plan ; Cæsar had to take refuge at Elea ; Taurus had to put back to Tarentum ; while, though he reached Sicily, Lepidus returned without effecting anything of importance. Another winter and spring had to be spent on preparations, and it was not till the autumn of B.C. 36 that the final engagements took place. At that time Pompeius's fleet was stationed along the Sicilian coast from Messana to Tyndaris, with headquarters at Mylæ. After reconnoitring the position from the Æolian islands, Cæsar left the main attack to Agrippa, while he himself joined Taurus at Leucopetra. Agrippa repulsed the enemy's ships, but not decisively enough to enable him to pursue them to their moorings. It was sufficient, however, to enable Cæsar to cross to Tauromenium, leaving his main body of men on the Italian shore under the command of Valerius Messalla. Here he soon found himself in the greatest danger. Pompeius's fleet was not held up by Agrippa, as Cæsar thought, but appeared off Tauromenium in force. Messalla was unable to cross to his relief, and a body of Pompeian cavalry attacked

Continued war with Sextus Pompeius, B.C. 37-36.

---

[1] The first period ended on the last day of B.C. 38 ; but neither Antony nor Cæsar had laid down their imperium of office. They now assumed that it went on from the first day of B.C. 37, the want of legal sanction during the intervening months being ignored. There is no certain trace of this second triumvirate having been confirmed by a *lex ;* yet one would think that they would have taken care to have that formality observed. See p. 143.

him while his men were making their camp. Cæsar himself managed to get back to Italy, but he left three legions, 500 cavalry, and 2,000 veterans, under Cornificius, encamped near Tauromenium, surrounded by enemies, and without means of supply. He himself landed in a forlorn condition, with only one attendant, and with great difficulty found his way to the camp of Messalla. Thence he sent urgent orders to Agrippa to despatch a force to the relief of Cornificius ; commanded Messalla to send for reinforcements from Puteoli ; while Mæcenas was sent to Rome with full powers to suppress the disorders likely to occur when the ill-success against Pompeius was known.

The force despatched by Agrippa found Cornificius and his men in a state of desperate suffering in the difficult district of Mount Ætna, and conveyed them to the fleet off Mylæ. So far, though Pompeius had maintained his reputation at sea, he had not shown himself able to follow up a success on land. And now the tide turned against him. Agrippa seized Tyndaris, in which Pompeius had large stores, and Cæsar landed twenty-one legions there, with 2,000 cavalry and 5,000 light-armed troops. His plan was to assault Messana while Agrippa engaged the fleet. There was a good road from Tyndaris to Messana (*via Valeria*), but Pompeius still held Mylæ and other places along the coast with the defiles leading to them. He was misled, however, by a report of an immediate attack by Agrippa, and, withdrawing his men from these defiles and strong posts, allowed Cæsar to occupy them. Finding the report to be false, he again attempted to intercept Cæsar as he was marching with some difficulty over the district of Mount Myconium. But his general (Tisienus) failed to take advantage of Cæsar's unfavourable position, who, having meanwhile been joined by Lepidus, encamped under the walls of Messana. He was now strong enough on land to send detachments to occupy the various towns from which Pompeius drew supplies ; and therefore it was necessary for the latter to abandon Sicily, or to scatter the fleet of Agrippa and so open the sea to his transports. In a second battle off Mylæ, however, the fleet of Pompeius was nearly annihilated, and though he escaped himself into Messana, his land forces under Tisienus surrendered to Cæsar. When he discovered this Pompeius, without waiting for the eight legions which he still had at Lilybæum, collected seventeen ships which had survived the battle and fled to Asia, hoping that Antony in gratitude for former services would save and possibly employ him.

The danger which for so many years had hung like a cloud about the shores of Italy was thus at an end. But there was one more danger still to be surmounted before Deposition of Lepidus. Cæsar's authority was fully established in Sicily. The eight Pompeian legions from Lilybæum under Plennius presently arrived at Messana. Finding Pompeius fled, as Cæsar happened to be absent, Plennius handed them over to Lepidus, who was on the spot. Lepidus added them to his own forces, and being thus strengthened, conceived the idea of adding Sicily to his province of Africa. It had not been definitely included in any of the triumviral agreements ; he had been the first to land there, and had in the course of his march forced or persuaded many cities to submit,— why should he have less authority to deal with it than Cæsar, whose office was the same as his own ? He had originally bargained for Narbonensis and Spain : he had been shifted to Africa without being consulted, and his provinces had been taken over by Cæsar. He was now at the head of twenty-two legions, and would no longer be treated as a subordinate. His arguments were sound ; but they needed to be backed by a determination as fixed as that of his rival, and, above all, by the loyalty of his army. Neither of these advantages were his. In a stormy interview with Cæsar he shewed that he could scold as loudly as another. But when they had parted, he failed from indolence or blindness to detect that Cæsar's agents were undermining the fidelity of his men, especially in the Pompeïan legions, by informing them that without Cæsar's assent the promises made them by Lepidus would not be held valid. On his next visit to the camp of Lepidus with a small body-guard, Cæsar was mobbed by the soldiers, and even had some of his guard killed, but when in revenge for this he invested Lepidus with his main army, the forces of the latter began quickly to melt away, and before many days he was compelled to throw himself at Cæsar's feet. He was forced to abdicate the triumvirate, and sent to reside in Italy, where he remained till his death (B.C. 13), in a private capacity and subject to constant mortifications. He retained indeed the office of Pontifex Maximus, because of certain religious difficulties as to its abdication, but he was never allowed to exercise any but the most formal functions. This treatment of a colleague was not generous ; but the whole career of Lepidus since the beginning of the civil war had been weak and shifty. He was " the greatest weathercock in the world " (*ventosissimus*),[1] as Decimus Brutus told Cicero, and he certainly presents the most pitiful figure of all the leading men of the day.

The old policy of Philippi and Perusia was followed as regards the forces of Pompeius. Senators and equites were,

The fate of Sextus Pompeius, B.C. 35.

it is to be feared, in many cases put to the sword ; while the rank and file were admitted into Cæsar's army, and an amnesty was granted to those Sicilian towns which had submitted either to Pompeius or Lepidus. Africa and Sicily Cæsar took over as his part of the Empire and appointed proprætors to each. He did not attempt to pursue Sextus Pompeius ; he preferred that Antony should have the responsibility and perhaps the odium of dealing with him. In fact, he did some years afterwards make his execution a ground of complaint against Antony. Yet Antony seems to have had little choice in the matter. For Pompeius

---

[1] Cicero, *ad Fam.* xi. 9 ; Cicero himself calls him *levissimus, ad Brut.* I, 15, § 9.

acted in Asia much as he had acted in Sicily and Italy, capturing towns and plundering ships, while sending peaceful embassies to Antony, offering to serve him against Cæsar. Being at last compelled to surrender to Amyntas (made king of Pisidia by Antony), and being by him delivered to Antony's legate Titius, he was taken to Miletus and there put to death. But it was, and still remains, uncertain whether this was done by Antony's order.

He was just forty, and had led a strange life since he witnessed his father's death from the ship off the coast of Egypt. He seems to have had some generous qualities which attached men to him. But the times were out of joint, and he was compelled to live the life of a pirate and freebooter, having a grievance against every successive party that gained power at Rome, trusting none, and feeling no obligation to treat them as fellow citizens or even as noble enemies. He seems to have missed more than one chance of crushing Cæsar; but his troops, though numerous, were fitted neither by spirit nor by discipline to encounter regularly trained legions in open fight. We cannot withhold a certain admiration for the courage and energy which maintained him as virtual ruler of no inconsiderable portion of the Roman Empire for nearly twelve years.

CHAPTER VII

ACTIUM

*Altera iam teritur bellis civilibus
aetas.
Sævis Liburnis, scilicet invidens,
privata deduci superbo
non humilis mulier triumpho.*

WHEN Sextus fled from Sicily Cæsar was about to complete his 27th year. It was nearly nine years since, while little more than a boy, he had first boldly asserted himself in opposition to men more than twice his own age, and had forced those who had been statesmen before he was born to regard him as their champion or respect him as their master. Since that time he had had little rest from grave anxieties or war. At Mutina, Philippi, Perusia, and in Sicily, he had tasted danger and disaster as well as victory; and had more than once been in imminent hazard. These fatigues had been made more trying by frequent illness, apparently arising from a sluggish liver, to which he had been subject from boyhood. Through all he had been supported by an indomitable persistence and a passionate resolve to avenge his adoptive father, all the more formidable perhaps in a character naturally cold and self-contained. As he went on there gradually awoke in him a nobler ambition, that of restoring and directing the distracted state. Neither now nor afterwards do the more vulgar attributes of supreme power—

The early manhood of Augustus and its fruits.

wealth, luxury,and adulation—seem to have had charms for him.
He felt the governing power in him, he believed in his "genius,"
what we might call his "mission," and the difficulties of a
divided rule became more and more clear to him. From this
time, therefore, he used every means which wise statesmanship or
crafty policy could suggest to rid himself of the remaining partner
in the Triumvirate, and to gain a free hand in the work of
restoration which he had already begun.

In private life he had taken a step which was the source of
a life-long happiness to him. The political marriage with
Scribonia in B.C. 40, contracted with the idea of

Marriage with Livia B.C. 38. conciliating Sextus Pompeius, had been ended by
divorce on the very day of the birth of his only
daughter Iulia. The reason alleged was her disagreeable
disposition ; but, besides the change in the political situation,
there was another reason of a more personal nature. The
peace of Misenum had permitted many partisans of Brutus,
Cassius, or Lucius Antonius, who had fled to Sextus Pompeius,
to return to Rome. Among others came Tiberius Nero,[1]
with his young wife, Livia Drusilla. Unless statues and coins
are more than usually false, she was possessed of rare beauty.
In B.C. 38 she was twenty years old, and had one son (the future
Emperor Tiberius) now in his fourth year, and was within
three months of the birth of her second son Drusus. Even
to the lax notions of divorce and re-marriage then current this
seemed somewhat scandalous. A year was held to be the
necessary interval for a woman between one marriage and
another. But the object of this convention was to prevent
ambiguity as to the paternity of children ; and when Cæsar
consulted the pontifices, they told him that, if there was no
doubt as to the paternity of the child with which Livia was
pregnant, the marriage might lawfully take place at once. No
opposition seems to have been made by Livia's husband, who was

---

[1] In B.C. 52 Cicero had wished to give his daughter Tullia in marriage
to Tiberius Claudius Nero (Cic., *Att.* 6, 6.).

at least twenty years her senior.[1] He acted as a father in
giving her to her new husband, and entertained the bridal pair
at a banquet. The marriage was so prompt that a favourite
page of Livia's, seeing her take her place on the same dinner
couch as Cæsar, whispered to his mistress that she had made a
mistake, for her husband was on the other couch. On the
birth of Drusus, Cæsar sent the infant to its father, thus com-
plying with the conditions of the pontifices. That the two
men should have been on good terms is not incredible in view
of the prevailing sentiment as to divorce. We find Cicero, for
instance, writing effusively to Dolabella almost directly after he
had compelled his daughter to divorce him for gross misconduct,
and there are other instances. At any rate Tiberius Nero, on
his death-bed in B.C. 33, left the guardianship of his sons to
Cæsar ; and in spite of such a beginning the marriage proved
permanently happy. Cæsar was devoted to Livia to the day of
his death ; his last conscious act was to kiss her lips.[2]

The victory in Sicily left him supreme in the West, and
he at once devoted himself to the re-establishment of order
and prosperity. The relief to Italy and Rome was
immense ; for with Pompeius master of the sea
the city was always in danger of famine, and the
Italian coast of devastation. This feeling of relief found
expression in the proceedings of the Senate, which now began
those votes of special honours and powers to Cæsar, which in
the course of the next ten or twelve years gradually clothed
him with every attribute of supremacy in the state. On his
return from Sicily he was decreed an ovation, as after Philippi,[3]

Honours voted to Cæsar.

---

[1] He was quæstor in B.C. 48, and therefore was not born later than
B.C. 78. Livia was born B.C. 58.

[2] Even Suetonius, not much inclined to speak good of Augustus, admits
that he *dilexit et probavit unice ac perseveranter.*

[3] Suetonius (C. 22) says that he had two ovations—after Philippi and after
the bellum Siculum. But if an ovation was decreed after Philippi, it was
not celebrated till B.C. 40, upon the reconciliation with Antony. The second
was this. Another had been voted in B.C. 43 after Mutina, but not
celebrated (C. I. L. I. p. 461). See also p. 100.

as well as statues and a triumphal arch. On the day of the victory over Pompeius (2nd of September), there were to be *feriæ* and *supplicationes* for ever; he and his wife and family were to be feasted on the Capitol; and he was to have the perpetual right of wearing the laurel wreath of victory. He refused the office of Pontifex Maximus, as long as Lepidus lived, but he accepted the privileges of the tribuneship—the personal sanctity which put any one injuring or molesting him under a curse, and the right of sitting with the tribunes in the Senate. This it seems gave him practically the full *tribunicia potestas* within the city. But it was a novel measure, and its full consequences were not perhaps foreseen.[1] He had twice before wished to be elected tribune, but his " patriciate " stood in his way. This was meant as a kind of compromise, and it furnishes the keynote to his later plans for absorbing the powers of the republican offices.

Cæsar's chief difficulties now came from the large military forces of which he found himself possessed, either by his own enlistment or from that of the various defeated leaders. To disband them was neither safe in view of possible complications with Antony, nor possible without finding large sums of money or great tracts of unoccupied land with which to reward the men; whereas his object now was to put an end to confiscation, fines, and unusual imposts, and to bring back confidence and security. After suppressing more than one incipient mutiny, he contrived to secure enough land for those who had served their full time, partly by purchases from Capua, where there was still a good deal of unassigned land. He repaid the colony by granting it

Measures of conciliation and restoration.

---

[1] Appian (b. c. v. 132) says that they elected him perpetual tribune (αὐτὸν · · εἵλοντο δήμαρχον ἐς ἀεί). Dio (49, 15) only says that they gave him the personal sacredness of the tribunes and the right of sitting on their bench. Orosius (6, 18, 34) says that the Senate voted *ut in perpetuum tribuniciæ potestatis esset.* We shall have to discuss this later on, but it must be said at once that Augustus was never tribune, and that it seems doubtful whether the *tribunicia potestas* was given in its full sense at this time.

revenues from lands at Cnossus in Crete, which had become *ager publicus* on the defeat of the pirates, and on some of which a Roman colony was not long afterwards established.[1] Some of the men, again, who had been most clamorous and mutinous he sent to Gaul as a *supplementum* to colonies already existing, or to found new colonies.[2] He was thus able to make remission of taxation, as well as of arrears due from the lists of forfeiture published by the triumvirs. His enemies said that his object was to throw the odium of their original imposition upon Antony and Lepidus ; or to make a merit of necessity, since in most cases it would have been impossible to collect the money. These motives may have had a share in his policy, but he doubtless also wished to restore confidence and cause an oblivion of the miseries of the civil wars. For the soldiers who remained various other employments were found. The weakness of the central government had long been shewn by the existence of marauding bands in various parts of Italy. The civil wars had aggravated the evil, till travelling had become dangerous almost everywhere, and even the streets of Rome were unsafe. Cæsar now organised a police force of soldiers under Sabinus Cotta to patrol the city and Italy, and within a few months the evil was much mitigated.[3] Besides this, Statilius

The wars for security of frontiers.

Taurus was sent with an army to restore order in the two African provinces—Proconsularis and Numidia.[4] Another expedition was sent against the Salassi, inhabiting the modern Val d'Aosta, who had for two years been holding out against Antistius Vetus. He had driven them into their mountain fastnesses ; but when he left the district they once more descended and expelled the Roman garrisons. The war was entrusted to Valerius Messalla, who

---

[1] Dio, 49, 14 ; Strabo, x. 4, 9.   [2] Dio, 49, 34.

[3] App., b. c. v. 132 ; Suet., *Aug.* 32.

[4] Or, as they were also called Vetus, and Nova Africa. The former was the old province formed of the territory of Carthage, the latter the new province formed after the battle of Thapsus (B.C. 46) of which the first governor was the historian Sallust. See pp. 23-4.

reduced them at least to temporary submission (B.C. 35-34).[1] Another similar war was that against the Iapydes, living in what is now Croatia, who in their marauding expeditions had come as far as Aquileia and plundered Roman colonies. To this Cæsar went in person. He destroyed their capital, Metulum, on the Colapis (mod. *Kolpa*), after a desperate resistance, in the course of which he was somewhat severely injured by the fall of a bridge. The rest of the country then submitted.[2] The Iapydes had no doubt provoked the attack. But that does not seem to be the case with the Pannonians, whom Cæsar proceeded to invade. They were a mixed Illyrian and Celtic tribe, dwelling in forests and detached villages without great towns, and appear to have lived peaceably. But Cæsar resolved to take their one important town, Siscia, at the junction of the Kolpa and Save, partly as a convenient magazine in wars against the Daci, and partly for the mere object of keeping his army employed and paid at the expense of a conquered country. The siege of the town lasted thirty days, and after its fall he returned to Rome, leaving Fufius Geminus to continue the campaign. So again in the spring of B.C. 34 Agrippa was sent against the Dalmatians, and when later in the season he was joined by Cæsar in person, their chief towns were taken and burnt; and this people, who since their defeat of Gabinius in B.C. 44-43, had been practically independent, had again to submit and pay tribute, with ten years' arrears, and restore the standards taken from Gabinius. Their submission was followed by that of other tribes, and by the middle of B.C. 33, the whole of Illyricum was restored to obedience.

These were the sort of successes to make a man popular at Rome; for they were not costly in blood or treasure, and they affected the interests of a large number of merchants and

---

[1] Appian, *Illyr.* 17 ; Dio, 49, 34, 38.

[2] Appian, *Illyr.* 18-21 ; Dio, 49, 37. The Iapydes (a wild tribe) had first been attacked in B.C. 129 by C. Sempronius and subdued after some disasters. (Livy, *Ep.* 59.)

men of business. Nor was this all. One of his legates, Statilius Taurus, was so successful in Africa, and another, C. Norbanus, in Spain, that both were decreed triumphs in B.C. 34, and in the same year Mauretania was made a Roman province. Cæsar had declined a triumph after the Pannonian war, but accepted honours for Octavia and Livia, who were exempted from the *tutela*, to which all women were subject; and during these two years his name was becoming associated with success and with the expansion of the Empire and of trade.

This was accompanied by restorations and improvements in the city calculated to appeal still more strongly to popular imagination. In B.C. 33 Agrippa as ædile re-

Improvements in the city. formed the water supply of Rome, constructing 700 basins, 500 fountains, and repairing the aqueducts.[1] He also cleansed the cloacæ, adorned the circus, distributed oil and salt free, and opened the baths gratis throughout his year of office, besides throwing among the spectators at the theatre *tesseræ* (tickets) entitling the holders to valuable presents. Cæsar himself, who was consul for a few months at the beginning of B.C. 33, erected the Porticus Octaviæ, named in honour of his sister, with the spoils of the Illyrian and Pannonian wars,[2] and began the building of the temple of Apollo and the two libraries, on the site bought for a house on the Palatine before B.C. 36, when that of Hortensius had been granted to him by the Senate,[3] and while he was still living in the house of Calvus near the Forum.

These successes in the Western provinces, combined with such costly improvements in the city, impressed

The contrast of Antony's career. (as it was intended that they should) the minds of the people in Rome with the feeling that Cæsar's name was the best guarantee for the era of peace and pros-

---

[1] Pliny, *N. H.* 36 § 121.

[2] The Porticus Octaviæ, of which an arch remains, was a rectangular cloister enclosing the temples of Jupiter Stator and Iuno Regina.

[3] Dio, 49, 15; Sueton., *Aug.* 72.

perity which seemed at last to be succeeding the ruin and horror of civil war. In strong contrast—carefully emphasized by Cæsar and his friends—were the military expeditions in the East, and the extravagance of Antony's infatuation for Cleopatra in Egypt. In B.C. 40 he had been roused from the intoxication of love and revelry in Alexandria to find Syria in the hands of the Parthian Pacorus, son of Orodes,

The Parthians. and of Labienus, son of the old legate of Iulius, who had joined the enemy after the battle of Philippi. They had defeated and killed his legate, Decidius Saxa, and taken possession of the province. It is true that next year, B.C. 39, P. Ventidius drove away Labienus, and in B.C. 38 defeated the Parthians and killed Pacorus. But Antony was jealous of Ventidius, deposed him from his command, and went in person to besiege the remains of the Parthian army in Samosata, where they had been received by Antiochus, king of Commagene. He failed to take the town, and though in his despatch he took all the credit of previous successes, the truth was well known in Rome. After his failure at Samosata he made somewhat inglorious terms with Antiochus, and going off to meet Cæsar at Tarentum left C. Sosius in charge of Syria. Sosius put down an insurrection in Judæa and established Herod as king (B.C. 38–7). But in B.C. 36 Antony suffered severe reverses in an expedition against Phraates, who had just succeeded his father Orodes as king of Parthia. One success, however, in the course of an inglorious campaign enabled him to send home laurelled despatches, the real value of which Cæsar and his friends took care should be known. In B.C. 35 he began carving out a kingdom for his elder son by Cleopatra, and making preparations for an expedition against the king of Armenia, whom he accused of failing in his duty of supporting him in the previous year. Having first made a treaty of friendship with the king of Media, in B.C. 34 he invaded Armenia, and getting possession of the person of the king by an act of treachery which shocked Roman sentiment—not very scrupulous in such matters—he brought him in silver chains to Alexandria.

Thus Antony's career as an administrator and defender of the Empire was rightly or wrongly looked upon as comparing unfavourably with that of Cæsar. But still more shocking to Roman feeling was his position in Cleopatra's court. Though the moral standard at Rome was far from high, it was rigid in regard to certain details. Just as a valid marriage could only be contracted with a woman who was a *civis*, so for a man in high position to live openly with a foreign mistress, however high her rank, was peculiarly scandalous. The beloved Emperor Titus, a hundred years later, had to give way to this sentiment and dismiss his Idumæan mistress. But that a Roman imperator should not only have such a connection with a "barbarous" queen, but should act as her officer and courtier; that she should have a bodyguard of Roman soldiers; should give the watchword to them as their sovereign; and should even employ them to deal with what in one sense or another was Roman territory—this seemed an outrage of the worst kind. In a poem written it seems while the campaign at Actium was still undecided, but when rumours of Antony's defeat were reaching Rome, Horace well expresses the disgust with which the position conceded to Cleopatra by Antony's fondness was regarded :

> False, false the tale our grandsons will declare—
> That Romans to a woman fealty sware ;
> Shouldered their pikes ; presented arms ; and did
> Whate'er her wrinkled eunuchs deigned to bid :
> Or that among our Roman flags were seen
> The gauzy curtains of her palanquin." [1]

Antony himself made no concealment as to the queen's connection with the army. After his disastrous expedition of B.C. 36–5, Cleopatra supplied him with money, and he told

[1] Horace, *Epod.* ix. ii. ; *cp.* Ov., *Met.* 15, 826.

his men when paying them that they were receiving it from her. The connection also involved a breach with Cæsar. Their friendship—always doubtful—had been patched up from time to time by formal reconciliations; in B.C. 43 after Mutina; in B.C. 40 at Brundisium; and in B.C. 37 at Tarentum. For a time Antony had found great pleasure in the society of Octavia, with whom he lived for a time at Athens. But after the meeting at Tarentum he left Octavia with her brother on his return to the East, and soon fell again under Cleopatra's spell, who, though not beautiful, fascinated him by her art and infinite variety. When in B.C. 35 Octavia, trying to effect another reconciliation, went to Athens, taking money and soldiers for him from her brother, Antony accepted the gifts, but sent her word that she was to return to Rome. Cæsar would have had her repudiate him at once, but she seems to have been sincerely attached to him, and to have shrunk from the idea of an insult to herself being made an occasion of civil war. She persisted in living in his town house, and in bringing up with liberality, not only her own children by him, but also Antony's children by Fulvia.

But after his return from the Armenian expedition (B.C. 34) Antony became still more infatuated with Cleopatra. He publicly gave her the title of "Queen of Queens," and her eldest son the name of Cæsarion and "King of Kings"; while to his two sons and daughter by Cleopatra he assigned kingdoms in Syria, Armenia, Libya, and Cyrene. He had the assurance to write to the Senate asking for the confirmation of these *acta*. When his two friends, C. Sosius and Cn. Domitius Ahenobarbus entered on their consulship (1st of January, B.C. 32), they resolved to suppress this despatch, in spite of Cæsar's wishes; but they communicated to the Senate his message that the second period of the Triumvirate having expired (on the last day of B.C. 33), he had no desire for its renewal. He did not, however, lay down his imperium, and the object of this

Final breach between Cæsar and Antony.

declaration was to embroil Cæsar with the Senate, should he wish to retain his extraordinary powers. Ahenobarbus, indeed, had had enough of civil war and wished to take no step likely to bring it about. But Sosius made an elaborate speech in praise of Antony, and attacking, or at least depreciating, Cæsar; and was only prevented from bringing in a motion in Antony's favour by the intervention of a tribune. A few days after this Cæsar (who had not been present on the 1st of January) summoned the Senate, and delivered a speech from the consular bench, which though studiously moderate as regards himself, was very outspoken as regards Sosius and Antony. No one ventured to reply, and the Senate was dismissed with the assurance that Cæsar would produce proofs of what he had said about Antony. The two consuls, without taking any farther step, left Rome privately and joined Antony in Alexandria. They were followed by a considerable number of Senators, Cæsar giving out that they went with his full consent, and declaring that others might go if they chose.

This was a division of the governing body similar to that of B.C. 49–8, and it was evident that a civil war was imminent.

The grievances of either side.

Sentiment was by no means all on one side at Rome, as is proved by the numbers of the Senate who crossed to Antony. Party feeling, in fact, was so keen that the very boys in the streets divided themselves into Cæsarians and Antonians;[1] and both leaders shewed great eagerness by arguments and declarations to put themselves in the right. Antony's grievances against Cæsar were:

---

[1] An anecdote has been preserved illustrating the policy of "sitting on the hedge," which must have prevailed among many while the contest between the two leaders was still undecided. After Actium, when Cæsar landed (the time and place are charmingly vague), a man offered a *cornix* which had been taught to say, "Ave, Cæsar, imperator et victor." He bought the bird at a large price, whereat the man's partner, being jealous, urged that he should be forced to bring another bird, which when brought repeated as it had been taught, "*Ave, Antoni, imperator et victor.*"

(1) that he deprived Lepidus of Africa without consulting him; (2) that he had not shared with him the countries formerly controlled by Sextus Pompeius; (3) that he enrolled soldiers in Italy without sending him the contingents due by their agreement. Cæsar's against Antony were that he was occupying Egypt (not a Roman province) without authority; had executed Sextus Pompeius, whom he (Cæsar) had wished to spare; had disgraced the Roman name by his conduct to the king of Armenia, by his connection with Cleopatra, and by bestowing kingdoms on his children by her; and, lastly, had wronged him by acknowledging Cæsarion as a son of Iulius Cæsar. Letters and messages were interchanged for some months on these and other points, both trying to justify themselves. Antony, in one letter at least, preserved by Suetonius, ridicules in the coarsest terms what he regards as Cæsar's hypocritical or prudish objection to his connection with the queen. But at length Cæsar found means to discredit Antony in the eyes of the Senators, and to convince them that they must prevent an invasion of Italy by a proclamation of war against Cleopatra, which would be understood to be against Antony. He did this by using two of Antony's officers who had quarrelled with him and returned to Rome— M. Titius and L. Munatius Plancus. The latter, Cicero's correspondent, the governor of Celtic Gaul in B.C. 44, and consul in B.C. 42, had joined Antony in Alexandria as his *legatus*, and had been much in his confidence. He is held up to scorn by contemporary writers as a monster of fickleness and an ingrained traitor, and his thus turning upon Antony was regarded with much contempt even by the Cæsarians. The story he and his companion had to tell, however, served Cæsar's turn. They brought word that, on hearing of his speech in the Senate, Antony had publicly divorced Octavia in the presence of the Senators, and had announced that he intended to undertake a war against him. They also told how Antony styled Cleopatra his queen and sovereign, gave her

a bodyguard of Roman soldiers, with her name on their shields; how he escorted her to the forum and sat by her side on the seat of justice; how, when she rode in her chair he walked on foot by her side among the eunuchs; how he called the general's quarters or prætorium "the Palace," wore an Egyptian scimitar and a robe embroidered with gold, and sat on a gilded chair; and how some religious mummeries had been played, in which he took the part of Osiris, she of the Moon and Isis. The Roman world believed that Antony was bewitched by Cleopatra; and the serious consequences likely to ensue were made more manifest by his will, of which Augustus got either a copy or an account of its contents from Plancus, and read it publicly from the Rostra. In it Antony affirmed the legitimacy of Cæsarion, gave enormous legacies to his children by Cleopatra, and ordered his body to be buried with that of the queen's in the royal mausoleum. Altogether people began to believe the report that he meant to hand over the Empire, even Rome itself, to Cleopatra, and to transfer the seat of government to Alexandria. There was one of those

War proclaimed against Cleopatra, B.C. 32.

outbursts of feeling which carries all before it. Even those who had been neutral, or inclined to be suspicious of Cæsar, turned violently against Antony. He was deposed from the consulship for B.C. 31, to which he had been elected, and declared to be divested of imperium. It seems probable that he was not at first declared a *hostis*,[1] but war was voted against Cleopatra. It was enough for his enemies that he should be found fighting with the Egyptians against Rome; and the vote was well understood to include him. Cæsar was appointed to proclaim the war with all the *Fetial* ceremonies, and the Senate assumed the *sagum*.[2]

---

[1] Dio, 50, 5 ; but Suetonius, *Aug.* 17, says that he was declared a *hostis*.

[2] Dio, 50, 5. Thus Horace, on hearing the rumours of Antony's defeat, exclaims (somewhat prematurely), *Epod.* ix. 27 :

> "*Terra marique victus hostis punico.*
> *lugubre mutavit sagum.*"

Both sides were now making preparations in earnest. Cæsar could draw forces from Italy, Gaul, Spain, Illyricum, Sardinia, Sicily, and other islands. Antony relied on Asia, the parts about Thrace, Greece and Macedonia, Egypt, Cyrene, and the islands of the Ægean, besides a large number of client kings who had owed their position to him.[1] He silenced their scruples, when gathered at Samos, by pointing out that they would not be formally at war with Rome, and promising that within two months of the victory he would lay down his imperium and remit all power to the Senate and people. Nor did he confine his exertions to the East. Agents were sent to cities in Italy carrying money, though Cæsar—who kept himself well informed—frustrated this attempt for the most part.

From Samos Antony removed his headquarters to Athens, whence in the winter of B.C. 32 he started to invade Italy. But at Corcyra he got intelligence of an advanced squadron of Cæsar's fleet near the Acroceraunian promontory, and thinking that Cæsar was there in full force, he decided to put off hostilities till the spring, by which time he expected to be joined by the forces of the client kings. He himself wintered at Patræ, distributing his forces so as to guard various points in Greece. He scornfully rejected Cæsar's proposal for an interview, on the ground that there was no one to decide between them, if either broke the terms upon which they might agree. The proposal was probably not seriously meant. It was only another means of putting Antony in the wrong.

Antony approaches Italy.

Nothing, however, was done before the end of the year, a storm having frustrated an attempt of Cæsar's to surprise some of the enemy's ships at Corcyra. In the early spring the

---

[1] Bocchus of Mauretania, Tarchondemus of Cilicia Aspera, Archilaus of Cappadocia, Amyntas of Lycaonia and Galatia, Philadelphus of Paphlagonia, Malchus of Arabia, Herod of Judæa, Sadalas of Thrace, Polemon of Pontus. (Plut., *Ant.* 61.)

first move was made by Agrippa, who swooped down upon
Methone in Messenia, killed Bogovas, late king of
Mauretania, and harassed the shores of Greece by
other descents, in order to divert Antony's attention; who was now with his main fleet in the
Ambracian gulf, having secured the narrow entrance to it by
towers on either side, and with ships stationed between. His
camp was close to the temple of Apollo, on the south side of the
strait. The successes of Agrippa encouraged Cæsar to move.
He landed troops in Ceraunia, making his own headquarters at
the "Sweet Haven," at the mouth of the Cocytus, and sent
a detachment by land round the Ambracian sea to threaten
Antony's camp. Having failed to entice the fleet from the
Ambracian gulf, or to tempt the men to abandon Antony, he
seized the high ground overlooking the strait, and opposite
Actium, where he entrenched himself, on the ground on which
he afterwards built Nicopolis. The summer months, however,
were wearing away without any decisive blow being struck by
either side, and the delay was irksome to both. Rome was in a
state of simmering revolt owing to distress and heavy taxes, a
discontent which found expression in the conspiracy of Lepidus,
son of the ex-triumvir. It was promptly suppressed, indeed,
and Lepidus was sent over to Cæsar to receive his condemnation; but, nevertheless, Mæcenas, who was in charge of Rome,
found that he had no sinecure. To Antony, again, delay
meant discontent among his Eastern followers, tottering loyalty,
and probable abandonment. Above all, Cleopatra was in a
highly nervous state, and was urging a return to Egypt. At
last on the 31st of August, a cavalry engagement going against
Antony, she became clamorous; and after long deliberation,
Antony determined to follow her advice. He ordered his ships
to be prepared for battle, but with the secret intention of
avoiding a fight and sailing away to Alexandria.[1]

Cæsar was kept informed of this, and resolved to prevent it.

[1] Dio, 50, 14-23.

Marginal note: B.C. 31, Con., C. Octavius Cæsar, Val. Messala. The beginning of hostilities.

His idea was to allow the Antonian fleet to issue out and begin
their course, and then to fall upon their rear. But
Agrippa thought that the superior sailing powers
of the Antonian fleet would render this impossible,
and urged an attack as soon as the ships cleared the straits.
There had been rough weather for four days, but on the 3rd of
September there was a calm,[1] or only some surf from the preceding storms; and when the trumpet rang out for the start
Antony's huge vessels, furnished with towers and filled with
armed men, began streaming out of the straits. They did not
at first show any signs of standing out to sea. The ships took
up a close order and waited to be attacked. There was a brief
pause on Cæsar's side. He or Agrippa hesitated to attack
these great galleons with their smaller craft. But before long
an order was issued to the vessels on the extremities of Cæsar's
fleet to exert their utmost powers in rowing in order to get
round Antony's two wings. To avoid this danger Antony was
forced against his will to order an attack.

Battle of Actium, Sept. 3, B.C. 31.

The battle raged all the afternoon without decisive result;
though the smallness of Cæsar's vessels proved in many points a
decided advantage. They could be rowed close up to bigger
ships and be rowed away again when a shower of javelins had
been poured in upon the enemy. Antony's men returned the
volleys and used grappling irons of great weight. If these irons
caught one of the smaller ships they were doubtless very
effective; but if the cast missed they either seriously damaged
their own ship, or caused so much confusion and delay that an
opportunity was given to the enemy to pour in fresh volleys of
darts. At length Cleopatra, whose ships were on the southern
fringe of the fleet, could bear the suspense no longer. She gave
the signal for retreat, and a favourable breeze springing up, the
Egyptian ships were soon fading out of sight. Antony thinking

---

[1] Dio, 50–31, says, ὑετός τε ἐν τούτῳ λαβρὸς καὶ ζάλη πολλή. But Plutarch,
Ant. 65, says that after four days of stormy weather on the day of battle
νηνεμίας καὶ γαλήνης γενομένης συνήεσαν.

that this was the result of a panic, and that the day was lost, hastened after the retiring squadron. The example of their leader was followed by many of the crews, who lightening their ships by throwing overboard the wooden towers and war tackle, fled with sails full spread. But others still maintained the struggle, and it was not until Cæsar's men began throwing lighted brands upon the enemy's ships that the rout became general. Even then the work was not over, for Cæsar spent the whole night on board endeavouring to rescue men from the burning ships.[1]

Antony got clear off from pursuit, but his camp on land was easily taken, and his army was intercepted while trying to retreat into Macedonia. For the most part the men took service in Cæsar's legions, the veterans being disbanded without pensions. Antony, however, was followed to Egypt by many of his adherents of rank, and still thought himself strong enough to make terms with Cæsar. But he could no longer hope for aid from the client kings. They all hastened to make their peace with Cæsar, or were captured and punished. Even Cleopatra was secretly prepared to betray him.

The finale of the civil war in Egypt, B.C. 31–30.

With the exception of one visit to Brundisium of seven days, to suppress the mutiny of some discontented veterans, Cæsar spent the winter at Samos and Athens, collecting an army and navy destined to deprive Egypt permanently of its independence. Cleopatra had indeed tried to brave it out. She returned to Alexandria with her prows decked with flowers and her pipers playing a triumphant tune. The people are not likely to have been deceived, but there was no sign of revolt. She was able to seize the property of those whose fidelity she suspected, and even put to death the captive king of Armenia to gratify her ally the king of Media. Messages were sent to the kings who had been allied with Antony, and for some gladiators whom he had in training at Trapezus.

[1] Suet., *Aug.* 17.

The gladiators started but were intercepted, and no help came from the client kings. A still worse disappointment awaited him in Cyrene, over which he had placed L. Pinarius Scarpus with four legions. When, leaving Cleopatra at Parætonium, he went to take over these legions, Pinarius refused to receive him and even put his messengers to death, and shortly afterwards handed over his province and army to Cæsar's legate, Cornelius Gallus. This was an unmistakable sign that Antony's day of influence was over. Cleopatra returned to Alexandria and made secret preparations for retiring into Asia, as far as Iberia (*Georgia*) if necessary, though still keeping up appearances and sending in every direction for aid. Cleopatra's son Cæsarion and Antony's son by Fulvia (Antyllus) were declared of man's estate and capable of governing, and messages were despatched to Cæsar proposing that Antony should retire to Athens as a *privatus*, and that Cleopatra should abdicate in favour of Cæsarion. The queen also, without Antony's knowledge, sent Cæsar a gold sceptre and crown. He made no reply to Antony, but answered in threatening terms to Cleopatra, while sending his freedman Thyrsus to give her privately a reassuring message. Antony suspected the purport of Thyrsus's mission, and with a last ebullition of his old swaggering humour had him flogged, and sent back with the message, that if Cæsar felt aggrieved he might put his freedman Hipparchus (who had joined Cæsar) to the torture in revenge. But things went from bad to worse with him. News came that the gladiators had been impounded, that his own legatus in Syria (Q. Didius) had bidden the Arabs burn the ships while he had prepared for his flight in the Red Sea, and that the only two client kings who had seemed inclined to stand by him—those of Cilicia and Galatia —had fallen off. He therefore tried once more to open communications with Cæsar. He sent him as a prisoner one of the assassins of Iulius, whom he had protected and employed, P. Turullius, and a considerable sum of money by the hands of his son Antyllus. Cæsar put Turullius to death and took the money, but returned no answer to Antony, though he again sent a private message to Cleopatra. Presently Antony was informed that Gallus had arrived at Parætonium with the four legions taken over from Pinarius; and believing that even now his personal influence was sufficient to win back the men, he hurried thither, accompanied by the remains of his fleet coasting along to guard him. But this only led to farther disaster. The soldiers refused to listen to him; and when his ships entered the harbour the chains were made fast across the mouth and they were trapped. On land he now found himself between two hostile forces; for Cæsar with Cleopatra's connivance had landed at Pelusium and was marchïng on Alexandria, and Gallus was attacking him from Parætonium. He once more executed one of those rapid movements for which he was famous. Hastening back to Alexandria he flung his cavalry upon Cæsar's vanguard when tired with its march. But the success of this movement encouraged him to make a general attack, in which he was decisively beaten. His last resource, the ships still remaining in the harbour of Alexandria, failed him. Acting under Cleopatra's orders the captains refused to receive him. The queen, it is said, had shut herself up in the Tomb-house or Ptolemæum, hoping to drive Antony to despair and suicide, as the only solution of the difficulty. If that was indeed her motive, she was both successful and repentant. Antony stabbed himself, and begged to be carried to the Tomb-house, where he died in her arms.

Cæsar was now eager to secure Cleopatra's person. He sent Gallus to her with soothing messages, which he delivered to her at the porch. But while he was speaking

Death of Cleopatra.

with her C. Proculeius entered by a window, seized the queen, and conveyed her to the Palace, where she was allowed her usual attendants and all the paraphernalia of royalty. Of the two accounts of Cæsar's interview with her the more picturesque one is given by the

usually prosaic Dio. He found her looking charming in her
mourning, surrounded by likenesses of various kinds of the
great Iulius, and in the bosom of her dress a packet of letters
received from him. On his entrance she rose with a blush
and greeted him as her lord and master. She pleaded that
Iulius had always honoured her and acknowledged her as
queen. She read affectionate passages from his letters, which
she kissed passionately with tears streaming from her eyes,
being at the same time careful to put respectful admiration and
affection for Cæsar himself into her looks and the tone of her
voice. Cæsar quite appreciated the drama thus played for his
behoof, but feigned unconsciousness, keeping his eyes fixed on
the ground and saying nothing but : " Courage, madam ! Do
not be alarmed, for no harm will happen to you." He said no
word, however, as to her retention of royal power, nor did
his voice betray the least tenderness. In an agony of disappointment she flung herself at his feet and besought him by
the memory of his father to allow her to die and share
Antony's tomb. Cæsar made no reply except once more to
bid her not be alarmed ; but he gave orders that though
allowed her usual attendants she was to be closely watched.
Cleopatra understood only too well that the intention was to
.take her to Rome that she might adorn the victor's triumph.
But in order to secure greater freedom she feigned submission
and to be busied in collecting presents to take to Livia.
Having thus diminished the vigilance of Epaphroditus and her
other guards, she some days afterwards made a parade of
writing a letter to Cæsar, which she induced Epaphroditus to
convey. When he returned, however, he found the queen,
decked in royal robes, lying dead with two of her waiting
women dead or dying by her side. " No one knows for
certain," says Dio, " how she died. Some say that a venomous
snake was conveyed to her in a water-vessel or in some
flowers. Others that the long pin with which she fastened
her hair had a poisoned point, with which she pricked her arm,"

Plutarch, with a like expression of doubt, says that the snake was conveyed in a basket of figs ; and that on receiving the letter brought by Epaphroditus Cæsar understood her purpose and hurried to the Palace to prevent it, and even summoned some of the mysterious Psylli—snake charmers and curers—to suck out the poison.[1] But in spite of his disappointment, he admired her spirit and gave her a royal funeral. Perhaps after all he felt relieved of a difficulty. According to Plutarch she had shown him that she was not to be easily managed. At the end of her conversation with Cæsar, he says, she handed him a schedule of the royal treasures. But when one of her stewards or treasurers remarked that she was keeping back certain sums, the enraged queen sprang up, clutched his hair, and beat his face with her fists. When Cæsar smiled and tried to pacify her, she exclaimed : " A pretty thing, Cæsar, that you should visit and address me with honour in my fallen state, and that one of my own slaves should malign me ! If I have set apart certain women's ornaments, it was not for myself, but for Octavia and Livia, that they might soften your heart to me."

It would be pleasanter if the death of Cleopatra and the confiscation of her treasury were the end of the story. But the executions of the two poor boys, Cæsarion and Antyllus, were acts of cold-blooded cruelty. The former, who could not have been more than sixteen, had been sent by his mother with a large supply of money to Æthiopia, but was betrayed by his *pædagogus*, overtaken by Cæsar's soldiers, and put to death. The young Antonius (or Antyllus) begged hard for his life, and fled for safety to the *heroum* of the divine Iulius, constructed by Cleopatra, but was dragged away and killed. He could at most have been no more than fourteen, and had in

---

[1] The earlier writers, Horace (*Od.* i. 37, 27) and Velleius (2, 87), seem to have no doubt about the snake story. Livy (as we have him) says nothing either way except that she died by suicide (*Ep.* 133). It is the later writers who express the doubt, Suet., *Aug.* 17 ; Plut., *Ant.* 86 ; Dio, 51 14.

childhood been betrothed to Cæsar's infant daughter, Iulia. Perhaps the pretensions of Cæsarion to the paternity of Cæsar, and his acknowledgment as heir to the throne of Egypt, made his death inevitable; but the extreme youth of Antyllus and his helplessness might have pleaded for him. The rest of Antony's children were protected by Octavia, and brought up as became their rank.

It is impossible not to feel some sympathy for Antony, who had thus flung away fame and life for a woman's love. But it was doubtless a happy thing for the world that the direction of affairs fell to the cautious Augustus rather than to him. He had some attractive qualities, but no virtues. Boundless self-indulgence in a ruler more than outweighs good-nature or liberality. It brings more suffering to subjects than the occasional gratification caused by the latter qualities can compensate. His scheme for erecting a series of semi-independent kingdoms in the East would almost certainly have been the cause of endless troubles. He was not more than fifty-three at his death, but there were signs of a great decay of energy and activity. The people thought of him—

> "As of a Prince whose manhood was all gone,
> And molten down in mere uxoriousness."

And undoubtedly, if instead of spending a winter in Samos in luxury and riot and part of another at Athens in much the same way, he had begun his attack on Cæsar a year earlier, the result might have been different. But he let the occasion slip and found, as others have done, that the head of Time is bald at the back.

CHAPTER VIII

Hic ames dici pater atque princeps.

THE seven years which followed the death of Antony and Cleopatra witnessed the settlement of the new constitution in
The new
constitution. its most important points. It has been called a *dyarchy*, the two parties to it being the Emperor and the Senate. They were not, however, at any time of equal power. As far as it was possible Augustus rested his various functions on the same foundation as those of the Republican magistrates, and treated the Senate with studious respect. But in spite of all professions, in spite even of himself, he became a monarch, whose will was only limited by those forces of circumstance and sentiment to which the most autocratic of sovereigns have at times been forced to bow. The important epochs in this reconstruction are the years B.C. 29, 27, 23 ; but it will be necessary sometimes to anticipate the course of events and to speak at once of what often took many years to develop.

The reduction of the vast armaments which the various phases of the civil war had called into existence was made
Reduction of
the army. possible by the wealth which the possession of Egypt put into Cæsar's hands. Though Egypt became a Roman province it was from the first in a peculiar position, governed by a "prefect" appointed by

the Emperor, who took as his private property both the treasures and domain lands of the Ptolemaic kings and the balance of the revenues over the expenses. This formed the nucleus of what was afterwards called the *fiscus*,[1] the imperial revenue as distinguished from the *ærarium* or public treasury. He was thus enabled to disband many legions at once, without the dangerous discontent of the veterans, or the irritation of fresh confiscations. It was imperatively necessary to do this if he wished to avoid the dangers which had so often threatened the State from leaders of overgrown military forces. The number of legions under arms during the preceding ten years was indeed formidable. In B.C. 36, when Cæsar took over those of Lepidus and Sextus Pompeius, he had forty-four or forty-five legions under his command.[2] Between that time and the war with Antony he had reduced the number to eighteen. But after the victory at Actium and the death of Antony, the legions taken over from him, along with those newly raised for the war, again amounted to fifty. Therefore Cæsar had twice to deal with a body of about 250,000 men. He says himself that in the course of his wars half a million citizens had taken the military oath to him. The wealth of Egypt served to purchase lands or compensate towns for such as were taken for the veterans. From first to last more than 300,000 men were provided for in this way.[3] An important purpose also served by this measure was the repeopling of Italy and the renovation of many towns which during the civil wars, or from other causes, had fallen into decay. Republican pre-

---

[1] This word—one of the financial terms borrowed from Sicily (lit. "a basket")—was perhaps not commonly used in the restricted sense in the time of Augustus, though the thing existed. Into the emperor's *fisc* went the revenues of the imperial provinces; but the balance in the case of most was not large. Cicero indeed (*pro lege Manil*, § 14) says that none of the provinces except Asia did much more than pay its expenses. This was probably an exaggeration, but not a very great one.

[2] This, it should be remembered, was exclusive of the legions regularly raised for certain provinces and stationed in them.

[3] *Mon. Ancyr.* 3, 16.

cedent was followed by recalling the ancient practice of settling
"colonies" in the Italian towns, but with this difference, that
the new colonists were usually treated as a *supplementum* of an
already existing colonia, lands being purchased for them from
private owners or from the communities. Augustus claims
twenty-eight of such Italian colonies, of which thirteen are
known to have been in past times " Roman " or "Latin"
colonies. Other towns, besides a money compensation, were
rewarded by being raised to the status of a colony, generally
with the addition of "Iulia" or "Augusta" to their name.
This system was presently extended beyond Italy—to Africa,
Spain, Sicily, Illyricum, Macedonia, Achaia, Gallia Narbonensis,
Asia, Syria, and Pisidia. Settlements in these countries were
all colonies of veterans, except Dyrrachium, which was filled
with dispossessed Italians. This was not altogether a novelty :
for extra-Italian colonies had been already established in
Cisalpine and Transalpine Gaul, at Carthage, and at Corinth.
Iulius Cæsar is said to have settled 80,000 citizens in this way
outside Italy. The extra-Italic colonies of Augustus, however,
differed from these last in regard to status. They had what
was called *Latinitas*, that is, citizenship without the right or
voting or holding office at Rome. In virtue of this citizenship they came under the Roman law and belonged to the
assize (*conventus*) of the provincial governors. Some of them,
again, had the special privileges which were summed up in the
general term "Italic right" (*ius Italicum*), and included freedom from the jurisdiction of the provincial governor (*libertas*),
and exemption from tribute (*immunitas*). The general aim
seems to have been to put the extra-Italic colonies as far as
possible in the same position as those in Italy. As a rule also
the veterans settled in a colony had been enlisted in the province, and had, therefore, already local connections. Augustus
took trouble in fostering and adorning these towns, whether in
Italy or the provinces, and records with pride that many had
become populous cities during his life-time. In many cases

their subsequent importance shewed that they had been well selected. Thus Carthage had a great mediæval history ; Durazzo and Philippi were long places of consequence ; Saragossa, Merida, Cordova, Aix, Patras, Beyroot, all trace their prosperity to the colonisation of Augustus.[1]

Nor did he meanwhile forget to encourage restoration at Rome, to which he had already given a strong impulse.

Improvements at Rome.

Nothing had damaged Antony in the eyes of the Romans more than the report of his intention to transfer the seat of Empire to Alexandria. A similar report as to the establishment of an imperial city for the East at Ilium caused a like uneasiness a few years later, which found expression in one of Horace's most spirited odes.[2] Cæsar prudently shewed not only that he held firmly by the Imperial position of Rome, but that he also wished to make it externally worthy to be the capital of the world. As in all his projects, no one co-operated more loyally than Agrippa. But others also were pressed into the service ; and those especially who had earned triumphs were encouraged to use a portion at least of their spoils in public works. In the next few years there was a great outburst of temple restoration,[3] and it became the fashion among the immediate friends and followers of Augustus to signalise their tenure of office or a military success by undertaking some important building. Horace again has reflected the view of such matters which the official classes were expected to take, and perhaps to a certain extent did take. The sufferings of the Romans in the revolutionary period had undoubtedly been great. The ruinous state of the temples was doubtless connected with the unsettled times—whether as cause or consequence, who could

---

[1] Traces of the work of Augustus in provincial towns may still be seen, as at Nismes and other towns in South-eastern France.

[2] Horace, *Odes* iii. 3.

[3] In the *Mon. Ancyr.* 20, he says that he repaired 82 temples in B.C. 28, and the Flaminian road with all but two of its bridges in B.C. 27.

exactly say ?   It was not unnatural to suppose that among the
other *delicta maiorum* this too had moved the wrath of the gods.
At any rate moral laxity went side by side with scepticism and
neglect of religious observances.   Nor need we regard either
poet or emperor as a monster of hypocrisy in supporting such
a doctrine.   Habit and tradition are stronger than philosophy.
There always remains the Incalculable after all our reasoning ;
and many to-day regret the decay of religious sentiment as a
public misfortune, who are yet profoundly uncertain as to
what they in truth believe themselves.

On his return from Asia and Greece, where he had spent
the winter and spring of B.C. 30–29, Cæsar was received with
enthusiasm by all classes.   Solemn sacrifice was
offered by the consul in the name of the people,
and every honour which the Senate could bestow
was awaiting his acceptance.   Those voted after Actium were
lavishly increased in September B.C. 30, on the news of Antony's
death and the occupation of Alexandria.   Two triumphal
arches were to be erected, one at Rome and another at
Brundisium ;[1] the temple of the divine Iulius was to be
adorned with the prows of captured ships ; his own birthday,
the day of the victory at Actium, and that of the entry into
Alexandria were to be for ever sacred ; the Vestal Virgins
and the whole people were to meet him on his return in
solemn procession ; he was to have the foremost seat at all
festivals ; and was to celebrate three triumphs—one for the
victory over the Dalmatian and neighbouring tribes, a second
for Actium, and a third for Egypt.   The *tribunicia potestas*

Honours bestowed on Cæsar, B.C. 30–27.

---

[1] The foundations of the triple arch at Rome were discovered in 1888
between the temple of Cæsar and that of the Castores.   For the inscription see C. I. L. vii. 872. SENATUS . POPULUSQUE . ROMANUS .
IMP . CÆSARI . DIVI . IULI . F . COS . QUINCT . COS . DESIG . SEXT .
IMP . SEPT . REPUBLICA . CONSERVATA. The date here indicated
is B.C. 29. See Lanciani, *Ruins of Ancient Rome*, p. 270. Middleton,
Remains of Ancient Rome, vol. i. p. 284. There does not appear to be
any record of the arch at Brundisium.

for life had again been voted to him with the right of exercising it within a mile radius beyond the walls. He was to have the right to hear all cases on appeal and to have a casting vote in all courts. His name was to be mentioned in public prayers for the state. On the 1st of January, B.C. 29, all his *acta* had been confirmed ; and when it became known that the Parthians had referred a disputed succession to the throne to his arbitration, some fresh honours were devised. The disasters under Crassus and Antony had made the Romans particularly sensitive in regard to the Parthians ; and this apparent acknowledgment by them of a superiority attaching to Augustus, however indefinite, was represented by the court party and the court poets, not only as a veritable triumph over the Parthians, but as a step in a career of Eastern conquest of almost unlimited extent.[1] Accordingly his name was now to be coupled with those of the gods in hymns ; a tribe was named *Iulia* in his honour ; he was to wear the chaplet of victory in all assemblies ; and to nominate as many members as he chose to all the sacred colleges. Cæsar accepted most of these honours, but begged to be excused the procession on his return. This was an honour which he always avoided if he could, preferring to enter the city quietly by night. It was no doubt a trying ordeal at the end of a long journey, and he may have felt like Cromwell that a larger crowd still would have come out to see him hanged. The three triumphs, however, were now celebrated with the greatest splendour, especially the third over Egypt, in which a figure of the dead queen

---

[1] Vergil, *Georg.* iv. 560, *Cæsar dum magnus ad altum fulminat Euphratem bello.* Horace, *Od.* I, 12, 53 :

> *Ille seu Parthos Latio imminentes*
> *Egerit iusto domitos triumpho,*
> *Sive subjectos Orientis oræ Seras et Indos.*

Similar exaggerations will be found scattered throughout the poems of Propertius (ii. 7, 3 ; iii. 1, 13 ; iii. 23, 5 ; iv. 3, 4 ; iv. 4, 48 ; iv. 11, 3). Still more exaggerated language was used afterwards on the restoration of the standards (B.C. 20).

lying upon a couch, with son and daughter beside her, was a prominent feature.

Cæsar now had ample powers for every purpose of government. The *tribunicia potestas* in itself gave him legislative initiative and control over other departments.

The increase of the Patriciate and the Census. It was afterwards regarded as the most important of his powers. But in his first measures of reform he availed himself rather of his powers as consul. The consulship was to be really, as it always remained nominally, the chief state office, combining all the prerogatives once centred in the *rex*. Thus in holding the Census of B.C. 28 he acted as Consul with his colleague Agrippa, exercising indeed a *censoria potestas*, though not one formally bestowed, but as inherent in the consulship.[1] He concluded it with the solemn *lustrum*, which had not been performed for forty-two years, the last Censors (B.C. 50) having apparently been prevented from performing this solemnity by the outbreak of civil war. The Census was made the occasion of a reform in the *ordines* and especially of the Senate. In the first place, he recruited the dwindling number of patrician *gentes* by raising certain plebeian families to the patriciate, as his own family had been raised by Iulius in B.C. 45 in virtue of a *lex Cassia*. The same power was now accorded to him by a law proposed by L. Sænius, who was consul during the last two months of B.C. 30. The

---

[1] A good deal of confusion in our authorities has arisen by a failure to distinguish between a *censoria potestas* granted like the *tribunicia* by special vote and the *censoria potestas* inherent in the consulship, from which it had been devolved in B.C. 444. In the *Monumentum*, ch. 8, Augustus himself says nothing about the *censoria potestas*, but in the Venusian fasti (C. I. L. ix. 422) we find *imp. Cæsar vi. M. Agrippa II. Cos. idem censoria potestate lustrum fecerunt.* Suetonius (c. 27) knew that he was not Censor, but supposed him to have acted under a decree granting him *morum legumque regimen perpetuum*, an office, however, which Augustus expressly says that he declined (*Mon.*, ch. 6). Dio (52, 42) describes him as τιμητεύσας σὺν τῷ Ἀγρίππᾳ, a direct confusion between the censorial power possessed by a Consul and that bestowed independently. He, however, apparently did receive *censoria potestas* (never the censorship) in B.C. 19 for five years.

object seems to have been to preserve a kind of nobility, which at the same time should have certain political disabilities. The patricians, indeed, still had the exclusive right of being appointed to certain religious offices, but, on the other hand, they were debarred from the tribuneship and the plebeian ædileship,[1] the two offices in which a man by legislative proposals or lavish expenditure might make himself politically conspicuous.

A similar desire to restore the ancient order of the State prompted his reformation of the Senate. The powers of this body had always been great precisely because they were not defined by law ; and by associating it with himself he would gain all the advantages ot this indefiniteness and prestige, while really keeping full control of it. Iulius Cæsar had made the mistake of treating it with studied disrespect, and his chief enemies were within its walls. The Triumvirs, though in reality despotic, had looked to it to give their *acta* an outward show of legality. Thus on Octavian's demand it had condemned Q. Gallius in B.C. 43, and Salvidienus in B.C. 40, for treason. It had confirmed the triumviral *acta* en bloc, giving Antony charge of the Parthian war and ratifying his arrangements in the East in advance. It had voted triumphs and other honours to the triumvirs and their agents. It was the Senate that in B.C. 41 voted L. Antonius an *hostis,* that in B.C. 32 decreed war against Cleopatra, deposed Antony from consulship and imperium, and in B.C. 31–30 voted the various honours and powers to the victorious Cæsar. The late civil war had in a way made the importance of the Senate more prominent. So many Senators had joined Antony at Alexandria that, like Sertorius in Spain and Pompey in Epirus, he had professed to have the Senate with him. The victory of Actium had pricked that bubble,

The lectiones Senatus.

---

[1] *Rex sacrorum*, the greater *flamens*, the Salii had still to be patricians. An *interrex* also must be a patrician, but that office was now practically at an end. The last case of an *interrex* was in B.C. 52.

and the Senate at Rome remained the only Senate of the Empire. Cæsar was wise to put himself under the ægis of this ancient and still respected body. But it was necessary to secure its dignity and effectiveness, which had suffered in various ways during the revolutionary period. Among other things its numbers had been swollen and often with men of inferior social standing. Iulius Cæsar had filled it with his creatures—provincials from Gaul and Spain, sons of freedmen, centurions, soldiers, and peregrini—so that a pasquinade was put up by some wit that "no one was to show a new Senator the way to the Senate House."[1] Another batch of Senators was introduced after Cæsar's death, chiefly by Antony, in virtue of real or fictitious entries found in Cæsar's papers, whom the populace nicknamed "post-mortem Senators" (*Senatores orcini*),[2] or sometimes even on their own initiative without any other formality than assuming the laticlave and senatorial shoe.[3] Many Senators no doubt perished in the proscriptions, in the subsequent battles of Philippi and Perusia, and in the contests with Sextus Pompeius, but the Triumvirs appear to have been lavish in enrolling new members without regard to fortune, origin, or official position ; and so careless were they in this matter that cases are recorded of unenfranchised slaves having obtained office and seats in the Senate and being then

---

[1] A jest that was reproduced in London when country peers came up to vote against the Home Rule Bill and were said by gossips to be obliged to ask their way to the House of Lords. A popular ballad also was sung about the streets—

"Cæsar leads the Gauls in triumph and guides them to the Senate house ;
Gauls have doffed their native brogues and donned the Senate's laticlave !"

Sueton., *Cæs.* 72, 80. See also Cicero, 9 *Phil.* § 12 ; 13 *Phil.* § 27 ; *ad Fam.* vi. 18 ; *Bell. Afr.* 28 ; Dio, 42, 51 ; 43, 27. Compare the career of P. Ventidius Bassus, brought a prisoner from Asculum to adorn the triumph of Pompey after the Social war, then a mule contractor to Cæsar, and afterwards going through all the offices to the consulship in B.C. 43.

[2] On the analogy of slaves enfranchised by will. Suet., *Aug.* 35 ; Plutarch, *Ant.* 15.

[3] Cicero calls such a man a *voluntarius Senator*, 13 *Phil.* § 28.

recognised and claimed by their masters.[1]   The result was that at the time of the battle of Actium there were more than a thousand Senators.[2]   This was too large a number for practical work, without taking into consideration inferiority of character. No doubt a good many who had sided with Antony disappeared in various ways ; but in now making a formal *lectio* Cæsar resolved to reduce the number still more.   Sixty voluntarily resigned and were allowed to retain the purple and certain social distinctions, but a hundred and forty were simply omitted from the new list.   By this means the roll was reduced to about six hundred, which continued to be the number in subsequent lectiones.

To secure their attendance and to prevent interference in the provinces the regulation was enforced which prohibited any Senator from leaving Italy (except for Sicily or Gallia Narbonensis) unless he had imperium or was on a legatio,[3] that is, practically, unless he was serving the state in some way on Cæsar's nomination.   In the next *lectio* (B.C. 19) Augustus tried an elaborate system of co-option, by nominating thirty on the existing roll, each of whom were to name five who were to draw lots for admission, and so on till the number was made

---

[1] Dio, 48, 34.

[2] Suet., *Aug.* 35 ; Dio, 52, 42.   In the *Monumentum* (c. 25) he reckons the number of Senators who had served under him as "more than 700." To them must be added those who had not taken active service and those who were with Antony.

[3] Dio, 52, 42.   The regulation had always existed because every Senator was bound to attend if called upon, and therefore must be within reach, unless he was one of those *qui reipublicæ causa abessent.* (Livy, 43, 11.) Thus Cicero, defending the Senators who crossed over to join Pompey in Epirus, says to Atticus (viii. 15) that there was hardly one who had not a legal right to cross, either as having imperium, or being legatus to an imperator.   The usual means of evading this was to obtain a *libera legatio* for a fixed time.   Occasionally a man got himself named an ordinary legatus to a provincial governor, but was allowed to go elsewhere with some colourable commission.   But this was an abuse.   See Cicero, *ad Fam.* xii. 21 ; *ad Q. Frat.* ii. 9 ; *ad Att.* xv. 11.   Sicily and Gallia Narbonensis were excepted as being practically Italy, or, as Cicero says, "suburban provinces."

up. But finding that it was not worked fairly he stopped this and made up the roll himself. This continued to be the system, but as time went on the difficulty was not so much to exclude unworthy men as to induce enough of the right sort to serve. Membership became less attractive as the imperial power developed, and the holding of profitable offices depended on the will of the Emperor, who was not bound to select from the Senate. Moreover, a property qualification was now required. None had existed under the republic by definite law, though a certain fortune was regarded as practically necessary ; and as the Senate was recruited from the *ordo equester,* a minimum was in the last century of the republic automatically secured. Cæsar fixed 800,000 sesterces, and later on a million sesterces as the Senatorial fortune, though in cases of special fitness he gave grants to enable men to maintain their position. Still the honour of membership was not found to make up for its disabilities—the difficulty of going abroad and the prohibition as to engaging in commerce. In B.C. 13 Augustus was obliged to compel men who had the property qualification to serve. Even then the attendance was so slack that in B.C. 11 the old quorum of four hundred was reduced. In B.C. 9 various regulations were introduced to facilitate business, such as the publication of an order of the day (λεύκωμα), fixed days of meeting, a variation as to the quorum required for different kinds of business, a scale of fines for non-attendance, the selection by lot of thirty-five Senators to attend during September and October, and an extension to the prætors of the power of bringing business before the house. Towards the end of the life of Augustus, when his age made it too much of an exertion to meet the full Senate, a committee of sixteen Senators was selected by lot to confer with him at his own house. The inevitable consequence was that this small committee practically settled most questions, which only came formally before the whole body, whose administrative function was farther lessened by the diminished importance of the

ærarium as compared with the imperial treasury or *fiscus.*
Finally, it lost the right of coining silver, retaining only the
bronze. On the whole, then, the tendency was towards
restricting the functions of the Senate and making membership
less attractive. But this does not appear to have been the
original design of Augustus. He habitually addressed it with
respect, referred all his powers to its confirmation, and took it
into his confidence on imperial affairs. He revived the ancient
dignity of *princeps Senatus*—in abeyance since the death of
Cicero—and held that rank himself all his life. Certain of the
provinces were still left to its management, and cases of
majestas were referred to its decision. The publication of the
Senate's *acta* had originated with Iulius Cæsar (B.C. 59), who
was not likely to have done anything to enhance its prestige.
The prohibition of this publication by Augustus was perhaps
intended partly to protect the proceedings from criticism, partly
to emphasise the fact that the Senate shared with him the
intimate secrets of government which it was not for the public
advantage to have generally known. The effect, however,
was not good ; what could not be ascertained with exactness
from official sources was often misrepresented by irresponsible
rumour, and one of the early measures of Tiberius was to reverse
this order.[1]

With a Senate purified by his first *lectio* Cæsar felt that the
constitution might in form, at any rate, be restored. But first
the end of the revolutionary period had to be
marked. On January 11, B.C. 29, the temple of
Ianus was closed, for the first time since B.C. 235,
for the third time in all Roman history. It was still shut
when Cæsar returned from Asia, and on the 1st of January,
B.C. 28, the *augurium salutis* was taken. This ceremony—
ascertaining by augury whether prayers for the people should
be offered to Salus—could only be performed in time of complete peace. At the same time a single edict annulled all the

The end of the
anarchy.

[1] Sueton., *Aug.* 36; Dio, 53, 19; Tacitus, *Ann.* 5, 4.

acta of the triumvirs, which were to have no force from his
sixth consulship (B.C. 28).[1] The constitutional significance of
this will be best seen by recalling some facts as to the triumvirs.
Whether its *acta* were good or bad, the triumvirate was in itself
a suspension of the constitution. Established by a *lex* on the
27th of November, B.C. 43, to hold office till the 31st of
December, B.C. 38, its authority had been renewed in the course
of B.C. 37 to the 31st of December, B.C. 33, whether by
another *lex* or by the will of the triumvirs themselves is a
moot point.[2] But, however appointed, the triumvirs were
like dictators in superseding all other magistrates, and more
powerful than dictators from the length of their tenure of
office, and because the terms of their appointment (*reipublicæ
constituendæ causa*) gave them absolute legislative powers.
They could abolish, modify, or grant dispensation from existing
laws. Their edicts had the force of laws, and such laws as
were passed in the regular way during their office either confirmed their powers, or were passed at their desire to give
formal permanence to their edicts. They had complete control of elections, and agreed between themselves as to the
nomination of magistrates, often for several years in advance.
They controlled the treasury, the domain lands, the raising or
removal of taxation in Rome and Italy. They divided among
themselves the command of the military forces and the government of the provinces. Each of them, personally or by a
legatus, exercised imperial powers in the provinces assigned
to him ; set up or put down client kings ; granted immunities
or freedom to cities, or abolished them ; bestowed or withdrew

---

[1] ὅρον τὴν ἕκτην ὑπάτειαν αὐτοῦ προσθείς. Dio, 53, 2. See Tacitus, *Ann.*
iii. 28.

[2] The doubt was an old one. Appian in one place affirms and in
another denies that there was a *lex* for the second period of the triumvirs
(*Illyr.* 28 ; b. c. v. 95). No other authority mentions one, and it certainly
was not passed in the early months of B.C. 37, that is, till after the triumvirs
had already continued their office without legal confirmation for some
time. Willems (*le Sénat*, ii. 761) holds that there was a plebiscitum ;
Mommsen that there was not.

the citizenship of individuals ; waged war with surrounding nations ; raised or remitted taxation.   At Rome also they had exercised the right of summoning, consulting, and presiding over the Senate, of vetoing the motion of other Senators, but without being subject to the tribunician veto themselves.   To abolish the *acta* of such a despotic body might with reason be regarded a considerable step towards a restoration of the constitution.   Even if some of his own *acta* were thereby abolished, Cæsar would have no difficulty in re-enacting them if desirable.   The point was to abolish the memory of a period of unconstitutional government, to prevent its enactments remaining as precedents or grounds of claim by citizen or subject, and to leave the field open for the new arrangement which Cæsar wished men to regard as a restoration of the republic.   For he had already conceived a plan, in virtue of which the people, magistrates, and Senate should resume their old functions, while he himself should be practically the colleague of the higher magistrates—endowed with their powers, though not necessarily with their office—and thereby practically direct the policy of the state.   The key to the policy—as he wished it to be regarded—is contained in his own comment : "After that time (January 1, 27) I was superior to all in rank, but of power I had no more than my colleagues in the several offices." [1]   There were some of his powers difficult to reconcile with this theory of a restored constitution ; but he was careful to rest these on votes of the people or Senate, to accept them only for fixed periods, or to profess to share them with his colleagues. [2]

The new constitution was now introduced in a characteristic scene, apparently designed to make it clear that Cæsar did not seek power, but undertook it under pressure.   In a meeting

[1] *Mon. Ancyr.* ch. 34.
[2] In B.C. 28 he took care to transfer the consular fasces to his colleague Agrippa in alternative months, and when with soldiers to give the watchword jointly with him.   (Dio, 53, 1.)

of the Senate, at the beginning of his seventh consulship, he
delivered from a written copy a carefully prepared
speech, in which he surrendered to the Senate all
the powers which it had bestowed upon him, as
well as those which he had acquired in any other
way—the command of troops, the powers of legislation, the
government of the provinces. He based his resolution on justice,
the inherent right of the people to manage its own affairs, and
on his own right to consult for his personal safety, health, and
ease. At the same time, he dwelt on his public services and
those of his adoptive father, the labours they had both endured,
the dangers to which both had been exposed, and justified the
exercise up to this time of his various powers. Finally, he
urged them to refrain from innovations, to give a hearty
obedience to the laws, to elect the best men for civil and
military offices without prejudice or favouritism, to deal
honestly with public money, to treat allies and subjects equit-
ably, to seek no wars but to be prepared for any, and to see
that he had no cause to regret his renunciation of power. The
speech was received with loud remonstrances, some sincere and
some perhaps cautious and time-serving, but so general that he
had to consent with real or feigned reluctance to receive back
his autocratic powers. Was he merely playing a part, or had
he any real wish to retire from public life? As in most cases
there was probably a division of feeling in his heart. He was
in weak health, and had had another illness a few months before.
For eighteen years—just half his life—he had been ceaselessly
engaged in fatiguing duties, in wars for which he had no
genius, and in civil adminstration which, though much better
suited to his tastes and abilities, had been carried out amidst
constant opposition and difficulty. One side of his mind may
well have been eager for rest. But, on the other hand, no man
who has tasted power and feels that he can wield it quits it
without pain. At no time did he find pleasure in the outward
trappings of state, or in the personal indulgences for which

Inauguration of the new constitution, 1 January, B.C. 27.

it gives opportunity, but he was ambitious in the best sense. He loved his country and desired to be remembered as the restorer of its prosperity and happiness, as the benefactor of the Empire and the guarantee of its peace and good government. Twenty-four years later when Valerius Messalla, speaking in the name of people and Senate, greeted him with the affectionate title of "Father of his country," he burst into tears and could only murmur that he had nothing more to pray for except to retain their affection to the end of his life. But whatever secret wish he may have had for rest he must have known that it was impossible. The elements of disorder and oppression were not destroyed. If the restraining hand were removed they would break out into new activity. Nor would it be safe for himself after years of steady working for this end, in the course of which he must have offended countless interests, to trust himself to a new generation of statesmen without the experience in the working of a free state possessed by their ancestors, and yet with the same passions and ambitions. A scheme had, in fact, been elaborated in conjunction with his faithful friends and ministers, Agrippa and Mæcenas. Dio represents the former as urging Cæsar to withdraw from power and frankly to restore the republic. He grounded his advice on the financial and political difficulties which he would have to face, on the uncertainty of his own health, on the impossibility of drawing back hereafter and the evil destiny of all those who in previous ages had attempted to gain absolute power. Mæcenas, on the other hand, not only urged him to retain his power, but went into most elaborate details as to the arrangements which it would be necessary to make. He did not deny the risks, but maintained that the glory was worth them, and that a withdrawal was neither safe for himself nor for the people. It is not clear how far we may regard these two speeches, as well as that of Augustus in the Senate, as representing what was really said. It is possible that as they were all written documents they may have been preserved, and that Dio is translating from them ; but at any rate they represent fairly well the two sides of the question which Augustus must have considered with care and anxiety.[1]

The arrangement actually made was of the nature of a compromise. The provinces were divided, as formerly between Antony and Cæsar, so now between Cæsar and the Senate. Those that required considerable military forces were to be under Cæsar, governed by his deputies with the rank of prætor (*legati pro prætore*), appointed by his sole authority, and holding office during his pleasure. The rest were to be still governed by proconsuls, selected as of old by ballot under the superintendence of the Senate from the ex-prætors or ex-consuls, subject to the existing laws as to length of tenure and the obligation of furnishing accounts, and liable with their staff to prosecution *de rebus repetundis* in the ordinary courts. The " primacy " of the Emperor, however, was apparent in this partnership with the Senate, no less than in that with colleagues in office. In the allotment of Senatorial provinces he retained the right of nominating the exact number required, so that no one of whom he disapproved could obtain a province. In both classes of province he appointed a procurator, with authority over the finances independent of the proconsul or legatus.[2] In both also the governor received a salary fixed by himself, and had to conform to certain general principles laid down by him. In all alike he

Division of the Provinces, B.C. 27.

---

[1] I do not myself see any good reason to doubt that Dio has given at any rate the substance of these documents. It is not perhaps natural to us to suppose two men like Mæcenas and Agrippa solemnly reading speeches to the Emperor ; but it was no unusual thing at Rome. Augustus himself is said to have done it, even to his wife, Livia, and frequently with others (Sueton., *Aug.* 84). Tacitus says it was the fashion of the time (*Ann.* 4, 37), as it seems to have been still earlier, for Cicero complains that his nephew, Quintus, had written an elaborate diatribe against him which he meant to deliver to Iulius Cæsar in Alexandria. (*Ad Att.* xi. 10. For similar documents see Dio, 52, 1–40 ; 53, 3 ; 55, 15–21.

[2] Dio, 52 15.

possessed a *majus imperium*, soon afterwards, if not at first, defined as a *proconsulare imperium*.[1]

For the rest he retained his right of being yearly elected consul, his tribunician power, his membership of the sacred colleges, his command of the army. But freedom of election was ostensibly restored to the people, and the Senate was still the fountain of honour, and had the control of the *ærarium*. But this last was no longer managed by two elected quæstors. but by two men of prætorian rank, nominated by the Emperor. It was, moreover, now of minor importance, as the *fiscus* (to use the later term) was entirely in the hands of Cæsar, and into it went the revenues of the imperial provinces, and, above all, of Egypt. The key of the position was that though the old republican magistrates still existed, Cæsar in various ways was their colleague, and of course the predominant partner. The Senate, however, accepted his view of the case, as afterwards expressed in the *Monumentum*, that he had " transferred the republic from his power to the authority of the Senate and people of Rome." To show their confidence in him the Senators voted him a bodyguard (the men drawing double pay), and confirmed his authority in the provinces. The latter, which made him *princeps* throughout the Empire, as he already

---

[1] The IMPERIAL provinces were : Hispania Tarraconensis, and Lusitania, the Galliæ (beyond the Alps), including the districts afterwards called Germania, superior and inferior, Cœle-Syria, Phœnicia, Cilicia, Cyprus, Ægypt.

The SENATORIAL were : Sicilia, Hispania Bætica, Sardinia, Africa, Numidia, Dalmatia, Greece and Epirus, Macedonia, Asia, Crete and Cyrene, Bithynia and Pontus.

Cisalpine Gaul ceased to be a province, and was included in Italy.

Subsequent changes were:

B.C. 24. Cyprus and Gallia Narbonensis were transferred to the Senate.

B.C. 21. Dalmatia was transferred to the Emperor.

B.C. 6. Sardinia was transferred to the Emperor for nine years. The provinces added during the life-time of Augustus : Galatia, Lycaonia, Mœsia, and the minor Alpine provinces were imperial.

All provinces added afterwards were imperial.

was in Rome, he refused to accept for more than ten years. But it was always renewed subsequently for periods of five or ten years; and when in B.C. 23, the *proconsulare imperium* was declared to be operative within, as well as beyond, the pomærium, he had, in fact, supreme control, military and financial, in all parts of the Empire. To mark his exceptional position without offending the prejudice against royalty, it was desired to give him a special title of honour. His own wish was for "Romulus," as second founder of the state. But objection was raised to it as recalling the odious position of *rex*, and he eventually accepted the title of AUGUSTUS, a word connected with religion and the science of augury, and thereby suggesting the kind of sentiment which he desired to be attached to his person and genius. This was voted by the Senate on the Ides (13th) of January, B.C. 27, and confirmed by a plebiscitum on the 16th. He was now "first" or *princeps* everywhere, whether in the Senate, or among his colleagues in the offices, or among the proconsuls in the provinces.[1] He was, therefore, spoken of as *princeps* in ordinary language, and the word gradually hardened into a title. It exactly suited the view which he himself wished to be taken of his political position, as giving a primacy of rank among colleagues of equal *legal* powers; though, of course, a primacy, supported by the power of the purse and the sword, made him a master while masquerading as a colleague. He, however, adopted the word as rightly expressing his position without giving needless offence, and his successors took it as a matter of course, though it less frequently occurs in inscriptions than their other titles.[2]

---

[1] Ovid (F. 1,587–616) says the Ides of January; the Calendarium Prænestinum gives the 16th. Possibly the one is the date of the SCtum, the other of the plebiscitum.

[2] Augustus himself uses it in the *Monumentum* (chs. 30, 32), "me principe," "ante me principem." Horace (*Od.* 1, 21, 13; 2, 30; *Ep.* 2, 1, 256), Propertius (v. 6, 46), both employ it when speaking of Augustus. It occurs in inscriptions referring to Tiberius, and is the common term used by Tacitus. If, therefore, it was not formally bestowed (as seems probable),

Closely connected with the bestowal of the title Augustus was another vote of the Senate, that the front of his house should not only be adorned with the laurels that told of victory over his enemies, but also with the oaken or "civic" crown which told of the lives of citizens preserved. This appears again and again on his coins with the legend—*ob cives servatos:* and it is mentioned by Augustus himself at the end of his record of achievements, as though—with the later title of Pater Patriæ—it indicated the chief glory of his career.

it soon grew into use as a title in ordinary language. Nor was it altogether a new idea ; Cicero had used it as a possible title of honour, with which Pompey or Cæsar, had they been moderate, might have been content. (Cic., *ad Fam.* vi. 6). Again, though it is not a mere extension of *princeps senatus*, yet it is clearly connected with it. As the Senatus is the first *ordo* in the state, the *princeps senatus* is also *princeps civitatis*. The two titles were soon confounded. Thus Pliny (*N.H.* xxxvi. § 116) speaks of M. Æmilius Scaurus as *totius princeps civitatis*, when he means that he had been several times entered by the Censors on the roll as *princeps senatus*. But a new connotation became attached to the word from the political powers of the *princeps*.

CHAPTER IX

> *Serves iturum Cæsarem in ultimos*
> *orbis Britannos et invenum recens*
> *examen Eois timendum*
> *partibus Oceanoque rubro.*

THE settlement of his official status at Rome left Augustus free to turn to other parts of the Empire. He had spent the greater part of two years after the victory at Actium in organising the East. His face was now turned northward and westward. In the spring of B.C. 27, he set out for Gaul to reorganise the provinces won by Iulius in B.C. 58–49, and farther secured by the operations of Agrippa in B.C. 37 and Messalla in B.C. 29. It was understood that he meant also to cross to Britain, and the court poets are dutifully anxious as to the dangers he will incur, and prophetically certain of the victories he will win. A British expedition had been for some years floating in Roman minds. It is true that Iulius Cæsar had invaded the island and imposed a tribute on some of the tribes. But the tribute does not seem to have been paid. The Briton was still *intactus*, and was classed with the Parthian as a danger to the frontier of the Empire.[1] He was chiefly known at Rome by the presence of certain stalwart slaves, and by the determination he displayed not to admit adventurous

Gaul and Britain.

---

[1] Horace, *Epode*, vii. 7 ; *Odes*, i. 21, 15 ; iii. 5, 2 ; Propert., iii. 23, 5.

Roman merchants.[1]   But, after all, Augustus found enough to
do in Gaul, and saw good reason for abstaining from such a
dangerous adventure.   The Britons, though they neglected
the *tributum*, yet paid a duty on exports and imports to and
from Gaul, principally ivory ornaments, and the better sorts of
glass and pottery ; and it was pointed out that the danger of a
British invasion of Gallia was small, that a military occupation
of the island would cost more than the tribute would bring in,
and that the *portoria* would be rather diminished than increased
by it.[2]   Augustus, at any rate, professed to be satisfied by
certain envoys sent to him from Britain.   They dedicated some
offerings on the Capitol, and received for their countrymen the
title of "Friends of Rome!"[3]

Augustus spent the summer and winter of B.C. 27-6 in
Narbo, finding enough to do in holding a census of the rest of
Gaul for purposes of taxation, and regularly
organising the country annexed by Iulius to
that ancient province, which had been Roman
long before his time.   Four provinces were created with
separate legati.   The original "province" was now called
Gallia Narbonensis ; the south-western district, extending from
the Pyrennees to the Loire, retained its old name of Aquitania ;
the central or "Celtic" Gaul was called Lugdunensis, from
its capital Lugdunum, made a *colonia* in B.C. 43 ; the northern
country up to the Rhine was Belgica, including the districts on
the left bank of the Rhine, in which Agrippa had settled certain
German tribes who had crossed the river.   Augustus was not
content with a merely political organisation.   He established
schools to spread the use of the Latin language, and everywhere
introduced the principles of Roman law.   He took especial

*Augustus
in Gaul,
B.C. 27-6.*

---

[1] Vergil, *Georg.* iii. 25 ; Horace, *Odes* iii. 4, 33.

[2] Strabo, ii. 5, 8 ; iv. 6, 4.

[3] Strabo, *l. c.* In the *Monument.* (ch. 32) Augustus records the visit of
two British princes, Dumnobellaunus and another, of whose name only the
letters *Tinn* remain (perhaps "Tincommius," a king of what is now
Sussex).

pains to adorn and promote the towns in Narbonensis, where traces of his buildings are still to be seen. The effect of his work now and ten years later was that Gaul became rapidly Romanised both in speech and manners, and that in learning and civilisation it soon rivalled Italy itself.

This was a work thoroughly congenial to Augustus, and in which his ability was conspicuous. But he now had to engage again in war, for which his genius was by no means so well suited. Ianus Quirinus was again open. The surrounding barbarians were again threatening Macedonia; the Salassi of the *Val d' Aosta* were again making raids, and there was imminent danger in Nothern Spain. The governor of Macedonia, M. Crassus (grandson of the triumvir) had been so successful over the Thracians and Getæ, that he was allowed a triumph in July, B.C. 27, but it appears that their incursions did not cease in spite of these victories.[1] The war with the Salassi was entrusted to Terentius Varro Muræna, who, after winning some victories in the field, sold many thousands of their men of military age into slavery, and established a colony of 3,000 veterans to overawe them, called Augusta Prætoria, the modern Aosta.[2]

From Narbo, Augustus next proceeded to Spain in the early part of B.C. 26, and spent the rest of the year in peaceful reforms and in the organisation of the province. But in B.C. 25 he was forced to enter upon a campaign against the Cantabri and Astures, those warlike tribes in the north-west, who, nominally included in

Augustus in Spain, B.C. 26-25.

---

[1] The triumph of M. Crassus is dated by the Tab. Triumph. C. I. L. I, 416; but the defeat of the "Dacian Cotiso" is classed with the Cantabrian war by Horace (*Od.* 3, 8, 18–24), and Livy, *Ep.* 135, mentions a second war of M. Crassus "against the Thracians," as contemporary with the Spanish war.

[2] The Salassi, who had for the last 100 years given much trouble, had twice in recent years been in arms: in B.C. 35 they defeated C. Antistius Vetus, and, in B.C. 34, had, with great difficulty, been partly subdued by Valerius Messalla. Their command of the principal Alpine pass made it important that they should be kept in check.

the upper province, were continually harassing the more obedient peoples, and showing their dislike of Roman supremacy.[1] The war was tantalising and difficult. The hardy highlanders knew every forest, mountain, and valley, and the Roman soldiers could neither provide against sudden attacks, not get at the enemy in their fastnesses. From fatigue and anxiety Augustus fell ill and was obliged to retire to Tarraco, leaving the conduct of the campaign to Gaius Antistius Vetus, who was able to win several engagements, because after the retirement of Augustus the natives ventured more frequently to appear in the open. Another of his legates, Titus Carisius, took Lance (*Sallanco*); and finally Augustus founded a colony of veterans among the Lusitani, called Augusta Emerita (*Merida*), and another called Cæsar-Augusta (*Zaragossa*) among the Editani, on the site of the ancient Salduba, from which all the great roads to the Pyrennees branch off. The Cantabri were not crushed, but they were quiet for a time. Ianus was closed, and Augustus returned at the beginning of B.C. 24; and the courtier Horace is again called on to celebrate a success, and to welcome the Emperor's home-coming as of a victor.[2] The Senate voted him a triumph, partly for the Spanish campaign and partly for some successes of his legate, M. Vinicius, in Gaul, who had caused his soldiers to proclaim Augustus imperator for the eighth time. Augustus refused the triumph, but accepted the acclamation of imperator—thus assuming as head of the army that what was everywhere done was, to use the technical expression, done "under his auspices," and was to be reckoned to his credit. He also accepted honours for his young nephew Marcellus, and his stepson Tiberius. The former was admitted to the Senate with prætorian rank, and with ten years seniority for office, in virtue of which he was at once elected ædile, though only in his twentieth year; the latter

---

[1] Hor., *Od.* 2, 6, 2, *Cantabrum indoctum iuga ferre nostra.*
[2] *Odes* iii. 8, 21, *servit Hispanæ vetus hostis oræ Cantaber sera domitus catena;* iii. 14, 3, *Cæsar Hispana repetit Penates Victor ab ora.*

was allowed five years' seniority, and at once elected quæstor in his nineteenth year. A triumphal arch was also erected in honour of Augustus in the Alpine region.[1] The temple of Ianus did not remain long closed, however. Soon after Augustus left Spain the Cantabri and Astures again rose; and in B.C. 24 took place the ill-judged and unfortunate expedition of Ælius Gallus into Arabia. A march of six months' duration, in which large numbers perished from heat and disease and only seven men in actual fighting, was followed by a retreat lasting sixty days. Gallus had been misled and duped by the satrap of the Nabatæans, and all the hopes of splendid booty were baffled. The expedition had been approved, if not suggested, by Augustus, partly on the pretext of preventing incursions into Egypt; but more, it would seem, because Arabia was regarded as an El Dorado, where vast treasures of gold and jewels were to be found, accumulated from the export of the rich spices of the country, which the inhabitants were believed to keep jealously in a country as yet never pillaged by an invader. As usual, the court poets echo the popular delusions, and eulogise the certain success of the Emperor; Horace harps on the rich "treasures of the Arabians," their "well-stocked houses," their "virgin stores." The Roman arms are to strike terror in the East and the Red Sea, and are at length being employed on what is their proper and natural foe.[2] Augustus, says another poet, is now a terror to the "homestead of the yet unplundered Arabia."[3] Happily this was an almost solitary instance of such wild schemes, prompted by greed, and promoted by ignorance and delusion. Augustus came to see that the frontiers of his great empire afforded sufficient work for its

The Arabian Expedition.

---

[1] Perhaps that of which remains exist at Aosta, and cannot now be dated. That at Turbia was built B.C. 6 (Pliny, *N. H.* 3 § 136). That at Susa in B.C. 8 [C. I. L. v. 7,231]. Horace may refer to it among the *Nova Augusti tropæa* (*Od.* 2, 9, 19).

[2] Horace, *Odes* i. 29, 1; ii. 12, 24; iii. 24, 1; i. 35, 32-40.

[3] Propert., 3, 1, 11.

military resources; but it was not till near the end of his long life that a great military disaster gave him a sharp reminder of the impolicy of pushing beyond them.

During these years the process of adorning Rome with splendid buildings or restorations of old ones had been steadily going on. For the largest number of these Augustus himself was responsible. In B.C. 28 the temple of Apollo on the Palatine, with its colonnades and libraries, had been dedicated. In the same year the restoration of 82 temples was begun on his initiative, and apparently at his expense. The new temple of Mars Ultor, vowed at Philippi, with its surrounding forum Augustum, was in process of erection, as well as another to Iupiter Tonans on the Capitol, vowed in the course of the Cantabrian expedition to commemorate a narrow escape from being struck by lightning. He also completed the forum and basilica partly erected by Iulius, had begun or projected the *porticus Liviæ et Octaviæ*, and had erected the imposing rotunda intended as the mortuary of the Iulian *gens:* while Statilius Taurus had built the first amphitheatre, Plancus a great temple of Saturn, and Cornelius Balbus was about to begin a new theatre. But most splendid of all were the benefactions of Agrippa. Baths, bridges, colonnades, garden, aqueducts, were all dedicated by him to the use of the public. Above all, by B.C. 25 he had completed the magnificent Pantheon, still in its decline one of the most striking buildings in the world. It was dedicated to Mars and Venus, mythical ancestors of the Iulian *gens*, but its name may be derived either from its numerous statues of the gods, or from the supposed likeness of its dome to the sky. Its purpose—beyond being a compliment to Augustus—is still a subject of dispute. Nor have we any record of its use except as the meeting-place of the Arval brothers.[1]

New buildings at Rome.

[1] Middleton (*Remains of Ancient Rome*, vol. ii. pp. 126–128) seems to have given good reasons against its connection with the Thermæ of

Great way, therefore, was already made towards justifying the boast of Augustus that he found Rome brick and left it marble. For these buildings were lined or paved with every kind of precious marble and stone. But the year following his return from Spain witnessed a crisis in his life as well as in his political position. He seems to have been in a feeble state of health all through B.C. 24, the effect probably of his fatigues and anxieties in Spain. But soon after entering on his eleventh consulship in B.C. 23, he became so much worse that he believed himself to be dying. It became necessary, therefore, to make provision for the continuance of the government. Augustus had no hereditary office, and no power of transmitting his authority. Still it was supposed that he was training his nephew and son-in-law Marcellus, or his stepson Tiberius, to be his successor. The former was curule-ædile, and seems to have conceived the ambition of succeeding his uncle. But when he thought death approaching, Augustus did not designate either of these young men. He handed his seal to Agrippa, and the official records of the army and revenue to Cn. Calpurnius Piso, his colleague in the consulship. He would play his part as constitutional magistrate to the last. To speculate on what might have been is not very profitable. Agrippa had advised a restoration of the republic in B.C. 30. But every year since then had made it more difficult ; and, if he had wished to do it, he would probably have found it as impossible as his master had done, and would have had to choose between supporting Marcellus and

The illness and recovery of Augustus, B.C. 23.

Agrippa. Lanciani (*Ruins and Excavations*, pp. 476–498) asserts that the structure as it now stands is of the age of Hadrian (about A.D. 129), and doubts Agrippa's original building being of the same shape. Even the portico with its inscription—M. AGRIPPA L. F. COS. TERT. FECIT—he thinks was taken to pieces and put up again by Hadrian. The history of the buildings, however, cannot be regarded as throughly ascertained. Agrippa's third consulship was in B.C. 27, whereas Dio places the completion of the Pantheon under B.C. 25 (53, 27). It may well have been that the external building was finished and dedicated in B.C. 27, and that the inside occupied two more years.

taking the direction of affairs into his own hands. The difficulty, however, did not arise ; for owing either to the goodness of his constitution, or the skill of his physician, Antonius Musa, Augustus recovered.

When he met the Senate once more he offered to read his will to prove that he had been true to his constitutional obligations, and had named no successor, but had left the decision in the hands of the Senate and people. The Senators, however, declined to hear it, but insisted that the powers which he had been exercising should be more clearly defined and placed on a better legal footing. Accordingly a *Senatus-consultum* was drawn up, to be afterwards submitted to the centuriate assembly, giving him a variety of powers, and forming a precedent which was followed in the case of subsequent emperors. It began with a confirmation of the *tribunicia potestas,* for life and unlimited as to place, with the right of bringing business of any kind before the Senate (*ius relationis*). It next gave him the *ius proconsulare,* both within and without the pomærium, involving a *maius imperium* in all provinces. Further, it gave him the right of making treaties ; the right of summoning, consulting, and dismissing the Senate (*ius consulare*) ; the confirmation of all his *acta,* "Whatever he shall think to be for the benefit and honour of the republic in things divine and human, whether public or private " ; finally, exemption from the provisions of certain laws and *plebiscita.* Some legal difficulty was apparently discovered afterwards as to the right of proposing laws to the centuriate assembly, which was remedied in B.C. 19 by his receiving the full consular power for life, with the right of having *lictors,* and sitting on the consular bench. This seems to have been a concession to legal purists. He doubtless exercised the full consular powers before ; but a distinction was drawn by some between the *ius consulare* and the *imperium consulare,* and whatever doubt there might be was now set at rest.

The new constitutional settlement, B.C. 23.

As the imperial powers may now be considered as fully developed, future extensions being merely logical deductions from the constitution as now established, it will The imperial powers. be convenient here once for all to point out their nature and extent. They may be classed under two headings—(1) *imperium*; (2) *potestas tribunicia*.

The first—*imperium*—embraces all those powers which Augustus obtained as representing the curule magistrates, or from special law and senatorial decrees. As imperator, then, he had supreme command of all forces by land or sea. The military oath was now taken in his name, no longer to individual officers raising legions. He alone had the right to enrol soldiers ; he nominated the officers ; his procurators paid the men in his name ; from him proceeded all rewards. The Senate, indeed, still awarded triumphs and *triumphalia orna-menta*, but it was at his suggestion, and the tendency was to confine the right of triumph to the Emperor himself.

By the same *imperium* he decided on questions of peace or war ; on the distribution of the *ager publicus*, and the assignation of lands to veterans and *coloni* generally.

Finally, the right of conferring the citizenship, complete or partial, and settling the status of all colonies and *municipia*, and of interpreting the laws by a *constitutio principis*, expressed in an edict or decree, which amounted, in fact, to legislative power.

The second—*potestas tribunicia*—was superior to the ordinary powers of the tribunes, because by it he could veto their proceedings, while they could not veto his. " It gave him "—to use Dio's words—" the means of absolutely putting a stop to any proceeding of which he disapproved ; it rendered his person inviolable, so that the least violence offered him by word or deed made a man liable to death without trial as being under a curse." From the ancient constitution of the office also it made him president of the *comitia tributa* (representing the old *consilia plebis*), gave him the right of interposing in all decisions of magistrates or Senate affecting the persons or civil status of citizens (*auxilii latio*), and that of compelling obedience by imprisonment or other means, as in the republic the tribunes had done even to the consuls in extreme cases (*coercitio*). Though this power was given the Emperor for life, it was also in a sense annual ; and it was in effect so much the most important of all his powers, while at the same time in origin and professed object so much the most popular, that it became the custom from henceforth to date all documents, inscriptions, and the like, by the year of the tribunician power from 27th of June this year (B.C. 23). The *imperium* was renewed at intervals of ten or five years, the tribunician power of Augustus went on from year to year without break. It was now unnecessary any longer to hold the consulship, for the *imperium* given him in other ways covered all, and more than all, which the consulship could give. It was convenient to use it for rewarding others, as it retained all its outward signs of dignity, and still in theory made its holder head of the state, though in reality its duties had become almost wholly ceremonial. He therefore abdicated the consulship, which he did not hold again till B.C. 5, when he desired to give *éclat* to his grandson's *deductio in forum*.

The clause in the *lex*, quoted above, also gave Augustus supreme control of all religious matters, and made him able, among other things, to nominate most of the members of the sacred colleges. He did not become Pontifex Maximus till the death of Lepidus (B.C. 13). When that took place he became official, as well as real, head of the Roman religion.

Certain other arrangements in regard to the city of Rome itself followed, all in the direction of centralisation. Thus Augustus presided at the review of the equites, which used to be held by the censors. Public works were mostly entrusted to *curators* appointed by him ; for the supply of corn he named a *præfectus annonæ* ; and for police a *præfectus urbi*, under whom were the *cohortes urbanæ*, the night-watch and fire brigade (*nocturni vigiles*). Each of these bodies had their own officers or *præfecti*; but Augustus from time to time appointed some one as *præfectus urbi*, to whom all alike would be subject. Such an officer, however, did not always assume the name, and really as well as theoretically the ultimate authority was Augustus himself, who later on, by dividing Rome into *regiones* and *vici*, made elaborate arrangements for the effective policing of the city.

Augustus might pose as a constitutional magistrate enjoying a life-tenure of his office, without the right of transmitting it to an heir. This view was strictly legal, but it
The succession.
was evident that such a power could not safely be left by its holder without any understanding as to a successor. The matter was indeed in the hands of Senate and people ; but in the minds of possible heirs, as well as of the Senate and people themselves, it began to be thought natural and necessary that some arrangement of the sort should be made. The cases are numerous in all history of rulers, whether new or hereditary, who have wished to found or continue a dynasty, or who have thought to prevent confusion and danger after their own death by naming a successor, or by taking him into present partnership. Such a scheme was not as yet fully developed, even if it was contemplated. But Marcellus, who had been adopted by Augustus on his marriage to Iulia, betrayed his hopes by protesting against the preference shewn by the apparently dying Emperor to Agrippa ; and Augustus yielded so far as to send Agrippa from Rome as governor of Syria.

A sudden disaster, however, put an end to any intention that may have been formed in regard to Marcellus. In the summer of B.C. 23, he was attacked by fever, and
Death of Marcellus.
Antonius Musa, who had successfully treated Augustus by a *régime* of cold baths, tried a similar treatment on the young man with fatal effect. His death was a great grief to Augustus and so severe a blow to Octavia, that she lived afterwards in complete retirement. It produced a sensation in Rome such as has been witnessed more

than once among us at the death of an heir to the throne;
and has been immortalised by a celebrated passage inserted by
Vergil in the sixth book of the *Æneid*, a work in which
Augustus was specially interested as a consecration of the
greatness of Rome and the hereditary dignity of the Iulian
gens. It is skilfully placed at the end of the catalogue of
Roman heroes whose souls are being reviewed by Anchises in
the Elysian realms, where they are waiting their time for
entering the bodies of men destined to make Roman history.
The Marcellus of the Punic war naturally introduces the
younger shade, whose brief tenure of life is even now foreshadowed by the cloud that hangs about his brow. When
Vergil recited the lines to the Emperor and his sorrowing
sister, Octavia fainted from emotion, and Augustus bestowed
a splendid reward upon the poet. It may help us to realise
the scene if we once more read the familiar lines. Æneas
notices the mysterious and melancholy shade and eagerly
questions his father :—

> "'What youth is this of glorious mien
> The noblest and the best between,
> Cheered to the echo? See, a cloud
> (The darkening shadow of the shroud)
> Hovers about him even now,
> And black night broods upon his brow.
> Is he some scion of the race,
> Destined our mighty line to grace?'
>
> Thus spake the son, the father sighed,
> And thus with rising tears replied :
> 'Seek not, my son, to learn the woe,
> Your progeny is doomed to know.
> The fates will show and then withdraw
> The gift men loved but hardly saw.
> Too mighty, gods! for so you deemed,
> With such a prince Rome's race had seemed!
> What sobs shall thrill the Martian plain!
> Ah, Tiber, what dark funeral train

Your waves shall see, as past the Mound
New-built you sweep your waters round!
No scion of the Ilian stock
Shall raise such hopes, such hopes shall mock.
Ah, Romulus, thy land shall see
No son to fire thy pride as he.
Oh loyalty! Oh faith unstained!
Oh strong right hand to yield untrained!
Whether on foot he grasped the sword,
Or charger's flank with rowel scored,
No foe would e'er have faced his steel
Nor learnt what 'tis the vanquished feel.
Oh child of many tears, if fate
Shall not prevent your living date,
Thou art Marcellus! Lilies fair
Scatter in handfuls on his bier!
Oh let me but his herse bestrew
With flowers bright with purple hue.
Vain gift! but let it still be paid
To grace my far-off grandson's shade.' "

The death of Marcellus had occurred in an unhealthy season when many shared the same fate. Yet there were found people who attributed it to Livia's jealousy on behalf of her son Tiberius, and her anger at the preference shown to the Emperor's nephew. Scarcely any death occurred in the imperial family that did not give rise to some such idle and malevolent gossip. But the Emperor soon had cause to regret the absence of Agrippa, who was living in Lesbos and administering Syria by his legate. The next year was a year of sickness and scarcity at Rome, and was also disturbed by more than one outbreak of political unrest, one of the few conspiracies against the life of Augustus being detected and punished. We do not know why Muræna and Fannius Cæpio plotted to kill Augustus, if they really did so. It may be that the change made in the principate in B.C. 23 seemed to them to be too much in the direction of autocracy, or that the consulship without Augustus as colleague suggested some idea that its old supremacy might be recovered. The violent party strife which occurred later at the election for B.C. 21, may have had some connection with the same feeling. Muræna had had a successful career, had been rewarded by an augurship and a consulship in B.C. 23, and there is nothing known which explains his conduct. It may be that his offence was chiefly intemperance of language. Dio says that he had a sharp tongue which spared no one, and Horace perhaps meant to give him a hint in the ode addressed to him. Velleius tells us that, unlike his fellow conspirator Fannius Cæpio, he was a man of high character.[1] At any rate their execution—for both are said to have been put to death—is one of the few instances of severity on the part of Augustus since the civil war. This trouble was followed by others—a renewed outbreak in Spain, riots at the elections, and a coldness between himself and his devoted friend and minister Mæcenas, caused, it is said, by his being supposed to have communicated to his wife Terentia, the sister of Muræna, some secret as to the detection of the plot. All these things must have caused Augustus much uneasiness. He had left Rome in the summer of B.C. 22 for Sicily, intending to start thence on another progress through the Eastern Provinces. There urgent messages came to him to return and put a stop to the disturbances. He did not wish to give up his Eastern journey and yet did not venture to leave the city without some control. His thoughts turned naturally to the support that had never failed him—to Agrippa. He was summoned home primarily to take charge of Rome; but he came back to what seemed the highest possible position next to that of the Emperor, and one that promised a still greater one in the future. Augustus insisted on his divorcing Marcella (daughter of Octavia) and marrying his own daughter Iulia, left a widow by Marcellus.

---

[1] A. Licinius Muræna was called A. Terentius Varro Muræna from being adopted by Terentius Varro. See Dio, 54, 3; Suet., *Aug.* 19; Hor., *Odes* 2, 10; Velleius Paterc. 2, 91. Of Fannius Cæpio nothing practically is known, he was prosecuted by Tiberius for *maiestas* and condemned.

As usual Agrippa did all that was imposed upon him well and thoroughly (B.C. 21–20). Having restored order in the city, he next went to Gallia Narbonensis, where he not only put a stop to some dangerous disturbances, but initiated great public works in the way of roads and aqueducts. Passing to Spain he finally crushed the Cantabri and Astures, who were again in arms. He seems indeed to have suffered reverses in this war, as his master had done before, but in the end he reduced them to submission. All this good work was done while Augustus was in the East (B.C. 21–19), and for it he refused the triumph offered him by the Senate at the instigation of the Emperor. But his succession, should he survive the Emperor, was now secured by his being associated with him in the *tribunicia potestas* and other prerogatives for five years at the first renewal of his powers in B.C. 17. Agrippa had now two sons by Iulia, Gaius born in B.C. 20, Lucius in B.C. 17 ; and Augustus adopted both of them by the ancient process of a fictitious purchase. He had now legitimate heirs and nothing farther was done about the succession for some years. Agrippa died in March, B.C. 12, just as his period of tribunician power was expiring. But during these years the two sons of Livia, Tiberius and Drusus, had begun those services on the German frontier and among the Rhæti and other powerful tribes which proved their vigour and ability. These services were renewed, after a few months' interval of quiet, in B.C. 13 and following years. Accordingly Augustus seems to have meditated putting Tiberius in much the same position as Agrippa had held. In B.C. 11 he compelled him to divorce his wife Vipsania (a daughter of Agrippa) and marry Agrippa's widow Iulia, the Emperor's only daughter. He thought still farther to secure a line of descendants to succeed if necessary to his power. But he made the mistake of neglecting sentiment. Tiberius was devotedly attached to Vipsania, by whom he had a son, and could feel neither affection nor respect for Iulia, who fancied that she lowered herself in marrying him.

The only thing that could compensate him for such a marriage was the chance of succession, and that was barred by the existence of Gaius and Lucius Cæsar. His only son by Iulia died, and before long her frivolity and debaucheries disgusted him, and therefore, though associated in the tribunician power for five years in B.C. 7, he sought and obtained permission in the next year to retire to Rhodes, where he stayed seven years in seclusion.

Meanwhile the boys were being brought up with a view to their splendid future under the eye of Augustus, when he was at home, and often under his personal instruction, Gaius and Lucius Cæsar. accompanied him as they grew older on his journeys, in a carriage preceding his own or riding by his side, and in fact were treated in every way as real and much beloved sons. In the year in which they assumed the *toga virilis* (B.C. 5 and B.C. 2) Augustus again entered upon the consulship, that the *deductio in forum* should be as brilliant and dignified as possible. The Senate was not behindhand; from the day of taking the *toga virilis* it voted that they should be capable of taking part in public business, and each of them in turn was designated consul, Gaius to enter upon his office that time five years. A new dignity moreover was invented, each in turn being named by the equites *princeps inventutis*. As Augustus was *princeps senatus* as well as *princeps civitatis*, each of these young men was to be the head of the next *ordo*, the original condition for belonging to which was that a man must be *iuvenis*. Both were members of the College of Augurs. They were, in fact, treated as we expect to see princes of the blood and heirs-apparent treated.[1] But whatever was the intention of Augustus or the expectation of the people, fate interposed ruthlessly. The younger—Lucius—died first, on the 20th of August, A.D. 2, at Marseilles, before he could

---

[1] In the *cenotaphia Pisana* Gaius is described after his death as iam *designatum* iustissimum ac simillimum parentis sui virtutibus *principem.*" But this is probably not an official title.

enter on the consulship to which he had been designated ; the elder Gaius was sent into Asia in B.C. 1, where he entered upon his consulship of A.D. 1. The object of his mission was to force Phraates IV., king of the Parthians, to evacuate Armenia which he had invaded. This was accomplished without fighting and by personal negotiation with the Parthian king ; but when he entered Armenia to take possession and arrange for its restoration to its recognised king, he was wounded by an act of treason under the walls of Artagera. Weakened by this wound, and being in other respects in a feeble state of health and spirits, he obtained leave from Augustus to lay down his command. He started on his homeward journey, but died on the way at Limyra in Lycia the 23rd of February, A.D. 4.

The succession was once more uncertain. The members of the imperial family at this time were few. Of the children

Tiberius finally
fixed upon as
successor.

of Agrippa and Iulia Agrippa Postumus was barely sixteen, and his two sisters, the younger Iulia and Agrippina a few years older. Drusus, the younger brother of Tiberius, had married Antonia, daughter of Marcus Antonius and Octavia, and had left three children, Germanicus, b. B.C. 15, Livia b. B.C. 12, and Claudius (afterwards Emperor) b. B.C. 10. Augustus meant to provide a new line of descendants by marrying Agrippina to Germanicus, but that did not take place till about A.D. 5. Meanwhile, probably on Livia's suggestion, he turned his thoughts to his stepson Tiberius, who had divorced Iulia and had a son (Drusus) by his former wife Vipsania, who was married to his cousin Livia. There is no good evidence that Augustus entertained any but warm feelings for Tiberius, and he certainly had had good reason to respect his military abilities and energy. He seems to have been hurt at his prolonged stay at Rhodes and to have regarded it as a sign that Tiberius cared nothing for him and his family. He had therefore discouraged his return two years before, though he had given him the position of legatus as a colourable pretext for staying abroad without loss of dignity. Upon the death of Lucius, however, he seems to have wished him to return to Rome. Tiberius did so, partly on the instigation of his mother, and partly, perhaps, because he had reason to expect the hostility of Gaius, and yet had judged from the latter's visit to him on his way to Syria that he was not likely to be a formidable rival ; for he was at once somewhat arrogant and weak, and was surrounded by injudicious and dishonest advisers. On his return he for some time lived in retirement and refrained from all public business. But when the death of Gaius was announced (A.D. 4) Augustus adopted Tiberius and Agrippa Postumus, having first arranged that Tiberius should adopt his nephew Germanicus. The adoption of Agrippa Postumus was shortly afterwards annulled, and he was banished to an island under surveillance.[1]

There was now therefore a regular line of succession. Tiberius indeed had no drop of Iulian blood in his veins, but adoption according to Roman law and sentiment placed him exactly in the same position as that of a naturally born son, and by his son's marriage to Antonia, his adoption of Germanicus, and the marriage of the latter to Agrippina, it seemed that there was security that after him must come some one who was collaterally or directly descended from Augustus. In the same year (A.D. 4) Tiberius was once more associated with Augustus in the tribunician power for ten years.[2] There could be no longer any doubt who would succeed. At the death of Augustus there would be, if Tiberius survived, a man already possessed of the most

---

[1] There seems little doubt that the character of Agrippa Postumus gave some ground for this measure ; but Augustus seems to have regretted and at times to have contemplated recalling him. His murder immediately after the death of Augustus is called by Tacitus "the first crime of the new reign." Whether Tiberius or Livia was responsible for it cannot be discussed here.

[2] So Dio (55, 5) says. Suetonius (*Tib.* 16) says five years. There may have been a renewal after five years.

important of his functions; and his position was still farther strengthened in the last year of the Emperor's life by being associated also in his *imperium proconsulare.* This gave him authority in the provinces and the command of all military forces; and we find him, in fact, upon the death of Augustus giving the watchword at once to the prætorian guard.

Augustus therefore is responsible for the principate of Tiberius, though some of its powers had to be formally bestowed by a decree of the Senate. Did he do ill or well in this? Hardly any emperor left behind him such an evil reputation as Tiberius. His funeral procession was greeted with shouts of "Tiberius to the Tiber," the Senate did not vote him the usual divine honours, and Tacitus has exerted all his skill to make his name infamous. A gallant attempt has been made by Mr. Tarver to plead for a rehearing of the case, and to shew that Tiberius was pure in private life and admirable as a ruler. I for one agree with with him in rejecting as unproved slander and often as physically impossible the charges of monstrous immoralities raked up both by Tacitus and Suetonius, often, no doubt, from the prurient gossip of Rome, which has never been surpassed for foulness. The same summary rejection cannot, I think, be applied to the formidable list of his cruelties. But these mainly fell upon members of the imperial family and their adherents; they did not affect the Empire at large. Augustus could not foresee these family and dynastic tragedies; but he judged, and apparently judged rightly, that he was leaving a successor whose prudence and sagacity, in spite of what seemed a sullen reserve, would secure the peace and prosperity of the Empire as a whole. There is nothing to prove that Augustus regarded him otherwise than affectionately. If he turned out to be the monster represented by his enemies, Augustus no doubt made a grave mistake. It is a ridiculous suggestion that he deliberately designated him his successor in order that people might regret himself. Such recondite snares for posthumous fame are more like the cunning of a madman than the motives influencing a reasonable being. Suetonius, who reports the suggestion, says that after mature reflection he is convinced that a man so careful and prudent as Augustus must have acted on better motives ; must have weighed the virtues and faults of Tiberius and decided that the former predominated. As a matter of fact Augustus had little choice. Agrippa Postumus was impossible ; Germanicus might have served, but he could never have displaced his uncle without a struggle. At the time of Tiberius' adoption he was only nineteen, and Augustus could not reckon on the ten more years of life which in fact remained for him. No doubt in these last years of his life Augustus had come to see that some sort of hereditary principle was necessary to prevent civil war at every vacancy. In B.C. 23 he had ignored that principle altogether, and as far as he could without naming an heir had put Agrippa in the way of the succession. But Agrippa had now been dead nearly sixteen years, and Augustus had had no minister since either so able or so faithful. Like Cromwell in his last hours, he was driven to recognise the conveniency of the hereditary principle ; and though the practical designation of Tiberius was apparently a breach of it, yet by means of the adoptions and marriages which he had arranged, it best prepared for its continuance hereafter. It was one of those politic compromises which had characterised his whole policy. It moreover best secured the position and safety of the beloved Livia ; and it set a precedent which was often followed with advantage in after-times, when military arrogance and violence did not over-power every other consideration, that an Emperor's natural heir should be his successor, or at any rate some one closely allied to him ; and that in case of the failure or complete unworthiness of such an heir a prudent emperor should provide for the succession by adoption.

CHAPTER X

THE IMPERIAL AND MILITARY POLICY OF AUGUSTUS

> *Tu regere imperio populos,*
> *Romane, memento.*

AT the end of his life Augustus left, among other memoirs, a roll containing certain maxims of state which he thought important for his successors to observe. Among them was an injunction not to seek to increase the Empire, for it would be difficult to guard an extended frontier. His own policy had been directed generally on this principle. Such additions as were made in his time were mainly those rendered inevitable by the necessity of securing the already existing frontiers. When his generals went beyond that they met with difficulties and sometimes with disaster. The additions actually made were (1) in Africa: Egypt was made a province in B.C. 30, at first almost as a private possession of the Emperor, though in B.C. 10 it was, nominally at any rate, put on the same footing as the other provinces. Mauretania, on the other hand, though made a province in B.C. 33, was restored to independence under King Iuba in B.C. 25. (2) In Asia a new province of Galatia was formed in B.C. 25, with a capital at Ancyra, and embracing several districts, such as Lycaonia, Isauria, Pamphylia, and parts of Phrygia. (3) In the West, sometime before A.D. 6, Mœsia, answering to the

The extension of the Empire under Augustus.

[1] *Monum. Ancyr.* 27 ; C.I.L. vi. 701.

171

modern Servia and Bulgaria, was made a province as a barrier of the Empire on the Danube. So also Illyricum, in B.C. 9–8, was extended to the Danube by the addition of Pannonia ; Noricum, also on the Danube, was held in subjection, if not fully organised as a province, after B.C. 16 ; and Rhætia (modern Bavaria) was put under a Roman procurator after B.C. 15. All these additions were clearly rendered necessary in order to protect the line of the Danube as the frontier of the Empire. Lastly, on the reorganisation of Gaul in four provinces (B.C. 16–14), two districts along the left bank of the Lower Rhine, called Germania Superior and Germania Inferior, were also occupied and partly organised, while some minor Alpine districts, Alpes Maritimæ (Savoy and Nice), Alpes Cottiæ (Susa and district), Alpes Penninæ (Canton du Valois) were taken over and administered sometimes independently and sometimes as part of other provinces. In these cases again the extension was merely consequential, the inevitable result of having a long frontier to defend against invading tribes.[1] The Rhine and the Danube then became the limits of the Empire. We shall have occasion to see immediately what dangers awaited an attempt to go beyond them.

Augustus twice spent periods of between two and three years in the East, engaged in resettling frontiers and re-organising the Roman provinces.

The East.

After the victory at Actium (B.C. 31) he remained in the East till B.C. 29. The changes then made chiefly consisted in upsetting most of the arrangements which had been made by Antony with various client kings, and in favour of the children of Cleopatra. Thus Cyprus, which had been restored to Cleopatra, was now separated from Egypt and made a province ; the coast towns of Syria and Palestine were reunited to the province of Syria ; certain cities of Crete and

---

[1] This is what Augustus means by saying " that he extended the frontiers of all the provinces bordering on tribes that had not submitted " (*Mon. Anc.* 26).

Cyrene, Iudæa and Ituræa, and of Cilicia, which Antony had assigned to Cleopatra's son, Cæsarion, were either reunited to the provinces or declared free, as was also the case with other districts and towns assigned by Antony to his own son by Cleopatra. Certain client kings, however, were allowed to retain their territory and dignity, such as Herod in Iudæa, Amyntas in Galatia, Archelaus in Cappadocia. But the eternal question in the East was that of the Parthians. They not only were resolved to maintain the Euphrates as the limit beyond which Roman power was not to pass, but they had frequently made raids upon Syria, and were always attempting to occupy Armenia, which was a Roman protectorate, and the intervening kingdom of Media. The disaster of Crassus in Mesopotamia, and the chequered operations of Antony, had all sprung from these facts. When Augustus arrived in Asia the state of things which had finally resulted from the operations of Antony was that Artaxes (whose father, Artavasdes, had been treacherously captured by Antony and afterwards put to death by Cleopatra) was king of Armenia, and had attacked Media and captured its king Artavasdes ; and that Phraates had recovered his kingdom of Parthia. Augustus had two or three advantages in dealing with these complications. He found the brothers of the Armenian Artaxes still prisoners at Alexandria, and sent them to Rome as hostages. Again the captured king of Media managed to escape and appealed to him for help ; and, lastly, Phraates of Parthia had only just recovered his throne, from which he had been expelled by a rebellion headed by Tiridates, and the latter escaped to Syria and sent to implore the help of Augustus, while legates from Phraates also arrived soliciting his support. Augustus availed himself skilfully of these complications to assume the position of a lord paramount and arbiter. He allowed Tiridates to remain in safety in Syria ; but he treated the legates of Phraates in a friendly manner, and cordially invited a son of that king to accompany him to Rome, where, however, he was kept as a hostage.   Artavasdes was set up in Lesser Armenia to form a check upon Artaxes.   These diplomatic successes were regarded in Rome, as we have seen, as veritable triumphs over the dangerous Parthians—the only name much known there. The abolition of the arrangements of Antony, which had involved the curtailment of the Roman Empire, was recorded on coins struck in B.C. 29, with a head of Augustus on the obverse, and on the reverse a figure of victory standing on the mystic cista, with the legend *Asia recepta*.   But it is with his second Eastern progress (B.C. 22–19) that the useful public works, such as roads and buildings, of which traces are still found, probably began.

Between these two visits there had been only two movements of serious importance—the useless and almost disastrous expedition of Ælius Gallus into Arabia (B.C. 24–3), and the invasion of Southern Egypt at Elephantine by Candace, queen of Æthiopia, encouraged by the diminution of the Roman forces in Egypt during the Arabian expedition.   The Æthiopians gained some minor successes over three Roman cohorts stationed near the frontier, but were eventually repulsed by the præfect Gaius Petronius, who pursued them to their capital town Nabata, which he took and plundered.[1]

Movements in the East between B.C. 24 and B.C. 22.

The second eastward progress of Augustus began with some months' residence in Sicily.   There he was busied in founding colonies, of which seven are named. The chief town of Sicily was still Syracuse, but it seems to have suffered in the time of Sextus Pompeius, and Augustus placed in it two thousand settlers, probably veterans.   It was the object of such colonies to provide for veterans and poor Italians, but also to Romanise countries more completely, and to introduce an industrial

Second Eastern progress, B.C. 22–19.

---

[1] The exact position of Nabata is uncertain.   It is described in the *Mon. Ancyr.* 26 as "close to Meroe."   Augustus takes the responsibility of both these campaigns as being *meo iussu et auspicio.*

class. Sicily needed above all things free cultivators. Its corn trade had suffered from the competition of Africa, Sardinia, and Egypt, and its pastoral farms were largely owned by Roman capitalists, who did not reside, but employed slave-labour directed by bailiffs or *villici*.[1] One object at least, therefore, of these measures of Augustus was to bring into the country a class of small landowners residing on their property. Land was found for them by purchase, where there was no *ager publicus* available.

From Sicily Augustus passed to Greece and wintered at Samos. Achaia was a senatorial province, but the Emperor,
Augustus in Greece B.C. 21. we may notice, exercised complete authority there. He had already established two colonies—at Actium and Patræ, and he seems to have devoted most of his attention to promoting their interests. He compelled the inhabitants of several townships in the neighbourhood of both towns to migrate to the new colonies, and he insisted on the colony at Actium being admitted to the Amphictyonic League. The places were well chosen for naval purposes, but the element of compulsion in his policy towards them was unfortunate. He does not appear to have done much for Greece generally. It was in a lamentably decaying state, the population declining, and old towns disappearing. Nearly the only exception was the Iulian colony at Corinth. Such changes as Augustus made on this visit rather tended to emphasise this state of things, and certainly did nothing to relieve it. Athens, which retained nothing of its greatness except its past and the still surviving reputation as a university town (though Marseilles was running it hard even in that), had disgraced itself in his eyes by the display of sympathy, first for the Pompeians against Iulius, again for Brutus and Cassius against the triumvirs, and lastly for Antony against himself.

---

[1] As, for instance, Agrippa. Hor., *Ep.* 1, 12, 1. The seven colonies mentioned are Syracuse, Tauromenium, Catana, Thermæ, Tyndaris, Lilybæum, Panormus.

A town always on the losing side can expect little favour. It was deprived of its few remaining extra-Attic dependencies, Ægina and Eretria, and was forbidden to avail itself of almost the only source of revenue left—the fees which certain persons were still willing to pay for the honour of being enrolled as its citizens. Sparta, indeed, was rewarded by the restoration of Cythera, in return, it is said, for hospitality to Livia when in exile with her former husband ; but, on the other hand, it was deprived of the control over its harbour town of Gythium. But though both Iulius and Augustus favoured Sparta, as against Athens—a fact commemorated by a temple to Iulius and an altar to Augustus—it remained completely insignificant.

Very different was his policy in Asia. There Augustus set himself to restore the prosperity of the towns by grants of money, by relief from or readjustment of tribute, and by the promotion of useful public works. Nor were details of local administration and internal reforms neglected. Edicts are preserved which touch on such matters as the age of local magistrates, or the succession to the property of intestates in Bithynia, shewing with what minute care he studied local interests and problems. It was now probably that schemes were set on foot for opening up the country by roads, afterwards carried out by his legates. Milestones are being now discovered along the *via Sebaste* connecting the six Pisidian colonies dated in the eighteenth year of his tribunician power (B.C. 6) and a marble temple to Augustus still stands at Ancyra (*Angora*), to witness the gratitude of these Asiatic cities. At the same time disorder or illegal conduct was sternly punished. Cyzicus was deprived of its *libertas* for having flogged and put to death some Roman citizens, and the same punishment was awarded for their internal disorders to Tyre and Sidon, whose ancient liberties had been secured to them by Antony when he handed over the country to Cleopatra.

But of all his achievements during this progress nothing

made such a sensation in the Roman world, or was so much celebrated by the poets of the day, as the fact that

Return of the standards by the Parthians. he received back from the Parthian king the Roman eagles and standards lost by Crassus in B.C. 53, by Antony's legate Decidius Saxa in B.C. 40, and by Antony himself in B.C. 36 in a battle with Parthians and Medes. Those taken by the Medes had been returned to him, but not those taken by the Parthians. In B.C. 23 Tiridates, who had been allowed to take refuge in Syria in B.C. 30, came to Rome, and Phraates, to counteract his appeal, sent ambassadors thither also. After consulting the Senate Augustus declined to give up Tiridates, but he sent back to Phraates the son whom he had kept at Rome for the last six years on condition that the king should restore the standards. Pressed though he was by the disaffection of his subjects, Phraates had not yet fulfilled his bargain. But perhaps this disaffection had by B.C. 20 become more acute, or he was alarmed by the promptness with which Augustus asserted Roman supremacy in Armenia. Artaxes had ruled ill and had been insubordinate. Augustus appears to have meditated an expedition against him, but his subjects anticipated the difficulty by assassinating him. Augustus says that he might have made Armenia a province, but preferred to allow the ancient kingdom to remain. Accordingly on his order Tiberius went to Armenia and with his own hand placed the diadem on the head of Tigranes, brother of the late king, who had been living in exile at Rome. Thus the supremacy of Augustus was acknowledged in Armenia and its king ruled by his permission. A coin struck in B.C. 19 represents it as a real capture of Armenia, having on its reverse *Cæsar Div. F. Armen. capt. Imp. viiii.* The Parthian king thought it well now to fulfil his bargain, and again Tiberius was commissioned to receive the captured standards in Syria. With the standards were also some prisoners; though there were others who had in the thirty-three years that had elapsed since the fall of Crassus settled peaceably in Parthian territory, married wives, and now refused to return.[1] Such a contented abandonment of their native land seemed shocking to the orthodox Roman, unable to suppose life worth living among barbarians for one who had once been a citizen of the Eternal City. Prisoners of war were never much valued at Rome. It was the traditional maxim that the state never paid ransom, though private friends might and did, and Horace's ode may be meant to support the Emperor's refusal of some demand of Phraates for ransom of prisoners to accompany the standards. This transaction, however, was the crown of the Emperor's work in the East. It is commemorated on coins of B.C. 19 bearing a triumphal arch, with Augustus receiving the standards, on the obverse, and the legend *civibus et signis militaribus a Parthis receptis* on the reverse. The poets were not behind with their compliments. Vergil, who was in Greece in this the last year of his life, seems to have inserted three lines in his description of opening the doors of Bellona to bring in an allusion to it.[2] Horace, who had for the time given up lyric poetry, yet contrives a compliment in one of his epistles ;[3] and, on returning to lyric poetry in B.C. 13–12, is careful to include it among the great services of Augustus ; and Propertius, after prophetic suggestions as to what will be done, at last burst out into a triumphant hymn of praise over the achievements of these years, and, above all, on the Nemesis that has come for the slaughtered Crassus.[4] Many years afterwards Ovid takes the opportunity in describing the temple of Mars Ultor, in which Augustus deposited the recovered standards, to glorify him for having wiped out an old and shameful stain upon the Roman arms.[5]

---

[1] Dio, 54, 8 ; Horace, *Od.* 3, 5 ; this ode was written several years before the restoration of the standards, but the fact of the *milites Crassi* having settled in Parthia was naturally known.

[2] Verg., *Æn.* vii. 604–606.   [3] Horace, *Ep.* i. 18, 56 ; *Odes* iv. 15, 6.

[4] Propert., 3, 10, 13 ; 4, 4, 16 ; 4, 5, 48 ; 4, 12, 3 ; 5, 6, 79.

[5] Ovid, *F.* v. 567–594. According to Mommsen there were two temples of Mars Ultor, one on the Capitol (Dio, 54, 8), the other in the Forum Augustum, vowed at Philippi, but not dedicated till B.C. 2. The *signa*

There were many other arrangements made with the client kings of Asia, all of which were accompanied by the strict condition that they were henceforth to confine themselves to the territories now assigned to them and were to make no wars of aggression. The *pax augusta* was to be strictly maintained everywhere.

All this had been done without any drop of blood shed in war, and Augustus was able to devote the winter of B.C. 20–19

Augustus returns from the East, B.C. 19.

at Samos to rest and enjoyment, receiving numerous embassies from all parts, as far as from India. The Indian envoys brought him a present of tigers, a beast never before seen in Greece or Italy, and a wonderful armless dwarf who could draw a bow and throw javelins with his feet. He returned next year by way of Athens, where he was initiated in the Eleusinian mysteries and where he met with Vergil. The poet joined the Emperor's train, visited Megara with him, and returned with him to Italy, only to fall ill at Brundisium and die (September 22).

Though Augustus returned to Rome amidst loud congratulations, the Western part of the Empire was not yet at peace, and

Troubles in the West. Defeat of Lollius, B.C. 16.

in fact there were many threatening signs of future trouble. Agrippa, indeed, in the very year of the Emperor's return from the East, crushed the rebellious Cantabri and Astures, not without severe fighting ; but though Augustus was able now to remain at home, passing laws, holding the secular games, and strengthening his family by adopting Agrippa's children, the Empire was not at peace, the Ianus Quirinus still stood open. There were, in fact, a number of "little wars," mostly frontier raids. Thus in B.C. 17–16, P. Silius Nerva was engaged with various Alpine tribes, and in repelling an inroad of Pannonians. There were also about the same time brief outbursts in Spain and Dalmatia, and

seem to have been deposited first in the former and then transferred to the latter. Ovid evidently speaks of them as in the temple in the Forum Augustum.

inroads of barbarous tribes (Dentheletæ and Scordisci) into Macedonia. In Thrace the guardian of the sons of Cotys had to be assisted against the Bessi, and the Sauromatæ had to be driven back across the Danube. These were comparatively unimportant affairs. But a more serious danger was caused by some warlike German tribes—Sugambri, Usipetes, and Tencteri —crossing the Rhine and invading Gallia Belgica. They defeated some Roman cavalry, and while pursuing them came up with Lollius and his main army, which they again defeated, capturing the eagle of the Fifth Legion. Suetonius says that the affair was rather disgraceful than really disastrous. But it seemed sufficiently serious to Augustus. Agrippa was away in the East looking after Syria and Asia, and did not return till B.C. 13; and he resolved to go to Gaul himself, taking with him Tiberius, and leaving Drusus to carry on the latter's prætorship. The Germans, however, had no wish to fight a regular imperial army, they therefore retired beyond the Rhine, and made terms and gave hostages.

Augustus nevertheless found enough to do without positive fighting in introducing improvements and reforms. At

Administration
of Gaul,
B.C. 16–14. Nemausus the old gate of the town walls still stands, inscribed with his name, and dated in the seventh year of his tribunician power (B.C. 16); he had, moreover, to listen to long tales of grievances caused by the extortions of Licinius, the procurator at Lugdunum. This man's career was an early example of that of the rich freedmen of later times. Brought as prisoner from Gaul by Iulius Cæsar, and apparently emancipated by Octavian in accordance with his uncle's will, he had by some means amassed an immense fortune, and retained the favour of Augustus by large contributions to the public works from time to time promoted by the Emperor. A millionaire disposed to such liberality is always welcome to a sovereign with a taste for expensive reforms. As a Gaul by birth, Augustus seems to have supposed that he would be a sympathetic officer. But he proved more

Roman than the Romans in exacting the last farthing. We are reminded of " Morton's fork " and of Empson and Dudley, when we are told that he insisted on certain monthly payments being made fourteen times in the year, on the ground that November and December meaning the ninth and tenth months, there must be two more to be accounted for ! The complaints were so serious, however, that Licinius thought it necessary to offer to surrender his whole property to Augustus, as though he had only amassed it for the public service, with the deliberate purpose of weakening the disloyal natives. We are not told whether he was left in power, but at any rate he escaped punishment and survived Augustus. He probably was recalled to Rome, where he tried to pacify public indignation by large contributions to the restoration of the Curia Iulia, which was re-dedicated in honour of the Emperor's grandsons about A.D. 12.

But another and more serious trouble had now to be faced. The Rhæti, inhabiting the modern Grisons, Tyrol, and parts of Lombardy, were making raids upon Gaul and Italy, burning and slaying and plundering. With them were allied the Vindelici (inhabiting parts of modern Baden, Wurtenburg, and S. Bavaria), with other Alpine tribes.[1] The campaign against these tribes was intrusted to Tiberius, who conceived a masterly plan which was crowned with brilliant success. Drusus was summoned from Rome to guard the passes into Lombardy, and in the valleys of the Tridentine Alps at the entrance of the Brenner pass, near the Lacus Benacus (Lago di Garda), he won a brilliant victory over them, and forced many of their mountain strongholds. Shut off thus from Italy they turned their armies towards Helvetic Gaul, but were met by Tiberius and again defeated between Bâle and the Lake of Constance. These two defeats seem practically to have annihilated these tribes, and they gave no further trouble. It was after this that Noricum was

Campaigns of Tiberius and Drusus, B.C. 15.

[1] Such as the Brenni and Genauni of Hor., *Od.* iv. 14, 10 ; cp. iv. 4, 18.

annexed, and Rhætia and Vindelicia conquered, and presently formed into the province Rhætia.

Still Augustus had to stay on another year in Gaul.   Risings had to be suppressed among the Ligurians of the Maritime Alps, and in Pannonia; while Agrippa, who had returned from Palestine accompanied or followed by Herod, went to Sinope, on the Pontus, to put down a disturbance that had arisen owing to a disputed claim to the crown of the Cimmerian Bosporus, which an usurper named Scribonius had seized.   At the end of B.C. 14, or the beginning of B.C. 13, Augustus returned to Rome with Tiberius, who entered then upon his first consulship, and there they were also joined by Agrippa.   Whether the temple of Ianus was now closed for the third time is not certain.   But there are some good reasons for supposing that it was.   In two passages, Horace, writing in B.C. 13, speaks of it as though it were a recent occurrence; Dio, in speaking of the return of Augustus, says that he came back after " having settled all the affairs of the Gauls, Germanies and Spains"; there was certainly a lull in the German trouble, where Drusus had been left in command; and lastly an inscription recording the extension of the great road to Gades in Southern Spain, has the date of this year, and records the closing of Ianus in honour of Augustus.   None of these are in themselves absolute proofs, but taken together they form a strong presumption.[1]

At the end of B.C. 14 Augustus returns to Rome.

B.C. 13.

At any rate, Augustus returned to Rome with the feeling that he had secured peace.   Though he, as usual, avoided meeting a complimentary procession by entering the city after nightfall, yet he came with laurelled fasces.   The next morning, after greeting a crowd of people on the Capitol, he caused the laurels to be taken off and solemnly laid on the

---

[1] *Mon. Ancyr.*, 13; Horace, *Epist.* 2, 1, 255; *Odes*, 4, 15, 9; Dio, 54, 25. For the inscription, see Clinton, *Fast. Hell.*, B.C. 14.   The tenth tribunician year is from June 27th, B.C. 14, to 26th June, B.C. 13.   The *ara pacis* was founded in this year (4th July), dedicated 30th January, B.C. 9.

knees of Jupiter, and the first business he transacted in the Senate was the settlement of the claims of his soldiers. But the peace did not last long. Augustus himself spent the next three years in Italy busied with the census, the lectio senatus, legislation, and various ceremonies. Lepidus died in the early part of this year, and he was at once declared Pontifex Maximus, though the *inauguratio* did not take place till the following February.

However, before the year was ended, news came of disturbances in Pannonia, and Agrippa—once more associated in the tribunician power—was sent thither. He had no

Death of Agrippa, B.C. 12. fighting, for the rising was abandoned at his approach.

It was his last journey. Next spring he was taken ill in one of his Campanian villas. Augustus threw all business aside and hastened to his house, but arrived too late. Never had ruler a more faithful or abler friend and servant. At every crisis of his life Agrippa had been by his side, and wherever danger was most threatening he had taken the post of difficulty and honour. If he gained wealth in his master's service, he was always ready to spend it in support of his master's aims. In the interests of the dynasty he had sunk all private wishes and ambitions. About Agrippa the passion for prurient scandal, characteristic of the age and people, for once is silent, and not a single line or inuendo survives to impeach his private or public life. Augustus shewed both his respect and deep feeling. He accompanied the body to Rome, pronounced the funeral oration himself, and deposited the ashes in the new mausoleum which he had erected for his own family.

The news of Agrippa's death seems to have encouraged the Pannonians once more to strike for freedom. Tiberius accordingly was appointed to succeed him in the com-

Tiberius in Pannonia. mand. He laid waste wide portions of their country, inflicted much slaughter upon the inhabitants, and seems quickly to have reduced them to obedience, though only for a time.

Meanwhile Drusus was not idle. The Sugambri and their allies crossed the Rhine into the district called Lower Germany,

Drusus in
Germania,
B.C. 12–9.

a part of Belgium (now North Brabant), where they would find tribes nearly allied to themselves, and willing to shake off the Roman yoke. Drusus had been engaged in the consecration of an altar to Augustus at Lugdunum, where he had invited the attendance of leading Gauls from all these provinces. He hurried back to the Rhine and drove the invaders over the river, and then throwing a bridge across it (somewhere below Cologne), he attacked the Usipites on the right bank of the Lupia, and then marched up the Rhine to attack the Sugambri. But there was a fleet of ships supporting him in the Rhine. He cut a canal from the River to Lake Flevo (Zuyder Zee), so that this fleet might sail up the coast to the mouths of the three rivers—the Amisia, Visurgis, and Albis (*Ems, Weser, Elbe*). He proposed to make the Elbe the limit of the Roman Empire, instead of the Rhine ; but in this first year only reduced the coast as far as the Visurgis. The next year (B.C. 11), he advanced by land to the same river, only farther inland, and occupied the country of the Cherusci (Westphalia), and though on their way home his men were nearly caught in an ambush, they got back safely to the banks of the Lupia, and several forts were established in various parts of the country. The next year (B.C. 10) he was engaged with the Chatti (Hessen), who endeavoured to regain the territories from which he had driven them in the previous year.[1] In B.C. 9, being now consul, he pushed as far as the Elbe, where he erected a trophy to mark the extreme limit of the Roman advance, through the land of the Chatti and Trevi. But on his return march he fell and broke his leg, and there being no skilled physician with

---

[1] But he does not seem to have had any fighting this year, and in fact the Senate voted to close the Ianus Quirinus, though that was prevented by an inroad of the Daci into Pannonia, with which Tiberius was sent to deal. Dio, 54, 36,

the army, he died after thirty days' suffering. Besides these marches into Germany, he had, during his command, established a line of fortresses on the Lower Rhine, to the number of fifty, as far up the stream as Argentoratum (Strassburg).

On hearing of his brother's accident, Tiberius, who was at Ticinum, hurried to his side, was with him when he died, and accompanied the corpse on foot back to Rome, where he delivered a funeral oration, and Augustus, who returned from Lugdunum at this time, another.

Tiberius in Germany B.C. 8–7.

The ashes were placed in the Mausoleum of Augustus. Tiberius was appointed to succeed him on the Rhine, and in B.C. 8 crossed the river to attack the Sugambri. But as the other tribes made their submission, the Sugambri were induced to send some of their leading men to negotiate also. Augustus then took a step which requires, at any rate, some explanation. He seized these legates and kept them in confinement in various towns as hostages. It had the immediate effect, however, of keeping the Sugambri quiet, large numbers of them were settled on the left bank of the Rhine, and Tiberius was able to come home for his triumph in B.C. 7, with which the name of Drusus was also associated.

No wars of any consequence disturbed the peace of the Empire for nearly nine years. Tiberius retired to Rhodes in B.C. 6, and his successors in the command of the army of the Rhine had the task of maintaining and strengthening the conquests of Drusus. The two districts on the left bank of the river, Germania Inferior and Superior, though for some purposes they belonged to Gallia Belgica, yet as military districts were distinct, and they included some fortresses on the right bank of the Rhine. The country between the Rhine and the Elbe was in an ambiguous position. It was not a province, and yet the commanders on the Rhine occupied as much of it as they could from time to time maintain.

But in A.D. 4 Tiberius, now returned from Rhodes, and

adopted son of Augustus, took over the command on the
Rhine, and immediately began a great forward
movement like that of his brother Drusus. He
too advanced to the Weser and reduced the
Cherusci who were in revolt; and after march-
ing to the Lippe again, advanced to the Elbe (A.D. 5), reducing
the Chauci and Longobardi, this time with the support of a
fleet that entered the mouth of the Elbe. Some others thought
it safer to send envoys and make terms of friendship with
Rome. Next year (A.D. 6) he was to attack the Marcomanni
under a powerful leader named Marobudus. The attack was
to be made from two sides. C. Sextius Saturninus, an able and
experienced officer, was to lead one army from the Rhine,
through the territory of the Chatti (near Cologne), while
Tiberius himself led another from Noricum across the Danube
The two were to converge upon the district now occupied by
the Marcomanni answering to the modern Bohemia. Tiberius
was accompanied by the governor of Pannonia (Valerius
Messalinus), and a large part of the troops stationed there.
But the expedition was prevented by a sudden rising in
Pannonia and Dalmatia. The inhabitants of these countries
had not become reconciled to Roman rule; they felt the
burden of the tribute, and the opportunity afforded by the
withdrawal of so many troops was eagerly seized. Tiberius
was forced to offer terms to Marobudus, which he accepted,
and hurry back to Pannonia, while Saturninus returned to
the Rhine for fear of an outbreak there. The rising in
Pannonia and Dalmatia was with difficulty suppressed after a
weary struggle lasting between three and four years. Many
legions had to be drafted into the country from other provinces
as well as large auxiliary forces. Germanicus was summoned
to assist with a new army, and Augustus himself came to
Ariminum to be near at hand. Suetonius affirms that it
was the most serious struggle in which the Romans had been
engaged since the Punic wars. In B.C. 9 Tiberius indeed

The marginal note reads: Tiberius again in Germany and Illyricum, A.D. 4-7.

returned to Rome to claim his triumph, but had to go back to put a last touch to the war.

Meanwhile the army of the Rhine had been under the command of P. Quintilius Varus. Velleius gives an unfavourable account of him. He was more a courtier than a soldier, and in his government of Syria had shown himself greedy of money. "He entered a rich province a poor man, and left a poor province a rich one." From the time of his accession to the command in B.C. 7 he seems to have regarded the country between the Rhine and Elbe as completely reduced to the form of a Roman province, and proceeded to levy tribute with the same strictness as he had been used to do in Syria. But the German tribes did not regard themselves as Roman subjects. The Romans were only masters of so much as their camps could control. While Varus was living in fancied security in his summer camp on the Weser, busied only with the usual legal administration of a provincial governor, four great German peoples, the Cherusci, Chatti, Marsi, and Bructeri, were secretly combining under the lead of the Cheruscan chief, Arminius, to strike a blow for liberty. As the autumn of A.D. 9 approached Varus prepared to return to the regular winter quarters on the Rhine (Castra Vetera). Arminius, who had served in the Roman army, and had been rewarded by the citizenship and the rank of eques, had ingratiated himself with Varus, and was fully acquainted with his plans, and though Varus had been warned of his treachery he seems to have taken no heed. In order to bring him through the difficult country where the ambush was to await him, a rising of a tribe off his direct road to the Lower Rhine was planned. He fell into the trap, and turning aside to chastise the rebellious tribe, was caught in a difficult pass, somewhere between the sources of the Lippe and Ems, and he and nearly the whole of his army perished. For three days the army struggled through a thick and almost pathless forest, encumbered by a heavy baggage train, and a

The fall of Varus, A.D. 9.

number of women and children, attacked and slaughtered at nearly every step by the Germans who were concealed in the woods, and continually made descents upon them. A miserable remnant was saved by the exertions of L. Asprenas, a legate of Varus, who had come to the rescue. Varus and some of his chief officers appear to have committed suicide. The loss of three legions and a large body of auxiliaries greatly affected the Emperor, now a man of over seventy. For many months he wore signs of mourning, and we are told that at times in his restless anxiety he beat his head upon the door, crying, " Varus, give me back my legions ! " Perhaps this is the picturesque imagination of anecdote mongers. Though alarmed for the possible consequences both at home and in the provinces, he acted with spirit and energy. He ordered the urban pickets to be carefully posted, suspended all changes in provincial governments, and held a levy of citizen soldiers, enforcing by threats and punishment the duty of giving in the names. For some time past service in the army had been regarded as a profession sufficiently attractive to draw volunteers, without having recourse to the legal right of conscription. But a sudden emergency like this seems to have found men apathetic or disinclined, and he had to resort to the old methods. He thought it necessary also to get rid for a time of Gauls or Germans who were serving in the city cohorts or residing in Rome. Tiberius, on the news of the disaster, hurried from his Pannonian quarters to Rome, and was appointed to the Rhine command, to which he went early in A.D. 10. The danger most to be feared was that the victorious Germans would at once cross the Rhine. But this had been averted partly because the Marcomanni had declined to join the insurrection, even when Arminius sent the head of Varus to their chief, Marobudus, and partly by the fact that the rebellious Germans themselves wasted time in blockading Aliso, the fort erected by Drusus on the Lippe, which was obstinately defended by its garrison under Lucius Cædicius.

It proved to be the Ladysmith of the German war, for the Germans, fearing to leave it on their rear, missed the opportunity of attacking the camps on the Rhine before they could be reinforced. The brave garrison, when their provisions were exhausted, escaped on a dark night and reached Castra Vetera in safety. Still, the result of the rising was to free Germany beyond the Rhine. When Tiberius arrived to take the command in A.D. 10, he spent the first year in strengthening the forts along that river ; and though in A.D. 11 he moved his summer camp beyond it, he never went far, or apparently engaged in any warlike operations then or in A.D. 12. In the next year he returned to Rome and was succeeded in the command by his nephew, Germanicus. The forward movements of this young prince belong to the next reign, but Tiberius no doubt learnt now what a few years later induced him to recall Germanicus and be content with the frontier of the Rhine.

The life of Augustus was now near its close, and there are no more military enterprises to record. He had never commanded in the field since the Cantabrian war of B.C. 25 ; but he had taken part in the most important wars by moving to within such a distance of the seat of war as to hear news quickly and to superintend the despatch of provisions and reinforcements. He was probably more usefully employed in this way, and was enabled to see, by personal observation, the needs of the provinces and the best methods of remedying abuses and promoting prosperity. In the course of his reign he is said to have visited every province except Sardinia and Africa, and hardly any is without some trace of his activity and liberality in the way of roads, bridges, or public buildings. He was anxious that all, however distant, should feel in touch with the central authority at Rome. Among other means to promote this was the establishment or improvement of an imperial post which should reach the most distant dependencies.

We must not think of this as being like the modern postal

service—meant for the general use of the public. It was purely official. Just as the main purpose of the great roads was to facilitate the rapid movement of armies and officials, so the post was a contrivance to expedite official despatches, to convey the Emperor's orders to remotest parts of the Empire, and to carry back news and warnings to the government at home. Along the great roads in Italy and the provinces there had long been posting houses where relays of horses, mules, or carriages could be obtained, but there was never what we should call a postal service for the transmission of private letters. Rich men kept slaves for this purpose (*tabellarii*), the magistrates had official messengers (*statores*), and the companies of *publicani* had their regular service of carriers. Private people could, as a favour, get their letters occasionally conveyed by some of these ; and it was considered a proper act of politeness at Rome when despatching a slave with letters to distant places, to send round to one's friends to know whether they wished to send any by him. Again, governors of provinces under the republic had arranged with certain scribes in Rome to copy out the *diurna acta* and transmit them by slaves or paid messengers. But for official purposes Augustus arranged a number of stations along the great roads with men, horses, and carriages, to convey to and from Rome all the news that it was needful for the government to know or all orders that emanated from the Emperor.[1] Private persons would have no right to use these public servants or conveyances ; but no doubt the organisation for the public service facilitated the transmission of private correspondence also.

This actual and material tightening of the bond which united distant parts of the Empire with the central government went side by side with the moral effect of the change in the position of the governors. No longer permitted to make what profit they could from excessive exactions, or percentages allowed

---

[1] Especially in camps, in which there seem to have been a regular service of *tabellarii castrenses*. (Wilmann's *Exempla* 1357.)

by usage though not by law, they all received a fixed salary, as did the lesser officials; and though extortion was still occasionally heard of, the provinces knew that they had a rapid means of appealing to the Emperor and a fair certainty of redress.

Another change that made at first for unity, though it afterwards had the contrary effect, concerned the army. In the time of the republic there was in theory no one standing army. There were many armies, all of which took the military oath to their respective commanders. Now the military oath was taken by all to one man—the Emperor. The commanders of legions were his *legati*. He regulated the pay, the years of service, the retiring allowance for all alike. Each of the republican imperators had a prætorian guard, generally consisting of auxiliary troops. Now there was one prætorian guard, naturally stationed at Rome, and though distinguished from the rest by increased pay and easier years of service, it, as well as the *cohortes vigilum*, was under the same command. This applies also to the fleet which was organised under Augustus chiefly to protect the coast and clear the sea of pirates : the two principal stations being at Misenum on the west, and Ravenna on the east coast, with a third maintained for a time at Forum Iulii (Fréjus). The men serving in these ships occupied the same position as citizen soldiers or auxiliaries, and like them took the oath to one man —the Emperor. But the very completeness of the organisation, it is right to notice here, eventually made for disruption. Certain legions became constantly attached to certain provinces, the auxiliaries serving with them being as a rule recruited from the same provinces. The several branches of the army thus came to feel an *esprit de corps*, and to regard themselves as a separate entity with separate interests and claims. Consequently, when in after-times the central authority was in dispute or in process of change, the legions in the different provinces spoke and thought of themselves as separate "armies," capable of taking an independent line and having a determining

The army under one commander-in-chief.

voice in deciding who should be their Imperator. In those troublous times the provinces which had no military establishment, or only a weak one, ceased to count for much, and had to follow the strongest army near them.[1] For the present such difficulties were not foreseen. Augustus was a strict disciplinarian, and little was heard as yet of any serious insubordination. When it did occur it was promptly punished. He disbanded the 10th legion for misconduct, and exercised at times the full vigour of military punishment for desertion of posts or lesser offences, and was careful in addressing his troops not to lower his dignity by affectation of equality. He called them "Soldiers!" not "Fellow-soldiers!" At the same time he kept up the traditional exclusiveness of the legions, and seldom employed freedmen, except as a kind of special constable in the city, and twice in times of great distress, the Illyrian and German wars: even then they were formed in separate cohorts, and armed in some way less complete than the legionaries.

The same conservative attachment to the ancient superiority of Rome made him chary of granting the citizenship either to individuals, or to masses of soldiers, or to states. This was one of the points in which his policy was opposite to that of Iulius. The latter by his large grants of citizenship to soldiers, professional men and communities, had helped to raise the number of citizens from about 450,000 in B.C. 70 to 4,063,000 (the number in the Census of B.C. 28). During the forty-five years that remained to Augustus the number had only gone up to 4,937,000 (the Census of A.D. 13). This is probably little more than can be accounted for by the growth of population; so that extensions of the franchise must have been insignificant. His idea was an empire, one in its military obligations and in

[1] The armed provinces were those on the frontier. Towards the end of the life of Augustus, the preponderance of the military force on the Rhine and Danube is the noteworthy fact. The Gauls and "Germany" had eight legions, Spain three, Africa two, Egypt two, Syria four, Pannonia two, Mœsia two, Dalmatia two. But those on the Rhine were more concentrated. (Tac., *Ann.* 4, 5.)

its subjection to one supreme head, and yet not divorced from the original city state. Rome was to be the imperial city, the seat of government ; the Populus Romanus was to be the inhabitants of Rome extended to the limits of Italy. There was to be a sharp line of division between the ruling and the ruled. It was one of those compromises that are without the elements of permanence. And yet it established a sentiment that has lasted, and is a reason that even to this day the centre of spiritual life to a large part of Europe is on the banks of the Tiber. In material matters the extension of the citizenship meant the gradual shifting of the centre of power, and when early in the third century Caracalla, for purposes of taxation, extended the citizenship to the whole Empire, though the Roman name and its historical prestige remained, Rome itself became only one of a number of cities in a widely spread empire, and politically by no means the most important. Such a conception was far from the mind of Augustus. It would have seemed to him to be more worthy of his rival Antony, who was for setting up a new Rome in Alexandria.

CHAPTER XI

O tutela præsens
Italiæ dominæque Romæ.

AFTER the settlement of the constitution in B.C. 23 Augustus was only absent from Italy three times, from B.C. 22 to B.C. 19 in Sicily and the East, from B.C. 16 to B.C. 13 in Gaul and Spain, and B.C. 9–10 in Gaul. At the outbreak of the Pannonian and Dalmatian wars A.D. 6–9 he stayed for some time at Ariminum. For the rest of the time he lived at Rome, with the usual visits to his country houses, made by land or yacht. His return to the city after any prolonged absence was celebrated with every sign of rejoicing, with sacrifices, music, and a general holiday. On his return from Gaul in B.C. 13 an altar was dedicated to *Fortuna redux.*[1] Nor was this mere adulation. The people had come to look upon him as the best guarantee of peace and security. The troubles of the days preceding the civil wars, the street fighting and massacres, the horrors of the civil war itself, were not forgotten : but his own part in them was ignored or forgiven ; it was only remembered that he had put an end to them ; that he had restored the ruinous city in unexampled splendour ; that it was owing to his liberality, or that of his friends acting under his influence, that at Rome

Popular feeling towards Augustus.

[1] C.I.L. x. 8375 ; *Mon. Ancyr.* 11.

there were luxurious baths, plentiful water, abundant food, streets free from robbers, help ready in case of fire, and cheerful festivals nearly always in progress. It was thanks to him that the roads in Italy were not beset by brigands, that the corn-ships from Egypt crowded the harbour of Puteoli unmolested by pirates on their course,[1] that not only the dreaded Parthian, but princes from the ends of the earth were sending embassies desiring the friendship of Rome. At the least sign of the old disorders they clamoured for his return and besought him to become Dictator, director of the corn trade, perpetual guardian of morals, anything, convinced that under his absolute rule there would be peace, plenty, and security. Horace exactly represents this feeling when he addresses Augustus in his absence in Gaul: "Oh scion of the gracious gods, oh best guardian ot the race of Romulus . . . return ! Your country calls for you with vows and prayer . . . for when you are here the ox plods up and down the fields in safety ; Ceres and bounteous blessing cheer our farms ; our sailors speed o'er seas that know no fear of pirates ; credit is unimpaired ; no foul adulteries stain the home ; punishment follows hard on crime. . . . Who fears Parthian, Scythian, German, or Spaniard with Cæsar safe ? Each man closes a day of peace on his native hills, trains his vines to the widowed trees, and home returning, light of heart, quaffs his wine and ends the feast with blessings on thee as a god indeed."[2]

These feelings found expression in a form which in our day

The worship of Augustus.

is apt to appear, according to our temperament, ridiculous or profane. In plain terms this was to treat Augustus as divine, a god on earth. The various expres-

---

[1] Suet., *Aug.* 98 : "As he chanced to be cruising in his yacht round the bay of Puteoli, the passengers and crew of an Alexandrine ship, which had just come to land, came with white robes, with garlands on their heads and burning censers in their hands, loudly blessing and praising him, and saying that they owed it to him that they were alive, that they sailed the sea, that they were enjoying their liberty and property."

[2] Horace, *Odes* iv. 5.

sions of Horace [1] may perhaps be put down to poetical exaggeration or conventional compliment, though there is a real meaning at their back ; but though Augustus refused to allow temples and altars to himself in Rome and Italy, [2] and even ordered certain silver statuettes to be melted down, the evidence of inscriptions makes it certain that the cult began in his lifetime in several places, as at Pompeii, Puteoli, Cumæ in Campania, and in other parts of Italy.[3] In Rome itself, when Augustus reorganised the *vici*, the old worship of the *Lares Compitales* at some consecrated spot in each *vicus* or " parish " was restored, but they were commonly spoken of as *Lares Augusti*, and the *Genius Augusti* was associated with them. It is this fact that, to a certain extent, explains and renders less irrational an attitude of mind which we are apt to dismiss as merely absurd. Each man had a *Genius*—a deity to whom he was a particular care. We speak of a man's " mission," implying by the word itself some external and directing power, probably divine. The step is not a long one which identifies the man and his genius, especially when his mission seems to be to bring us peace and prosperity. " Oh Melibæus, 'twas a god that wrought this ease for us ! " exclaims the countryman in Vergil, who had got back his lands. This confusion between the inspirer and the inspired, between the mission and the man, was everywhere apparent. Among the statues in the temples, and in the sacred hymns and other acts of worship, the figure or the name of Augustus was associated with those of the gods in a way that admitted, indeed, of a distinction being drawn between a memorial to an almost divine man and an act of devotion

---

[1] See, among others, *Ep.* ii. 1-16 ; *Odes* 3, 5, 2 ; 4, 5, 32.

[2] Suet., *Aug.* 52 ; Dio, 51, 20.

[3] The Latin inscriptions bearing on this point have been collected in a convenient form by Mr. Rushforth, *Latin Historical Inscriptions*, pp. 51-61. Other places in Italy thus shewn to have adopted the cult in some form or other during the lifetime of Augustus are Asisium, Beneventum, Fanum Fortunæ, Pisa, Tibur, Verona, possibly Ancona, and Forum Clodii, and some unnamed place in Latium.

to a god, but often obscured that distinction for ordinary folk. When we dedicate a church to a saint, or "to the glory of God and in memory of So-and-so," the distinction is of course clear, but the confusion which has from time to time resulted is also notorious. Thus in the Cuman Calendar of a sacred year, in which the anniversaries of striking events in the career of Augustus are marked for some act of worship, sometimes the *supplicatio* is bluntly stated as *Augusto;* sometimes in honour of some abstract idea as *imperio Augusti, Fortunæ reduci, Victoriæ Augustæ;* at others to a god—*Iovi sempiterno, Vestæ, Marti Ultori, Veneri.* In fact, the *supplicatio* always had a double reference, it was an act of prayer or thanksgiving to a god, but it was also an honour to a successful man. The two ideas properly distinct easily coalesced. A *supplicatio* in honour of Augustus, without much violence, became a *supplicatio* to him.

Of the still more formal cult which arose after his death with a temple regularly dedicated to him by Livia on the Palatine, and a new college of Augustales to keep up the worship in all parts of the Empire, an explanation somewhat analogous may be given. He was declared *divus* by the Senate, he was the late Emperor of blessed memory, a sainted soul, the very spirit or genius of eternal Rome. The traditions in early Roman history of the god-born and deified founder, the hero-worship of Greece, the veil which concealed (as it still conceals) the state of the departed, combined with the tolerant spirit of polytheism to make it almost as easy for the men of that time to admit a new deity into the Olympian hierarchy, as for mediæval Europe to admit a new saint into the Calendar.

Augustus, as we said, had the good sense and modesty to put difficulties in the way of this worship in Rome and Italy. It was another matter in the provinces. The divine, or semi-divine, honours paid him there were closely bound up with loyalty to Rome and a belief in her eternal mission. He therefore allowed temples and altars to be built, but always on the understanding that the name of Rome should be associated with his own. Such a method of expressing devotion to Rome and reverence for her magistrates had not been unknown in earlier times. In the second century B.C. a colossal statue of Rome had been set up by the Rhodians in a temple of Athena ; the people of Chalcis had erected a temple in honour of Flamininus ; and Cicero implies that in his time it was not an uncommon thing to do in the Asiatic provinces. At Smyrna a temple to Rome had been erected in B.C. 195 ;[1] and even before these the communities in Asia and Greece had been accustomed to honour the Ptolemies in a similar manner. The new cult therefore had nothing strange to the feelings and habits of the time. It began early in his career of success— not later at most than B.C. 36, after the defeat of Sextus Pompeius [2]—and it spread rapidly. We hear of temples "to Rome and Augustus," or altars, at Cyme, Ancyra, Pergamus, Nicomedia, Alexandria, Paneas, Sparta, and elsewhere in the East. Connected with them were yearly festivals and games, as at Athens, Ancyra, and in Cilicia.[3] Nor was it in the East only that this worship began in the lifetime of Augustus. We hear of temples or altars in Spain, Mœsia, Pannonia, Narbonne ; and the altar at Lugdunum (Lyon), consecrated by Drusus in B.C. 12, was deliberately intended to supersede the Druidical religion which was national and separatist.

For forming an estimate of Augustus himself it is of great interest to decide, if possible, how far he was deluded, how far he was acting from deliberate policy in countenancing these things. When some people of Tarraco reported to him, as an omen of his

The attitude of Augustus to this worship.

---

[1] Plut., *Flamin.* 16 ; Cicero, *ad Q. Fr.* 1, 1, 9 ; *ad Att.* 5, 21 ; Tac., *Ann.* 4, 56. Polyb. 31, 15.

[2] Appian, b. c. 5, 132, "and the cities began placing his image side by side with those of their gods."

[3] Information as to these is mostly to be found in Greek inscriptions, C.I.G. 3,524, 3,604, 3,831, 4,039. See also Dio, 51, 10 ; Strabo, 27, 1, 9 Joseph., *Antiq.* 15, 10, 3 ; Livy, *Ep.* 137 ; Pausan., iii. 25.

victorious career, that a palm had grown on the mound of his altar in that city, he replied with half-grave, half-playful irony, "That shews how often you use it!"[1] But there is no note of disapproval or abnegation in the answer. He accepts it as a natural fact that there should be such an altar, as a modern sovereign might accept the compliment of a statue. Can we explain it, except as a case of conscious fraud or blinding vanity? I believe we may. We must notice first that Augustus had been zealous in the apotheosis of Iulius, had urged Antony to become his flamen, had built a temple to him in Rome, and encouraged the building of temples and altars elsewhere. Now this apotheosis and worship of Iulius had begun before his death,[2] as Augustus knew perfectly well. But in spite of the manifestly party spirit of the packed Senate that voted the divine honours to Iulius, he gave no sign of revulsion or incredulity. On the contrary, he professed himself the heir not only of his wealth and honours, but also of his religious obligations and political purposes. It is clear, again, that Augustus believed in the gods, that is, in some immortal being or beings who governed and controlled the world. The restorer of a hundred temples, of sacred writings and ancient religious rites, the pious fulfiller of vows made in the hour of danger or escape, may have had crude or uncertain beliefs, have held views philosophical or superstitious, wise or foolish, but he could hardly have been an atheist.

He was too busy a man to be much troubled with philosophic doubts, and perhaps—obvious as it may be—the answer of Napoleon would have represented his view: who after listening for a time to certain atheistic arguments, said,

---

[1] Quintilian, vi. 377.

[2] For this and his statue in the temple of Quirinus, with legend of *Deo invicto*, the vote of the Senate giving him a temple, flamen, and other divine honours, see Dio, 43, 45; 44, 6; Cicero, 2 *Phil.* § 110; *ad Att.* 13, 44; Sueton., *Cæs.* 76. It was worse than the case of Augustus, more insincere and less spontaneous. The Senate was filled with the protégés of Iulius at the time.

pointing to the starry heavens, "All very well, gentlemen, but who made all that?" Given a belief in oneself and in Providence, the next step is to believe that Providence is on our side, as Cromwell saw the hand of God even in his most questionable achievements. If we can translate this into the language of an age accustomed to hear at any rate with acquiescence of heroic men, sons of the gods and destined to be enrolled among their peaceful ranks, of the genius which attended each man from the cradle to the grave, of the care of the gods for the welfare of the state in its darkest hours, manifested by omens, warnings, and even material appearances: if again we consider how much it adds to the strength of a belief to find it shared by others and to see that it makes for the moral good of the world, we may come faintly to conceive a frame of mind in Augustus on this subject which need not— in view of his age and its sentiments—be set down either as wholly irrational or wholly hypocritical. "The Roman Empire," he might say to himself, "is all that really matters in the world. I am divinely appointed to restore and defend it. I have in fact secured its peace and prosperity. If the people call me god, it is their way of honouring the Genius that directs me, the Providence that has selected me to be their benefactor and saviour. If they believe in that, they must also believe in the sanctity and eternal authority of Rome and the Empire. Religion and loyalty are but different words for the same virtue." In his eyes the state was divinely appointed, even in itself divine, and in so far as he represented the state he was a divinity to its subjects. Stability was its first requisite. "My highest ambition," he said in an edict, "is to be called the author of an ideally good constitution, and to carry with me to the grave a hope that the foundations I have laid will remain unmoved." Goodness, and loyalty to the state, had become convertible terms to him. Once as he was looking at a villa formerly belonging to Cato, one of his companions, thinking to please him by denouncing an anti-

Cæsarean, spoke of the "obstinate wrong-headedness of Cato." But he answered gravely "any one who is opposed to revolution is a good man as well as a good citizen." At another time he came upon one of his grandsons reading a book of Cicero. The boy, thinking he was on forbidden ground, tried to conceal the book ; but Augustus took it into his hand, read in it a short time, and handed it back with the remark, " A true scholar, my boy, and a patriot." Perhaps he thought with remorse of his own part in the great man's death, perhaps of the time when he believed him to have been false to himself, but "patriot"—"a lover of his country"—made up for all.[1]

It is clear, again, that it was not personal vanity or a desire for adulation that actuated Augustus. He disliked fulsome compliments or overstrained titles of respect, and laughed at cringing attitudes, as when he said of some obsequious petitioner that "he held out his billet and then snatched it away again like a man giving a penny to an elephant." He specially objected to be called *dominus*, a word properly applying to a master of slaves, and forbade the word to be used even in jest in his own family. He wished to be regarded as a citizen among citizens. He took care to shew interest (unlike Iulius) in the games and shows that were liked by the people, and disapproved of special marks of respect being paid to his young grandsons by the people rising and cheering when they entered the circus. He went through the streets on foot even when Consul, or rode with the curtains of his sedan drawn back, that he might not seem to avoid the looks or approach of the crowd; he admitted all kinds of people without distinction of rank to his morning levees ; forbade the Senators to rise when he entered or left the house ; visited friends without state, and was careful to attend family festivities such as betrothal parties. At elections he went round with his candidates and canvassed for

The civilitas of Augustus.

[1] Macrob., *Sat.* 2, 4, 18 ; Plut., *Cic.* 49 ; Suet., *Aug.* 28.

votes, and appeared for his clients in the courts (though anxious not to allow his presence to exercise an unfair influence) and shewed no annoyance at being cross-questioned and refuted. In the Senate he allowed great freedom of speech without resentment. He was interrupted while speaking by cries of "We don't understand," "I would contradict you if it were of any use." On one occasion, when he was leaving the house with some signs of anger after a tiresome debate, he was followed by cries, "Senators should be allowed to speak freely on public affairs," something like the shouts of "Privilege" that greeted Charles I. on a famous occasion. When he mildly remonstrated with Antistius Labeo for nominating Lepidus (whom he particularly disliked and treated with great contumely) to the Senate, Antistius retorted rudely, "Every one is entitled to his own opinion." He was tolerant of such language and wrote a soothing note to Tiberius, who expressed himself vehemently about some occurrence of the sort : "My dear Tiberius, don't give way to youthful excitement, or be so very indignant at some one being found to speak harm of me. It is quite enough if we can prevent their *doing* us any harm." In matters more personal or private he could stand a telling or rough retort. When holding a review of the equites he brought up a number of charges against a certain eques, who rebutted them one after the other and ended with the contemptuous remark : "Next time, sir, you cause inquiries to be made about a respectable man, you had better intrust the business to respectable people." Seeing another eques eating in the circus he sent a message to him, "When I want to lunch, I go home." "Yes," was the answer, "but you are not afraid of losing your place." Another eques was rebuked by him for squandering his patrimony, and deigned no further remark than, "Oh well, I was under the impression that it was my own property." He once paid a Senator's debts, and got no more thanks than a note with the words, "Not a farthing for myself !" A young man was once noticed at Court with an extraordinary likeness to himself. Augustus ordered him to be introduced and said : " Young gentleman, was your mother ever at Rome ? " " No," he replied, " but my father was." In this case it must be acknowledged that the Emperor richly deserved the retort. The point, however, in all these stories is that he was content to give and take and be a man among men. There would be no longer any ground for Pollio's remark, when Augustus wrote some satirical epigrams upon that incarnation of all the talents : " I say nothing. It is not easy to write against a man who can write one's name in a proscription list." There are other anecdotes which still farther illustrate this human side of Augustus. A veteran begged him to appear for him in court, and Augustus named one of his friends to undertake the case. The veteran cried out, " But when you were in danger at Actium, Cæsar, I did not get a substitute ; I fought for you myself ! " With a blush Augustus consented to appear. The troubles and tragedies of life interested him. On hearing of one of Herod's family executions, he remarked, " I had rather be Herod's pig than his son ! " And when a man supposed to be rich was found on his death to be overwhelmed with debt, he sent to purchase his pillow at the auction, which had enabled him to sleep when he owed such enormous sums. He could bear to have the laugh turned against himself. The story of the man with the two ravens, one taught to greet himself and the other Antony, has been already referred to (p. 119). Another is of a similar kind. A poor Greek poet was in the habit of waylaying him as he left his house for the forum with complimentary epigrams to thrust into his hand. Augustus took no notice for sometime, but one day seeing the inevitable tablet held out he took it and hastily scribbled a Greek epigram of his own upon it. The poet by voice and look affected to be overpowered with admiration, and running up to the Emperor's sedan handed him a few pence, crying, " By heaven above

you, Augustus, if I had had more I would have given it you!"
Everybody laughed and Augustus ordered his steward to give
him a substantial sum of money.

It is curious that though Augustus was unmoved by rough
retorts or offensive speeches he shewed considerable sensitive-
ness to attacks which took the form of lampoons and epigrams.
He went so far on some occasions as to refute them in an
edict. But he used the "edict" as a means of communication with the citizens and provinces on all sorts of subjects,
such as for explaining his purpose in putting up the bust of
distinguished men, or to draw attention to what he thought
useful in ancient writers. But he shrank not only from
offensive poems, but from being the subject of any poetry
or history composed by incompetent people. Before all
things he was not to be made to look ridiculous by witty
attacks or clumsy praise. The prize poem or declamation
was an abomination to him, and the prætors were charged
to prevent the public use of his name in such compositions.
Connected with this sensitive refinement of taste may be
mentioned the simplicity of his manners and way of life.

The Palace of Augustus, though in a group of great splendour, was not in itself on a scale approaching the huge con-
structions of later Emperors. He appears at first
to have occupied a modest house close to the
forum, which had once belonged to the orator
Licinius Calvus, who died B.C. 47. He then purchased a site
on the Palatine on which to erect a new house; but in B.C. 36,
after the final defeat of Sextus Pompeius, the Senate voted
him the house of Hortensius. In a chamber of this house he
slept summer and winter for the rest of his life, though
occasionally when unwell he would pass the night in the
house of Mæcenas on the Esquiline which was regarded as a
healthier situation. On receiving this house from the Senate,
he devoted the site already purchased to the temple of Apollo
and its libraries, which with its peristyle was filled with the

The residences of Augustus.

most precious specimens of Greek art, and in which under the statue of Apollo by Scopas the Sibylline books were preserved in gilded caskets. In B. C. 12, upon becoming Pontifex Maximus, he built a small temple of Vesta between these buildings and his house, to keep up the tradition of the Pontiff residing near the shrine of Vesta in the forum, while he handed over the official residence of the Pontiff to the Vestal Virgins themselves. The house of Hortensius was afterwards partly destroyed by fire and rebuilt with greater magnificence, the neighbouring house once owned by Catiline being taken in ; but even then it was on a moderate scale compared with the later palaces. Its entrance, however, was conspicuously marked by the laurels, the civic crown, and gilded shields which were placed there by vote of the Senate since B.C. 27. Besides this town-house, which has furnished the name for a royal residence to this day, he had of course various villas in different parts of Italy. But they were not numerous in comparison with the number we know to have been owned by nobles at the end of the republic. There was one at the ninth milestone on the Flaminian Way called *ad gallinas*, in the gardens of which was the bay tree, from the leaves of which Augustus had his garland made when celebrating his triumphs ; as it became the traditional habit of succeeding Emperors to do also. The others near Rome were selected for their coolness and healthy position—Lanuvium twenty miles from the city on a lofty spur of the Alban Mountains, "cold Præneste" twenty-five miles, and "sloping Tibur" about twenty miles away. These, however, were suburban residences and gave no escape from society or business. They were full of Roman villas,[1] and in the temple of Hercules at Tibur he frequently sat to administer justice. When he could get a real holiday he preferred a yachting voyage among the islands on the Campanian coast.

---

[1] See Horace, *Odes* iii. 4, 22 : vester, Camenæ, vester in arduos | tollor Sabinos, seu mihi frigidum | Præneste seu Tibur supinum | seu liquidæ pacuere Baiæ,

For one of them (Ænaria) he took in exchange from the municipality of Naples the beautiful Capreæ, destined for greater notoriety under his successor. He used to call it or some small island in the bay his " Castle of Idleness." [1] His villas were on a modest scale. He greatly disapproved of the vast country palaces which were becoming the fashion, and forced his granddaughter to demolish one which she was building.[2] Earlier in life he was accused of extravagance in the matter of rich furniture and antique bronzes. But he seems to have shaken off this weakness later on. The furniture of his villas was extremely simple, and there were no costly pictures and statues in them, but the gardens were carefully laid out with terraces and shrubberies, and generally adorned with various curiosities, as at Capreæ with the huge bones of a whale.

His table was simple and the dinners never long. He was careful in selecting his company, but knew how to make graceful concessions as to the rank of his guests when occasion required it. He drank little wine, and generally not of the best vintages ; but he exerted himself to promote conversation and to draw out the silent and shy. He would sometimes come late and retire early without breaking up the party ; sometimes talked instead of eating, taking his own simple food before or after the meal. Before all he does not appear to have adopted the unsociable habit, often mentioned by Cicero and especially characteristic of Iulius, of reading and answering his letters at table. The dinner was generally a family function and his young grandsons were always present at it. Sometimes conversation was varied by reciters, readers, actors or professors of philosophy. But at the Saturnalia and other festivals the

---

Apragopolis. In Suetonius (c. 97) it is doubtful whether he means Capreæ or some other island. Perhaps it is *Nesis*, where M. Brutus had a villa which might have come into his hands as confiscated property (Cic., *ad Att.* xvi. 1-4.)

[2] An echo of his master's feelings on this point is as usual found in Horace, *Od.* ii. 15.

quiet and decorum of these meals gave way to the spirit of the hour. The table was better furnished and the Emperor presented his guests with all kinds of gifts, or amused himself by holding a kind of blind auction, putting together lots of widely different value which the guests bid for without knowing what they were purchasing. On such occasions gambling with dice was permitted, though in family parties the Emperor took care to lose or to surrender his winnings, and sometimes he supplied each member of the party with a sum of money beforehand with which to make their stakes. But games of chance had a fascination for him at all times of his life, and his real gambling was not confined to festival days. He made no secret of it, and we hear nothing of any great loss or gain. Social life at Rome began early in the day, visitors at a levee would arrive soon after daybreak, and a magistrate would sometimes have to be up immediately after midnight, to take omens or perform some other religious rite. But as Augustus worked late at night, and was not a good sleeper, early rising was painful to him, and resulted in his falling fast asleep in his sedan. If any of these night duties became imperative he took the precaution of sleeping in some lodging near the place. But his normal habit was to work up to noon, then after the light luncheon or prandium, often consisting of bread and a few grapes, to sleep for a short time fully dressed. Having finished the morning's work and bath, dinner (cena) would come between 3 and 4, though busy men like the Emperor often pushed it on to 6 or 7; after dinner he went to his study, and there finished off what was left of the day's work, his memoranda and accounts, sitting or reclining on his couch far into the night. The amount of work which he must have bestowed upon his official business is shewn by the state of readiness and completeness in which the various schedules of the finances of the Empire and the army, and the book of political maxims were found at his death. In early youth he had dabbled in literature, and composed a tragedy in the Greek fashion called "Ajax"; but coming in later years to estimate its value more truly he destroyed it, and when some friend or flatterer inquired for it, he said, "Ajax has fallen on his own sponge."[1] He composed also memoirs of his own life, but they were interrupted by his serious illness after the Spanish War (B.C. 25–3), and never resumed. They were used by Suetonius and other writers, as well as collections of his letters, edicts, and speeches, but have not been preserved. Only one of his epigrams has survived, of which I shall speak hereafter. These excursions into literature, never very serious, seem to have ceased as he got on in life. In the third book of his *Odes* (written between B.C. 30–25), Horace tells the Muses that " they afford a recreation to high Cæsar when he has put his troops into winter quarters and seeks a rest from toil,"[2] but in the fourth book (B.C. 13–12) it is the statesman, the conqueror, and reformer that he addresses, not the man of letters. The Epistle addressed to Augustus in B.C. 12, though it deals with literary criticism and explicitly supports the Emperor's well-known dislike of being the theme of inferior writers, while it dwells upon his numerous employments and warmly compliments him on his successful achievements, contains no word or hint of his authorship.[3] The principate was a most laborious profession, absorbing all his energies and occupying all his time, and though he might enjoy the company of literary men, despatches, edicts, and state papers would now be the limit of his literary ambition.

The heavy work of his lofty position was performed under painful conditions of health. Besides at least four serious

---

[1] Another tragedy " Achilles " is mentioned by Suidas.

[2] Hor., *Od.* 3, 136. Suetonius (*Aug.* 85) mentions others, "An answer to Brutus about Cato," evidently a youthful essay ; " Exhortations to Philosophy," no doubt youthful too ; an hexameter poem called *Sicilia*. When he tried to read them in later life to a family audience they bored him so much that he handed the rolls over to Tiberius to finish. Lastly, a short volume of Epigrams which he used to compose in the bath.

[3] Hor., *Epist.* 2, 1.

illnesses [1] of which we hear, he was subject to periodical complaints, generally recurring at the beginning of spring and autumn. Soon after B.C. 30 he gave up the martial exercises of the Campus, then the less fatiguing ball games, and finally confined himself to getting out of his sedan to take short runs or walks. As he grew old his only outdoor amusements (except yachting) seem to have been fishing and playing games with little children.

In the last years of his life he gave up going into Roman society. In the earlier part of his principate he dined out freely, and not always in select company. He seems to have been rather inclined to the vulgar millionaire, perhaps because he could reckon on contributions to the public objects which he had at heart. He did not expect splendid entertainments, and was content with the wine of the district, still he did not like being treated with too little ceremony. To one man who gave him a dinner ostentatiously plain and common, he remarked on leaving—"I did not know that I was such an intimate friend of yours." At times, too, he had occasion to assume the Emperor with some of these *nouveaux riches*, as in the celebrated case of Vedius Pollio. This man had a stew-pond of lampreys, which he fed with flesh. When he was entertaining Augustus on one occasion the cup-bearer dropped a valuable crystal cup, and his master ordered him at once to be thrown to the lampreys. Augustus tried to beg him off, but when Pollio refused, he ceased to entreat ; assuming imperial airs he ordered all the cups of the same sort in the house, and all others of value, to be brought into the room and broken. Licinius, the grasping procurator of Gaul, was another of these rich vulgar people, with whom Augustus was somewhat too intimate, and expected in return for that honour large contributions to his works. On one occasion he even took the liberty of altering the figure in the promissory note

[1] In B.C. 46, 42, 25, and 23. From that time, however, though generally delicate he seems not to have had any serious attack.

sent by him so as to double the sum. Licinius said nothing, but on the next occasion he sent a note thus expressed : "I promise towards the expense of the new work—whatever your Highness pleases."

Wit is seldom kind, and some of the retorts attributed to him are not always exceptions to the rule. To a hump-backed advocate pleading before him, and often repeating the expression, "If you think I am wrong in any way, pray set me straight," he said, "I can give you some advice, but I can't set you *straight*." To an officer who made rather too much fuss about his services, and kept pointing to an ugly scar on his forehead, he said, "When you run away you shouldn't look behind you." More good-natured are the following. To a young prefect who was being sent home from camp for misbehaviour, and who exclaimed, "How can I go home? What am I to say to my father?" he replied, "Tell him that you did not like me." To another who was being cashiered, and pleaded to have the usual good-service pension, that people might think he had left the service in the usual way, he said, "Well, give out that you have received the money ; I won't say that I haven't paid it."

Though affable to all, and neither an unkind nor un-reasonable master to his slaves, or patron to his freedmen, he was enough a man of his age not to hesitate to inflict cruel punishment for certain offences. A secretary who had taken a bribe to disclose some confidential paper, he ordered to have his legs broken. A favourite freedman was forced to commit suicide when detected in intrigues with Roman married ladies. He ordered the personal servants of his grandson Caius, who had taken advantage of his illness and death to enrich themselves in the province of Syria, to be thrown into the sea with weights attached to their feet. To those who had been his friends there is hardly any instance of extreme severity after the end of the civil wars.

It is possible that Muræna died before trial, though his fellow-conspirator was put to death. Cornelius Gallus, the first prefectus of Egypt, committed suicide rather than confront the accusations brought against him and the evident animus of the Senate ; but Augustus did not wish it, and exclaimed with tears in his eyes that it was hard that he should be the only man who might not be angry with his friends without the matter going farther than he intended. The coldness that arose between him and his ministers Agrippa and Mæcenas was only temporary and never very grave. He deeply deplored their loss at their death. We shall have to discuss his conduct to his daughter and grand-daughter and their paramours in another chapter. But neither in regard to these persons nor the conspirators against his life did he ever act in a way that his contemporaries would think cruel.

These anecdotes of Augustus do not suggest a very heroic figure, very quick wit, or great warmth of heart. They rather indicate what I conceive to be the truer picture, a cool and cautious character, not unkindly and not without a sense of humour ; but at the same time as inevitable and unmoved by pity or remorse as nature herself. No one accuses him of having neglected or hurried any task that it was his duty to perform. But neither friend, relation, nor minister ever really influenced him. He issues orders, and they all obey instinctively, without remonstrance, and generally with success. He is providence to them all. Everything succeeds under his hands. He is no soldier, though he knows one when he sees him, but all the nations of the earth seek his friendship. Till the last decade of his life no serious reverse befel his armies ; at home all opposition melted away, as the difficulties in a road or course disappear before a skilful driver or steerer. He is not godlike, but there is an air of calm success about him which swayed men's wills and awakened their reverence.

CHAPTER XII

THE REFORMER AND LEGISLATOR

*Quid leges sine moribus
vanæ proficiunt ?*

THE activity of Augustus as reformer in the city and Italy,
and to a great extent in the provinces also, was subsequent to
the settlement of his constitutional position in B.C.
The earliest
reforms in the 23, after which date changes in it were generally
Empire. consequential, and in matters of detail. But it
began long before. In B.C. 36 he had taken effective measures
to suppress the brigandage which had pushed its audacity
nearly up to the very gates of Rome. In B.C. 34–3 Agrippa,
under his influence, had started the improvement in the
water supply of Rome by restoring the Aqua Marcia ; had
cleansed and enlarged the cloacæ, repaired the streets, and
begun many important buildings. In B.C. 31 we have
evidence that Augustus was turning his attention to the
details of administration in the provinces,[1] and in the next
year, in his resettlement of Asia, he restored to Samos,
Ephesus, Pergamus, and the Troad, works of art which
Antony had taken from them to bestow upon Cleopatra.[2]

---

[1] The *lex Iulia et Titia*, enabling the provincial governor to assign
guardians to such persons as were legally bound to have them, was passed
between the 1st of May and 1st of October, B.C. 31, the period during
which M. Titius was consul.

[2] Authorities will be found in Mommsen, *res gestæ*, p. 96.

In B.C. 28, measures of relief were adopted for state debtors, and a term fixed beyond which those who were in actual possession of properties could not be disturbed by legal proceedings.

The first need of the country was security. How difficult this had long been to maintain, and how ill the senatorial government at the end of the Re-

The roads and police patrols, B.C. 27.

public had been able to cope with the evil is shewn by the fact that remnants of the bands of Spartacus and Catiline were in B.C. 61 still infesting the district of Thurii. In spite of the repressive measures of B.C. 36, which seem to have been successful as far as the immediate neighbourhood of Rome was concerned, at the end of the civil war armed bands still openly appeared in various parts of Italy, seized and carried off travellers, confined them in the slave-barracks, or *ergastula*, or put them to ransom. These *ergastula* were originally slave-prisons used for keeping refractory slaves, who worked during the day in chains, and were shut up in separate cells at night, often underground or only lighted by windows high up and out of reach of the inmates. In some parts of Italy —chiefly the north—they were not known, and chained slaves were not employed; but in other parts they were numerous, and afforded convenient hiding-places. The chief abuse connected with them was that men properly free could be carried off and concealed in them as though they were slaves, while they afforded a leader in rebellion convenient sources from which to draw recruits; the miserable inmates being only too ready to join any one who gave them a hope of freedom and release from those horrible dens. Accordingly a review of the *ergastula* is constantly heard of, till they were finally abolished by Hadrian. Among the measures for the suppression of brigandage now taken was a visitation of these places. It was not done in mercy to the slaves. Augustus, though he treated his own servants

with kindness, took the sternest Roman view of the absolute
power of a master, and boasts that after the war with Sextus
Pompeius he handed over 30,000 slaves—who had been
serving with the enemy—to their masters "to be punished." [1]
When we remember what the "punishment" of a Roman
slave meant, it is difficult to think without horror of the
sum total of human misery which this implies.

A more effective and permanent measure, however, was to
secure the roads and make them fit for rapid military move-

The great
roads of Italy
secured.

ments. A system of road commissions (*curæ
viarum*) was started in B.C. 27, commissioners
(*curatores*) being appointed to superintend each
of the great roads leading from Rome to various parts of
Italy. The duty at first was usually imposed upon men
who had enjoyed triumphs, and Augustus himself, after his
triple triumph, undertook the *via Flaminia*, the great north
road from Rome to Ariminum on the Adriatic, from which
place other roads branched off through the valley of the Po,
and to the Alpine passes. The pavement of the road was
relaid, the bridges repaired, and the completion of the work
was commemorated by the still existing arch at Rimini,
with its partially surviving inscription.[2] For greater safety,
also, military pickets were stationed at convenient points along
the roads, which put a stop to brigandage.

In close connection with the roads were the twenty-eight
military colonies established by Augustus in Italy. Of these
seven were along the line of the Flaminia, or near it ; one of
them (Bononia) was the point where the main roads to Rome
converge. Others guarded the entrances to the Alpine passes,
or the road through Venetia to Istria—which Augustus included in Italy—while another group protected the main

---

[1] *Mon. Ancyr.*, 25.

[2] C. I. L. xi. 365; *Mon. Ancyr.* 20. "In my seventh consulship I remade
the Flaminian road from the city to Ariminum, and all the bridges except
the Mulvian and Minucian."

roads through Campania. Thus these colonies were not only centres of loyalty to the Empire, but served to keep open the great routes. The object of the division of Italy into eleven regions, the exact date of which is not known, was probably for the purpose of the census, and the taxation which was connected with it, but it was also for other administrative purposes, as for the regulation of the military service of the young men in each of them.[1] The regions followed the natural divisions of the country and of nationalities, but the importance of the roads in connection with them is shown by the fact that before long they became known in many cases by the name of the chief road that traversed them, as Æmilia, Flaminia, and others. What Augustus was doing for Italy his legates under his authority were doing for the most important provinces. Great roads—*viæ Augustæ*— were being laid everywhere. We have evidence of them from inscribed tablets in Dalmatia, Pisidia, and Cilicia, Bætica, Northern Spain, Gallia Narbonensis, and elsewhere.[2] These works went on throughout his reign, but in B.C. 20 he commemorated his formal appointment as head commissioner of all roads by placing a pillar covered with gilded bronze in the forum near the temple of Saturn, with the distances of all the chief places along the great roads from one of the thirty-seven city gates from which these roads branch out. The base of this *milliarium aureum* is still in its place.

Another source of mischief were the *collegia*, or guilds. Under cover of promoting the interests of certain trades and professions these guilds were used, or were believed to be used, for all kinds of illegal purposes. Some of them were of great antiquity, but they had come to be so often

The collegia.

---

[1] See Suet., *Aug.* 46. The regions are described by Pliny alone, *N.H.* iii. 46–128.

[2] The inscription on the road to Salonæ in Dalmatia is dated A.D. 19, but it must have been begun much earlier. For the other roads see Willmanns 832, 829, 830, 832 ; Clinton's *Fasti*, anno B.C. 14 ; *Journal of Hellenic Studies*, xii. part i. p. 109 *sq.* C. I. L. iii. 6,974.

misused for political terrorism (especially the *collegia opificum*) that the Senate had suppressed many of them in B.C. 63. But Clodius shortly afterwards got a law passed authorising their meetings, and he employed them freely for promoting his own riotous proceedings. Iulius Cæsar had dissolved all except the most ancient and respectable, but during the civil wars they seem to have revived. Under a law passed in B.C. 22 Augustus held a visitation of them. Some were dissolved and some reformed, and a licence was henceforth required from Senate and Emperor for their meetings.

In the city itself the first need was food. It depended very largely on imported corn. Again and again we hear of dearth and famine prices at Rome. The people, often, no doubt, rightly, believed that this dearness of provisions arose from artificial causes. When Sextus Pompeius and his confederates were scouring the seas and pouncing upon corn-ships the cause was clear enough, and the gratitude to Augustus for crushing him was very natural. But even when there was no such evident danger great distress was often caused by sudden rise of prices. The idea had always been in such times to appoint some powerful man *præfectus annonæ*, with a naval force enabling him to secure that the corn fleets should have free passage to Italy, should be able to unload their cargoes without difficulty, and dispose of them at a moderate price. A well-known instance of this was the appointment of Pompey in B.C. 57. But in less troublous times a separate commissioner was appointed to watch the several places of corn export, Sicily, Sardinia, and Africa. These were not posts of very great dignity, and Brutus and Cassius in B.C. 44 looked upon their nomination to them as a kind of insult. But besides the dangers of the sea and of pirates certain merchants had hit upon means—practised long before at Athens—of artificially raising the price. They made what we should call " a corner " in corn. Either they bought it up and kept it

Feeding the city.

back from the market, or they contrived various ways of delaying the ships and producing a panic among the dealers. As in all difficulties, the people looked to Augustus for help, and in B.C. 22 begged him to accept the office of *præfectus annonæ*, "chief commissioner of the corn market." While declining the dictatorship offered him at the same time with passionate vehemence, he accepted this commissionership; and the law which he caused to be passed now or some time later on shews how necessary some State interference was. By this law penalties were inflicted on any one " who did anything to hinder the corn supply, or entered into any combination with the object of raising its price; or who hindered the sailing of a corn-ship, or did anything of *malice propense* whereby its voyage was delayed." [1]

But besides a free and unmolested corn market, the Roman populace had long come to look for another means of support —a distribution of corn either altogether free or considerably below the market price. Detached instances of this practice occur in the earlier history of Rome, the corn sometimes coming as a present from some foreign sovereign, sometimes being distributed by private liberality. It had always been objected to by the wiser part of the Senate, and had laid the donors open to the charge of trying to establish a tyranny. It was reserved for the tribune Gaius Gracchus to make it into a system (B.C. 122). Since his time it had been submitted to as a matter of course by nearly all magistrates. Sulla, indeed, seems to have suspended it for a time, but the first measure of the counter revolution that followed his death was to re-establish it. Iulius Cæsar had restricted it to citizens below a certain census, but had not the courage to abolish it. It was, indeed, a kind of poor-law relief, but of the worst possible sort. It not only induced a number of idle and use-

Distribution of corn free or below market value.

---

[1] Digest, 47, 11, 6. The penalties varied from a fine to exclusion from the corn trade, *relegatio*, and condemnation to public works.

less people to prefer the chances of city life to labour in the country, but it unnaturally depressed the price of corn, and therefore discouraged the Italian farmer, already nearly ruined by the competition of foreign corn ; it exhausted the treasury, and, after all, did not relieve the poor. Livy regards it as one of the causes which denuded Italy of free cultivators, and left all the work to slaves. Cicero always denounced it on much the same grounds, and Appian points out how it brought the indigent, careless, and idle flocking into the city.[1] The system, moreover, was open to gross abuses, slaves being manumitted that they might take their share, under contract to transfer it to their late masters. Augustus saw that by these distributions injustice was done both to farmers and merchants, and that agriculture in Italy was being depressed by it. He says in his memoirs[2] that he had at one time almost resolved to put a stop to the practice, but refrained from doing so because he felt sure that the necessity of courting the favour of the populace would induce his successors to restore it. However unsound this reasoning may be, it would no doubt have been an heroic measure for one in his position to have carried out the half-formed resolution. As a matter of fact, his distributions were on a large scale, and in times of distress were entirely gratis. *Tesseræ*, or tickets, entitling the holders to a certain amount of corn or money, were distributed again and again. The value of the corn tickets was generally supplied from the *fiscus* or his private revenue ; but that after all was only a question of accounts, it did not affect the economical or moral results in any way.

A better economical measure was a system of State loans. Immediately after the end of the civil war the transference to the

State loans.   Roman treasury of the enormous wealth in money and jewels of the Ptolemies at Alexandria caused the price of money to go down and the money value of

---

[1] Cicero, pro Sest. § 103 ; *ad Att.* vi. 6 ; Livy, vi. 12 ; Appian, b. c. ii. 120. Dionys. H. xii. 24.   [2] Quoted by Sueton., *Aug.* 42.

landed property consequently to go up. For a time at least the common rate of interest sank from 12 to 4 per cent. Augustus took advantage of this state of things to relieve land-owners who were in difficulties, by lending them money free of interest, if they could show property of double the value as security for repayment.

There were other reforms equally beneficial. Among the many *curæ* (commissions) which he established was one for superintending public works, which would thus not depend on private munificence; another of the streets; of the water supply; and, above all, of the Tiber. Rome was, as it still is, extremely subject to floods. Quite recently there were five or six feet of water in the Pantheon, and in B.C. 27 the rise of the Tiber was so serious that the lower parts of the city were covered, and the augurs declared it to be an omen of the universal prevalence of the power of the new *princeps*. In B.C. 23 it swept away the *pons Sublicius*.[1] He could not of course prevent these floods, but he gave some relief by dredging and widening the river-bed, which was choked with rubbish and narrowed by encroachments. The commission thus established remained an important one for many generations, but in B.C. 8 he superintended the business himself.

The Tiber.

A danger at Rome, more frequent and no less formidable than flood, was fire. So frequent were fires that the most stringent laws had been passed against arson, which it seems was even punishable by burning alive. In B.C. 23 Augustus formed a kind of fire brigade of public slaves under the control of the curule-ædiles. But the old magistracies were no longer objects of desire, and it was difficult to get men of energy to fill them, a state of things which was one of the chief blots in the new imperial system. At any rate in this case they were not found efficient, and in the later years of his reign (A.D. 6), a new brigade in four divisions was

Fire brigades.

[1] Dio, 53, 20, 33; Horace, *Odes* I, 2.

formed of freedmen with an equestrian præfect, who turned out to be so effective that they became regularly established.

Another part in the scheme of Augustus for the reconstruction of society was to revive the influence of the Sacred Colleges and brotherhoods, and to renew the ceremonies with which they were connected.

The Sibylline Books and Sacred Colleges.

One method of doing this was to become a member of them all himself, much as the king of England is sovereign of all the Orders. Thus according to the *Monumentum* (ch. 7) he was pontifex, augur, quindecemvir for religious rites, septemvir of the Epulones, an Arval brother, a fetial and a sodalis Titius. Nor was he only an honorary or idle member. He attended their meetings and joined in their business, and took part in whatever rites they were intended to perform. Thus his membership of the Arval brethren is recorded in the still existing *acta* ; as a fetial he proclaimed war against Cleopatra. The *sodales Titii*, a college of priests of immemorial antiquity, had almost disappeared until the entrance of Augustus into their college revived them and their ritual. He not only joined these colleges, but revived and even increased their endowments,[1] and, above all, those of the six Vestal Virgins, to whom he presented the *regia*, once the official residence of the Pontifex Maximus, and an estate at Lanuvium. The restoration of the College of Luperci, which had celebrated on the 15th of February the old ceremony of " beating the bounds " almost from the foundation of the city, was more or less a political matter. It had gone out of fashion, and its ceremonies had got to be looked upon as undignified. Iulius Cæsar had revived and re-endowed them. The Senate for that very reason in the reaction after his death

---

[1] The Sacred Colleges (1) were exempt from military service, imposts and public services of all kinds ; (2) had a charge on the *ager publicus* for sacrifices, feasts, &c. ; (3) in most cases had estates besides ; (4) received special grants from time to time for repairs of buildings.

had deprived them of these endowments, which Augustus now restored. We have already noticed his renewal of the *augurium salutis*, the old ceremonial prayer at the beginning of the year that could only be offered in time of peace. He also induced some one to accept the office of *flamen Dialis* in B.C. 11, after it had been vacant since B.C. 87, because the restrictions under which its holder laboured were so numerous and tiresome that in spite of its dignity—its seat in the Senate and curule chair and lictor—no one would accept it. He took pains again to restore the Sibylline Books to their old place of importance. The originals were lost in the fire of B.C. 82, and a commission had at once been issued to collect others from towns in Greece and Greek Italy. But some of them were getting illegible from age, and some were of doubtful authenticity, and consequently all kinds of prophetic verses got into circulation, giving rise at times to undesirable rumours and panics. Augustus in B.C. 18 ordered them to be re-copied and edited, and the authorised edition was then deposited in his new temple of Apollo on the Palatine, and continued to be consulted till late in the third century. After an attempt by Iulian to revive its authority it was finally burnt by Stilicho about A.D. 400.

As one of the quindecemvirs Augustus had charge of these books, but he formally took the official headship of Roman religion by becoming Pontifex Maximus. He was

Pontifex
Maximus.

elected and ordained to that office in March B.C. 12. The people had wished him to take it in B.C. 30, but he would not violate what was a traditional and sacred rule that the office was lifelong, and though Lepidus was degraded from the triumvirate in B.C. 36, he was still Pontifex Maximus. It is true that he was not allowed to do any of the duties, or only those of the most formal kind, but still he had the office. The ground for asking Augustus to take it was that the election of Lepidus had been irregular ; he had managed to get put in during the confusion following the assassination of Cæsar, and therefore might be deposed. Augustus however takes credit for his scrupulous observance of a religious rule, and was particularly gratified by the crowds of people who came up to vote for him, a sort of ecclesiastical coronation.[1]

In B.C. 17 he gave an emphasis to some of these religious revivals by celebrating the *ludi sæculares*, the centenary of the city, in virtue of some verses found in this Sibylline volume. We need not trouble ourselves as to whether his calculation of the year was a right one (the *sæculum* was really 110 years), it is enough to note that they were meant, like a centenary of a college or university, to call out patriotic and loyal feelings which should embrace both the country and the country's religion. They are made interesting to us by the fact that Horace—always ready to further his master's purposes—was selected to write the Anthem or Ode to be sung by a chorus of twenty-seven boys and twenty-seven girls. An inscription, found in 1871 in the bed of the Tiber, gives the official program of this festival, and ends with the words *Carmen composuit Q. Horatius Flaccus.*[2] The poet probably had before him, when he wrote it, the general scheme of the festival, which included solemn sacrifices and prayer to Iuno, Diana, Iupiter, and Ilithyia. Augustus and Agrippa took the leading part in the religious functions— as members of quindicemviri—and both repeated the prayers, which in the case of all these deities invoked a blessing on the "Populus Romanus Quiritium." In short, everything was done to mark it as a national festival, to make the Romans recall their glorious inheritance and unique position, and at the same time to show that the *princeps* represented that greatness before gods and men. Whatever else Augustus may have thought of the national religion, he evidently regarded it as the surest

The ludi sæculares, May 31—June 2. B.C. 27.

---

[1] *Mon. Ancy.,* 10 ; Livy, *Ep.* 117 ; Vell., ii. 63 ; App., b. c. v. 131 ; Dio, 44, 53. All these authorities speak of the irregularity of the election of Lepidus.

[2] *Ephemeris Epigraphica,* viii. 2 ; Lindsay's *Latin Inscriptions,* p. 102.

bond of national life, and the inclusion of a prayer to Ilithyia, goddess of childbirth, joined with his contemporaneous attempt to encourage marriage and the production of children (which the obedient Horace echoes [1]), shews that he also connected that religion with morality. The restoration of religion, in fact, in his mind, goes side by side with the purification of morals. It is the practical statesman's view of religion as a necessary police force and perhaps something more. Napoleon restored the Catholic Church in France with a similar sagacity, and the people blessed him, as they did Augustus, for giving them back *le bon Dieu*.

But the state of things required in his judgment, not only a religious revival, but more stringent laws. Horace again reflects his master's views in the making, before *The reformation of morals.* they find expression in act. The sixth ode of the first book (written about B.C. 25) joins to the necessity of a restoration of the temples and a return to religion a warning as to the relaxation of morals, tracing the progress in vice of the young girl and wife, with the shameful connivance of the interested husband, and exclaims: "Not from such parents as these sprang the youth that dyed the sea with Punic blood, and brake the might of Pyrrhus and great Antiochus and Hannibal, scourge of God." Again in the twenty-fourth ode of the same book, also written about B.C. 25, he warmly urges a return to the old morality, and promises immortality to the statesman who shall secure it : " If there be one who would stay unnatural bloodshed and civic fury, if there be one who seeks to have inscribed on his statue the title of 'Father of the Cities,' let him pluck up heart to curb licentiousness. His shall be a name for the ages ! " And when Augustus has acted on the resolution, to the formation of which the poet was privy, he tells him ten years later that by his presence family life is cleansed from its foul stains, that he has curbed the licence of the age and recalled the old morality.[2] This he would repre-

---

[1] *Carmen Sæcul.* 13.   [2] Horace, *Odes* iv. 5, 21 ; iv. 15, 9-12.

sent as the result of the Emperor's legislation, the *lex marita* of the secular hymn.

It was after his return from the East in B.C. 19 that Augustus first received censorial powers for five years. Whether this amounted to a definite office—a *præfectura moribus* or *regimen morum*, as Dio and Suetonius assert—does not much matter. The experiment of appointing censors in the ordinary way had been tried in B.C. 22 for the last time and had not been successful, and the *censoria potestas* now given to Augustus practically put into his hands that control over the conduct of private citizens which the censors had exercised by their power of inflicting "ignominy" upon them. The ancient censorial stigma had been applied to irregularities in almost every department of life, but it depended on the will of the censors themselves, not on laws. Feeling now directly responsible for the morals and general habits of the citizens he began a series of legislative measures designed to suppress extravagance and debauchery, and to encourage marriage and family life, which would have permanent validity. He believed in externals, even trivial ones, as indicating a growing laxity; making, for instance, a point of men appearing in the forum and on official occasions in the old Roman toga. The lighter and more comfortable *lacerna* or *pallium* was as abominable in his eyes as a suit of flannels would seem to a martinet of to-day in the Park or on parade.[1] Before all things the Romans were to be national, in dress no less than in other respects.

But the failure which always attends such regulations was no

---

[1] We frequently hear in earlier times of the scandal caused by certain people abandoning the heavy and not very comfortable toga for lighter dress, Greek or Gallic. Those who care to trace the history of such a matter will find references to it in Cicero, *pro Rab. Post.* § 27 ; 2 *Phil.* § 76 ; Livy, 29, 19 ; Tac., *Ann.* ii. 59 ; Hor., *Ep.* 1, 7, 65. And if it is desired to see how futile such orders are against a prevailing fashion, the continued disuse of it may be traced in Juvenal 1, 119 ; 3, 172 ; Mart. 1, 49, 31 ; 12, 18, 17 ; Suet., *Aug.* 40 ; and as late as Hadrian we find that the order needed renewal, Spart. *Had.* 22. George III. insisting that Bishops should wear wigs is a case in point.

less inevitable in regard to the first of his new reforming
Sumptuary laws. measures, his sumptuary laws, regulating the exact
amount that it was legal to spend on a *cena* in
ordinary days, on festivals, and at wedding feasts, or the *repotia*
which the bridegroom gave on the afternoon following his
marriage. This was no new thing. It had been tried at
various times throughout Roman history. Beginning with
a very ancient law regulating the amount of silver plate each
man might legally possess, the rent he might pay for his house,
and the provisions of the Twelve Tables, we have laws in the
third and second centuries B.C., limiting the cost of dress and
jewels for women, the number of guests that might be entertained at banquets, and the amount that might be spent upon
them. Sulla had also a sumptuary law, among his other acts,
of the same kind. But Iulius Cæsar had gone farther than
any one in B.C. 46. He had not only regulated the cost of
furniture and jewels, according to the rank of the owners, and
the amounts to be spent upon the table, but he had sent agents
into the provision markets, who seized all dainties beyond the
legal price, and even entered private houses and removed dishes
from the table. Of course such measures were not only
annoying, they were ineffective also. Directly he left Rome
the rules were neglected. Our own Statute Book has many
laws of the same kind, which rapidly became dead letters.
Nearly the one and only permanent effect of the old
sumptuary laws had been to create a sentiment against large
and crowded dinner parties as vulgar.[1] Nor did Augustus
succeed much better. Towards the end of his reign he
issued an edict extending the legal amount which might
be spent on banquets, hoping to secure some obedience
to the law. But nothing that we know of Roman life
afterwards leads us to think that this form of paternal government—though quite in harmony with Roman ideas—ever

---

[1] Cicero (*in Pis.* § 67) speaks with scorn of the vulgar rich man who
had five, or sometimes more, guests on each couch.

attained its object. Human nature was stronger than political theory.

Nor were the laws, carried about the same time,[1] on marriage, divorce, and kindred subjects, much more effective.

The Iulian laws of marriage, adultery and divorce.

In part they re-enacted rules which had always been acknowledged and always disobeyed, and so far as they did not punish a crime, but endeavoured to enforce marriage, they were continually resisted or effectually evaded. They consisted of a series of enactments— whether we regard them as separate laws or chapters in the same law—for restraining adultery and libitinage, for regulating divorce, and for encouraging the marriage of all ranks.[2] They were passed in B.C. 18–17, and were supplemented by a law of A.D. 9, called the *lex Papia Poppæa*. The text of none of them survives, and we have to trust to scattered notices in the later legal writers. They may be roughly classed as restrictive, penal, and beneficiary. In the first may be placed the regulation that no senator or member of a senatorial family might marry a freed-woman, courtesan, actress, or the daughter of an actor ; though other men might marry a freed-woman or even emancipate a slave in order to marry her. And under the same head came the regulations as to divorce. The legal doctrine appears to have been that marriage contracted with the old religious ceremony called *confarreatio* was indissoluble, except in the case of the wife's adultery, on whose condemnation to death the execution was preceded by a solemn dissolution of the marriage or *diffareatio*. It was also a common belief that no divorce had ever taken place at Rome until that of Carvilius in B.C. 231. Yet the laws of the Twelve Tables (B.C. 450) contained provisions as to divorce, so that it had certainly been known before ; and perhaps the truth was that

---

[1] Though in making regulations on these subjects Augustus acted on his censorial powers, when it came to enacting laws he would propose them to the tribes in virtue of his tribunician powers.

[2] *De adulteriis coercendis; de pudicitia; de maritandis ordinibus.*

Carvilius was the first to divorce his wife without any plea of adultery, in which case he would have to give security for the repayment of her dowry. Since that time the religious *confarreatio* had become extremely rare. Both men and women avoided an indissoluble tie. The fashion was to be married *sine manu*, that is, without the woman passing into the *manus* or power of her husband. She still remained subject to the *patria potestas*, or to that of her guardian, or was *sui iuris* according to her circumstances at the time. Such marriages could be dissolved by either party, and without charge of misconduct. Public opinion seems to have restrained both men and women for some time from taking advantage of their freedom, but its force steadily diminished, till towards the end of the republic divorce became so common as to provoke little remark. It was an arrangement—as in the case of Augustus and his family—governed almost entirely by considerations of convenience or advantage, and generally left all parties concerned on a friendly footing. This of course was not always the case when the divorce was the result of misconduct, or at least of misconduct on the wife's part, nor even if it resulted from incompatibility of temper or money disputes, which left a feeling of soreness behind them. It was a system—however disastrous to family life—too deeply rooted for Augustus to attempt to change it, even if he had wished to do so. His law seems to have dealt only with certain formalities and conditions of divorce—such as the necessity of having witnesses, and in case of a charge of misconduct a kind of family council or court of inquiry —not with the freedom of divorce itself, except that in the case of a freed-woman, she was prevented from divorcing her husband or marrying again without his consent. That, however, rested on the idea of the rights of a patronus rather than on the sanctity of marriage. Otherwise the law chiefly dealt with questions of property, restraining the husband from alienating his wife's estate without her consent, and re-enacting (with what modifications we do not know) the provisions for the repayment of dowry.

The *penal* enactments affected (1) those guilty of adultery or seduction (*stuprum*), and (2) those who remained unmarried or without children. In adultery both parties were

<small>Penalties (1) for adultery or seduction.</small>

punished by transportation (*deportatio in insulam*) and a partial confiscation of property. A husband's unfaithfulness incurred no penalty except that he lost all claim to retain any part of the wife's dowry, even for the benefit of children. But the old barbarous principle of the injured husband's right to kill both wife and paramour, if detected by himself, was retained, though under certain conditions. If he allowed the guilty wife to remain with him, he was bound to release the man ; and if he connived at the adultery for gain, he was subject to a fine. *Stuprum* was formerly defined as the forcible detention of a free woman for immoral purposes, and could be punished by flogging or imprisonment. Under the Iulian law it was extended to the seduction of an unmarried woman or a widow who had been living chastely.

The penalties upon those who remained unmarried between certain ages were in the form of a direct tax or of certain

<small>(2) For remaining unmarried.</small>

disabilities. The former, under the name of *uxorium*, was of great antiquity, and had been levied by the censors of B.C. 404, but it was light and intermittent ; the Iulian law revived and increased it. The disabilities were that an unmarried man between the legal ages could not take a legacy from a testator not related to him within the sixth degree, unless he married within a hundred days of being informed of the legacy. This was extended by the *lex Papia Poppæa* (A.D. 9) to the childless, who could only take half any legacy from a testator unconnected with them within the sixth degree. One child saved a man from coming under this law, three children a freeborn woman, four a freed-woman. Again, a husband and wife who were childless could only receive a tenth of a legacy left by one to the other, though, if there were children by another marriage, a tenth was added for each, or if they had had children who had died. For all alike there were numerous exemptions founded on absence from home on public service, age, or ill-health; and a certain time of grace (*vacatio*) was given between the attainment of the legal age and the actual marriage, or between two marriages, or after a divorce.

The beneficiary clauses of the law were those which relieved married men or women and men or women with

Privileges to parents. The *ius trium liberorum.*

children from these disabilities, and gave them exemption from certain onerous public duties and special places of honour in the theatres. The fathers of three children at Rome, four in Italy, five in the provinces, had also certain preferences for offices and employments and other honorary distinctions, such as taking precedence of a colleague in the consulship. This was not a new idea, for it had in one shape or another existed in many Greek states, and in B.C. 59 Iulius Cæsar had in his agrarian law given the preference to fathers of three children in the distribution of land.

The disabilities imposed on the unmarried were met with vehement resistance, in consequence of which the clause was

Opposition to the law.

introduced giving the three years' grace between the attainment of the legal age and the actual marriage. After the passing of the Papia Poppæa (A.D. 9) the Emperor in the theatre or circus was received with loud shouts from the equestrian seats demanding its repeal. He is said to have sent for the children of Germanicus and held them up as an example for all to follow; and he afterwards summoned two meetings of the equites, one of those married, and the other of the single. To each he delivered a speech, which Dio reports or invents. He pointed with dismay to the fact that the first meeting was so much less numerous than the second. He commended the married men for having done their duty to the State, but to the unmarried he addressed a longer and more vehement appeal. He argued that they were defeating the purpose of the Creator, were contributing to the disappearance of the Roman race, which was being replaced by foreigners necessarily admitted to the franchise in order to keep up the numbers of the citizens; that he had only followed in his legislation the precedent of ancient laws with increased penalties and rewards, and that while he acknowledged that marriage was not without its troubles, yet that was true of everything else, and they were compensated by other advantages and the consciousness of duty done.[1]

But though the Emperor carried his point at the time and passed a law which remained in force for more than three centuries, it did not really benefit morality. It was constantly evaded by colourable marriages, often with quite young children. "Men did not marry to have heirs, but in order to become heirs," it was said. And though Augustus attempted to prevent this by an edict enacting that no betrothal was to count which was not followed by a marriage within two years, other means of evading the law were found which gave rise to the intrusion of spies and informers who made their profit by thus violating the secrets of the family. Again, the granting of the *ius trium liberorum* became gradually a matter of form, and the idea of the superiority of the married state necessarily disappeared with the rise of certain Christian ideals. The law was repealed by the sons of Constantine.

Though a line is often drawn between a man's public and private character, it still remains hard to reconcile the earnestness of Augustus in pressing these laws and his severity in punishing offences of this nature with the reports of his own personal habits. I have already expressed my disbelief in the stories of his youthful immoralities. Suetonius, who spares no emperor the inevitable chapter summing up his sins of the flesh, asserts that

The character of Augustus in view of this legislation.

[1] Dio, 56, 2-10; Suet., *Aug.* 34.

not even his friends deny the intrigues of his later years, but merely urge that they were conducted not for the gratification of his passions, but for motives of policy, that he might gain information of secret plots. He mentions no names and gives no evidence ; the only names that have come down are those mentioned in Antony's extraordinary letter justifying his own connection with Cleopatra. Antony, however, could only have known Roman gossip at second or third hand in Alexandria, and the whole tone of the letter is so reckless and violently coarse that it goes for very little by way of evidence. Dio indeed mentions the wife of Mæcenas. But his statements do not hang together or amount to very much. In one place he tells us that Augustus was annoyed with Mæcenas because the latter had told his wife something as to measures being taken against her brother Muræna. At another he says that some gossips attributed his journey to Gaul in B.C. 16 to a wish to enjoy her society without exciting popular remark, "for he was so much in love with her that he once made her dispute with Livia as to the superiority in beauty." Even if the gossip was worth anything, this hardly looks like a secret intrigue. Nor is it a confirmation of it that Mæcenas at his death left Augustus his heir. However, the fact may nevertheless be so. Livia is said elsewhere by Dio to have explained her lasting influence over Augustus by the fact that she was always careful not to interfere in his affairs, and, while remaining strictly chaste herself, always pretended not to know anything of his amours. If Livia did say this, it would of course be a sufficiently strong proof of the allegations against him. But such reported sayings rest ultimately on gossip and tittle-tattle, and do not go for much. The story told by Dio, and amplified by Zonaras, of Athenodorus of Tarsus getting himself conveyed into his chamber in the covered sedan intended for some mistress, and springing out of it sword in hand and then appealing to Augustus as to whether he did not often run such risks, is not very likely in itself, and at any rate must refer to the triumviral days. For about B.C. 30 Atheno-dorus was sent back to govern Tarsus. The one epigram by the hand of Augustus, which has been preserved by Martial,[1] is undeniably outspoken and coarse, but it is the coarseness of disgust, not of lubricity, and to my mind is evidence—so far as it may be called so—for him rather than against him. If, however, all that Suetonius and Dio allege against his middle life is true, we must still remember that in the eyes of his contemporaries, and indeed in Roman society generally from Cato downwards, such indulgence in itself was not reprehensible. It entirely depended on circumstances, and whether other obligations—such as friendship, public duty, family honour—were or were not violated. From that point of view the only crime of Augustus would be in the case of Terentia, wife of Mæcenas, if the tale is true. As among the other emperors whose life Suetonius wrote, with the exception of Vespasian, the character of Augustus stands out clear. One age cannot judge fairly of another, and it is not seldom that we find ourselves at as great a loss to reconcile theory and practice, as to account for lives such as those of Augustus and Horace in conjunction with the legislation of the former and the moral sentiments occasionally expressed by the latter.

[1] Martial, *Epigr.*, xi. 20.

CHAPTER XIII

LATER LIFE AND FAMILY TROUBLES

*Edepol, Senectus, si nil quidquam
aliud viti apportes tecum, cum
advenis, unum id sat est quod diu
vivendo multa quæ non volt videt.*

AFTER the restoration of the standards and prisoners from the
Parthians in B.C. 20, and when the peaceful settlement of the
Eastern provinces and subordinate kingdoms had
been carried through or fairly started, Augustus
appears to have thought that the greater part of
his life's work had been accomplished. The frontiers of the
Empire had been settled and secured. The Eastern provinces
had been visited, necessary reforms introduced, and great works
of public utility set on foot. He wrote word to the Senate
that the Empire was sufficiently extensive, and that he had
no intention of adding to it by further annexations. He
returned to Rome the following year (B.C. 19) to find that
the renewed trouble in Northern Spain had been settled, or
was on the point of being settled, by Agrippa. He proposed
to devote himself henceforth to internal reforms and the
superintendence of the peaceful improvements which he
contemplated in the provinces. He no doubt had in mind
the necessity of a personal visitation of distant parts of the
Empire from time to time ; but by associating the able and
trustworthy Agrippa with himself in the tribunician power

(B.C. 18) he might feel that he would always have a support in the administration at home or abroad on which he could rely. It was at this time, therefore, that the reforms and restorations were accomplished which have been described in the last chapter, crowned by the national festival, the *ludi sæculares*, in which he and Agrippa stood side by side as mouth-pieces of the whole people before the gods.

We have seen, however, how these peaceful hopes were disappointed. Scarcely were the secular games over than news came of the serious disturbances in Gaul, Pannonia, Dalmatia, and Thrace, which led to his three years' absence from Rome and his long residence in Gaul and Spain. He had only returned to Rome from this absence little more than a year when he lost Agrippa, who died in March, B.C. 12, and he was obliged to fall back upon the support of Tiberius, as his two grandsons were only eight and five years old respectively. It was in B.C. 11 that he compelled him to divorce his wife, Vipsania, to whom he was devotedly attached, and marry Iulia, left a widow by Agrippa. The change was thoroughly distasteful to Tiberius. He loved Vipsania, and he had good reason to suspect Iulia of at least levity. So strong were his feelings for his divorced wife that means had to be taken to prevent the two meeting, for on a chance *rencontre* he was observed to follow her with straining eyes and tears. The arrangement, indeed, was wholly the work of Augustus, with a view to a possible failure in the succession (which did actually occur), for by this time he had evidently imbibed the idea of a dynasty, and of the necessity of having some one connected with him to take his place, who would be regarded as a natural successor by all classes of citizens. But it proved the origin of a sorrow and mortification which did much to overcloud his later days.

At first, we are told, the marriage seemed likely to be a happy one. Iulia accompanied her husband on his campaigns in Dalmatia (B.C. 11–10), or at any rate awaited him at Aquileia,

where a child was born and died. But from that time
forward the breach between them was always
Iulia, b. B.C. 39;
ob. A.D. 14. widening. Tiberius seems to have remembered
certain passages that had passed between them
while she was still the wife of Agrippa, and she regarded him
as her social inferior, and wrote a violent complaint of his character and habits to Augustus—supposed to have been composed
for her by her lover, Sempronius Gracchus, who paid for that
service by his life in the first year of the next reign ; and
when in B.C. 6 Tiberius retired to Rhodes, his motive seems
to have been as much to escape her company as to avoid the
awkwardness of his political position. Left thus to her own
devices in the midst of a corrupt society, she seems soon to
have outdone all former excesses. She was beautiful—except
that she early had grey hair—witty and wilful : so wilful
and capricious that Augustus used to say that he had "two
fanciful daughters whom he was obliged to put up with—the
state and Iulia." She drew round her all the rich and extravagant youth. At the amphitheatre, on one occasion, some
one pointed out the contrast between the respectable elderly
personages who surrounded Livia and the wild youth who
formed her own train. "Oh! they will grow old along with
me!" she replied. To a graver friend, who suggested that
she would do better to imitate the economical habits of her
father, she retorted : "He forgets that he is a Cæsar ; I
remember that I am Cæsar's daughter." Once the Emperor
entered the room while she was at her toilet and noticed that
her tire women had been plucking out her grey hairs. He
stayed chatting on all kinds of subjects, and insensibly led the
conversation to the subject of old age. "Which would you
prefer ?" he asked, "to be grey or bald ?" "Oh, grey," she
replied. "Then I wonder," said he, "that you let these
women make you bald so soon." She had at times given him
some unpleasant doubts as to her conduct. She came to see
him once dressed in a meretricious style, which she knew

would vex him. Next day she reappeared dressed with complete decorum. He had said nothing the day before, but now exclaimed, "Isn't this a style more becoming to a daughter of Augustus ?" "Oh," said she, "I dressed to-day for my father to see, yesterday for my husband."

He had never liked her mixing in general society as a girl. She and his granddaughters, who lived in his house, were trained to spend their time in women's work, spinning wool, and the like, and to have no secret conversations or idle talk ; and he once wrote to a young noble who had called on her while staying at Baiæ that "he had taken a great liberty." But in spite of such seclusion she had developed a considerable knowledge of and taste for literature, and her cheerful good nature made her popular at court and in society. Her father watched her career as a married woman, and from time to time gave her half-grave and half-playful hints as to her extravagance in dress and the style of people that surrounded her. But he does not seem to have entertained serious suspicions. Meanwhile she is said by our authorities not only to have been indulging in numerous intrigues, but to have violated all propriety and decency by joining in noisy revelry at night in the streets and forum, and to have been present at parties where men stayed late and drank deep. The crash came at a moment that seemed a culminating one in the Emperor's career, when a scandal must have been peculiarly trying.

Since the beginning of B.C. 8 Augustus had been at home. In that year a fresh period of his various powers had been duly renewed by a vote of the Senate, which had also

Pater patriæ, B.C. 2.

honoured him by naming the month Sextilis after him as "August," and he had had the gratification of welcoming Tiberius home from Germany victorious, and witnessing his triumph. His young grandson Gaius was designated consul in B.C. 5 for the sixth year from that time, and the next year he himself took that office after an interval of eighteen years, that he might add dignity to the ceremony

of Gaius taking the *toga virilis*. Though vexed at Tiberius's
retirement to Rhodes, he had good reason to hope that in the
two young Cæsars the succession was well provided for. In
spite of some uneasiness on the German frontier and among
the Parthians, there was for the time profound peace. At the
beginning of B.C. 2 he was again consul, in order to introduce
the second grandson to the forum ; and to show their apprecia-
tion of his achievements, and their affection for his person, the
Senate at length voted to give him the title of "*pater patriæ.*"
It was first offered him by a popular deputation in his villa at
Antium. He made some difficulty about accepting it ; but
the next time he appeared at the theatre or circus he was met
by loud shouts, the whole people addressing him by that title,
and at the following meeting of the Senate on the 5th of February
Valerius Messala was put up to address him formally : "With
prayers for your person and your house, Cæsar Augustus—for
in offering them we deem ourselves to be praying for the
perpetual felicity of the Republic and the prosperity of this
city—we, the Senate, in full accord with the Roman people,
unanimously salute you as *Father of your country.*" Augustus,
rising with tears in his eyes and voice, could just answer briefly,
"My dearest wishes have been fulfilled, Fathers of the Senate,
and what is there left for me to ask of the immortal gods
except that I may retain this unanimous feeling of yours to the
last day of my life ? "

Though the title had long been popularly applied to
Augustus, this was the first official recognition of it. It had
very old historical precedent, from Romulus to Iulius Cæsar.
It was meant to be the highest compliment which could be
paid, but it conferred no new powers, though in after-times
some of the Emperors regarded it as giving them a kind of
paternal authority. Augustus was evidently highly gratified.
The shows given at his expense this year were of unusual
magnificence : gladiators, wild beast hunts, sham sea-fights on
the flooded Transtiberine fields, had all roused great enthusiasm,

and a special festival in his honour had been held at Naples—in the Greek fashion—as an expression of thanks to him for assistance rendered in the distress caused by a recent earthquake and eruption of Vesuvius. The year thus opened with unusual cheerfulness, and though now past sixty he might feel encouraged by the popular enthusiasm to continue his work with unabated energy.

Suddenly the disgrace that had been gathering round his house was revealed to him. We are not told who enlightened him and turned the suspicions which he had per-

Detection of Iulia. sistently put away into certainty. Of course the natural suggestion is that it was Livia, between whom and Iulia, as mother of the two young heirs who stood in the way of Livia's son Tiberius, there was no cordial feeling. The contrast in their ways of life, and the remarks caused by it, no doubt reported by good-natured friends, had not helped to make these relations any more pleasant. But whoever was the informant, Augustus was at last thoroughly roused, and thrown into the greatest state of agitation. Whatever may have been his own private vices in the past, the decorum of the palace in which Livia presided was unimpeached and highly valued by him. The pure atmosphere of the Augustan house—Horace says—and the paternal care of the Emperor were mainly the causes of the manly characters of Tiberius and Drusus, and Horace always echoes what Augustus at any rate wished to be thought true. To have the secrets of the family thus revealed to the multitude, to the scorn of the hostile and the pity of the well-disposed, was no doubt galling. He shunned society for some time and kept away from Rome. He had also the additional annoyance of reflecting that the publicity was greatly his own fault. In the heat of his anger he wrote to the Senate and put the affair, more or less, in its hands. In cooler moments he repented of this, and exclaimed that "it would never have happened if Agrippa and Mæcenas had been alive." Several men are said to have suffered death on the charge, though we only know of two names, Iulius Antonius and Sempronius Gracchus, the former of whom committed suicide, while the latter was banished to an island on the African coast. Seneca, who generally makes the worst of Augustus, says that he spared their lives and punished them by banishment. The case of Iulius Antonius was particularly bad. He was the son of Antony by Fulvia, had been brought up by Octavia, married to her daughter Marcella, and by her influence and the kindness of Augustus, had been prætor (B.C. 13) and consul (B.C. 10). He had therefore been treated as a member of the family, and a highly favoured one. Gracchus is said to have begun his intrigue while Iulia was the wife of Agrippa, and to have helped to irritate her against her husband Tiberius. But however guilty Iulia may have been, she did not forfeit the popular affections. Again and again Augustus was assailed by petitions to recall her. He passionately refused, exclaiming at last to a more than usually persistent meeting, that he "would wish them all daughters and wives like her." The most that he could be persuaded to grant was that at the end of five years she should be allowed to exchange her island (Pandateria) for Rhegium, and to live under less stringent conditions as to dress and food, and the servants who attended her. Her mother, Scribonia, accompanied her into exile, and though Tiberius, acting under the authority of Augustus, sent from Rhodes a message of divorce, he made a formal request that she might be allowed to retain whatever he had given her. The sincerity of such an intercession was illustrated by the fact that on the death of Augustus he immediately deprived her of all allowances. She, however, only survived her father a few weeks. All this severity is perhaps best accounted for if we accept the statement of Dio and Pliny, that she was charged not only with adultery, but with joining in some plot against her father in favour of her lover, Iulius Antonius.[1] At any rate it is difficult not to feel

[1] Pliny, *N. H.* 7 § 149 ; Dio, 54, 9.

some sympathy with a woman, married and re-married without choice on her part or any question of affection, for nine years the wife of a man as old as her father, and then transferred to another, whose heart was fixed elsewhere, and whom his warmest admirers cannot describe as one likely to be sympathetic or expansive, one in fact who began with a strong prejudice against her. She knew also that her own mother, with whom she seems to have kept up affectionate relations, had been turned off immediately after her birth for no assignable reason, just as she had been married for a momentary political object. She could have grown up with no very deep reverence for her father's morality or lofty ideas of the marriage relationship.

From this time forward family misfortunes seemed to dog the steps of Augustus for some years to come. The next blow was the death of the two young sons of Iulia, Gaius and Lucius, whom he had adopted, had personally educated in their childhood, and was training for their great future. When the elder was only 15 (B.C. 5) he had been designated consul for A.D. 1, and the Senate had voted that he and his brother might at that age "take part in public business," that is, might be employed in any capacity the Emperor might choose directly they assumed the *toga virilis*. Accordingly, in B.C. 1, Gaius was sent to the East, with a pretty wide commission to visit the Eastern provinces. He seems to have travelled considerable distances, and even entered Arabia. Tiberius, who was then at Rhodes, crossed to Samos to greet him. The meeting, however, was not a happy one. M. Lollius, the head of Gaius's staff, seems to have influenced the young prince against Tiberius, and induced him to send home a report to the Emperor of certain indications that he was contemplating some treasonable measures. Augustus candidly informed Tiberius of this, and it was it seems partly from the necessity of clearing himself, that at the earnest entreaty of his mother, he, two years later,

Death of Gaius
and Lucius
Cæsar,
A.D. 2–4.

sought and obtained the permission of Augustus to return to Rome. Meanwhile there had been wild talk among the staff of Gaius, one of them expressing his readiness to sail to Rhodes and bring the head of "the exile" back. He does not, however, appear to have forfeited the confidence or affection of Augustus, who writes to him on the 23rd September, A.D. 1 : "Good day to you, Gaius, apple of my eye, whom by heaven I continually miss when away. But it is especially on days such as this one that my eyes seek for my Gaius ; and wherever you have spent it I hope that you have kept my sixty-fourth birthday in good health and spirits. For you see I have safely passed the grand climacteric, which for all old men is their 63rd year. Pray heaven that whatever time remains for me I may spend with the knowledge that you and your brother are safe and sound and the republic supremely prosperous, with you playing the man and preparing to take up my work." But these hopes were doomed to be disappointed, as we have seen, by the treacherous wound received at Artagera in Armenia in A.D. 4. Two years earlier his younger brother, Lucius, had died suddenly and somewhat mysteriously at Marseilles at the beginning of a progress through the Western provinces, which was to form part of his political education. The fact that his death corresponded nearly with the return of Tiberius from Rhodes gave rise to suspicions that it had been caused by the machinations of Livia, anxious to secure the succession for her son. Even the death of Gaius, though so far away, was put down to the same malignant influence ; for it was argued that his wound was slight and had not been expected to end fatally. Tacitus records that the detractors of the imperial family were accustomed to remark that "Livia had been a fatal mother to the republic, a fatal stepdame to the family of the Cæsars." There is, however, no scrap of evidence to connect her with either event. It is doubtful whether the young men had shewn much promise ; but their death was treated as a matter for public mourning. At Pisæ, of which colony they were "patrons," there still exist two long and pompous inscriptions (*Cenotaphia*) recording their death, speaking of the successful campaign of Gaius in the East, ordering mourning "in view of the magnitude of so great and unexpected a calamity," and decreeing various honours to the memory of Lucius "princeps iuventutis," and of Gaius "princeps designate."

These losses were followed by the adoption of Tiberius by Augustus, and that of Germanicus by Tiberius. The former had already several children, so that the sons and grandsons and great-grandsons—by adoption—of Augustus in A.D. 7, as recorded on the arch at Pavia, were Tiberius ; Germanicus ; Drusus, son of Tiberius ; Nero and Drusus, sons of Germanicus, and Claudius, his brother. All these survived Augustus. But Tiberius and Claudius alone reigned, Caligula was not born till five years later (A.D. 12).

The succession.

Augustus thus felt that the succession was well secured ; but the last decade of his life was destined in some ways to be the most troubled of all. The German wars began again in A.D. 4, and culminated in the Varian disaster of A.D. 9 ; while the difficulties and alarm were increased by the dangerous risings in Pannonia and Dalmatia (A.D. 6–9), during which Augustus remained for some time at Ariminum, to be within moderate distance of the seat of war. A renewed outbreak of piracy also compelled him to take over the management of Sardinia from the Senate for three years (A.D. 6–9). This was partly the cause, perhaps, of the distress at Rome in B.C. 6 from a rise in the price of corn, intensified by various disastrous fires. The unrest thus created led to some more or less dangerous conspiracies, such as that of Plautius Rufus, who was accused of abetting disturbances and spreading seditious libels. Others were connected with attempts to rescue Iulia at Rhegium and Agrippa Postumus in Planasia, an island near Elba. We also hear of a plot of one Cornelius Cinna, who however was pardoned and allowed to be consul in A.D. 4.

Fresh troubles. The younger Iulia.

Seneca asserts that after this act of clemency the life of Augustus was never attempted again ; and Dio has recorded a conversation between him and Livia in that year, in which, seeing her husband sleepless and torn with continued anxieties, she recommended this policy of leniency. But one last mortification remained for him. In A.D. 9 his granddaughter Iulia was discovered to have followed her mother's example. She was married to Æmilius Paulus Lepidus, and had a son and a daughter Lepida, once betrothed to the future Emperor Claudius, but never married to him. Her lover, D. Silanus, was not banished to any definite place, but was obliged to leave Rome, to which he was not allowed to return till A.D. 20, and then under disabilities for State employment. Iulia herself was banished to the island Tremesus (*St. Domenico*), on the coast of Apulia, where she remained till her death in A.D. 27, supported by an allowance from Livia. We do not know enough of the affair to judge of her guilt ; but in some mysterious way her husband was involved in a charge of treason about this time. In the same year the poet Ovid was banished to Tomi, forty miles south of the mouth of the Danube, in a district exposed to constant raids of the Sarmatians and Dacians. It has always been supposed that this severity was connected with the affair of Iulia, and that either he was one of her lovers, or was privy to some of her intrigues, amatory or political. The reason assigned in the edict appears to have been the licentiousness of his verse, and as Augustus was just then engaged in reinforcing his laws against various forms of immorality, and trying to encourage marriage as against concubinage, this may have been partly the reason. Only as his most licentious poems had been published seven years before it seems a little late in the day. His own account of his misfortune—never outspoken—goes through two phases. At first he seems to wish to attribute it all to his amatory poems. " He is a poet destroyed by his own genius : his verses have been his undoing : they deserved punishment, but sure not so heavy a one." But presently he began to own that there was something else : " Not," he says, " any political offence, no plot against the Emperor, no plan of violence against the state. He had seen something he should not have seen. He is ruined by his own simplicity and want of prudence, combined with treachery on the part of friends and slaves. The exact cause he dare not reveal, and yet it is well known at Rome." Ovid was now fifty-two and married for a third time to a wife connected distantly with the imperial family. The chances are therefore against an intrigue with Iulia. There is one other possible explanation ; Ovid was at Elba when he got notice of the edict, staying with his wife's connection, Paulus Fabius Maximus, who afterwards incurred the suspicion of Livia as favouring Agrippa Postumus, confined in the neighbouring island of Planasia since B.C. 7. We know from Suetonius that there was at least one plot to remove him, and it may be that Ovid knew of it and even saw some of the conspirators.

However that may be, the other explanation is also possible : that Augustus meant what he said, and regarded Ovid's works as unwholesome. He was what would be called in our time a " decadent " poet. He represents the worst side of Roman society, as it began to be unfavourably affected by that abstention from practical politics, which came to be the fashion in the latter half of the reign of Augustus. He had himself refused to take any office that would give him a seat in the Senate, and seemed to think that to be the natural conduct of a man of taste and literature. He was the mouthpiece of the gilded youth who sought in amorous intrigue, and a fastidious dalliance with the Muses, a more congenial employment than the performance of those duties to the state which no longer held out promises of unlimited wealth or power. He was only cleverer than the ruck of such men, and Augustus may possibly have selected him as the representative of a tendency at which he was alarmed. Ovid was precisely the sort of man to create the tone of society which had been the ruin of his daughter and granddaughter. It is quite possible that being intimate with such circles the poet may have known, or been supposed to know, something inconvenient about the last scandal, and, at any rate, he would be on the side of Iulia as against her grandfather. At the time of his exile he was engaged, at the Emperor's suggestion or request, on the composition of the poetical Calendar or Fasti, which was incidentally to celebrate the chief events of Roman history, and it has been suggested that the story of Claudia's vindication of her chastity (*Fast.* iv. 305 *sqq.*) was intended as a veiled defence of the elder or younger Iulia. Whatever the offence given, neither Augustus nor Tiberius could ever be induced to allow his recall.

The poet's abject language in praying to be allowed to return illustrates incidentally the absolute supremacy of the Emperor, and the attribution to him of divine honours and powers, the steady progress of which has been noted in a previous chapter. We may also note that what Paris is to the Parisians, Rome is to Ovid. Augustus and his ministers or friends had made it the home of splendour and luxury. The poet fondly dwells on all its beauties, pleasures, and conveniences, and, like a true Parisian, can hardly conceive of life away from it, its games, its theatres, the sports on the Campus, the lounge in the forum, or the wit and poetry heard at the tables of the great. As the spring comes round in his dreary, treeless dwelling on the Pontus, he thinks of the flowers and vines of Italy, but, above all, of the pleasures of the city in April, the month of festivals : "It is holiday with you now, and the wordy war of the wrangling forum is giving place to the unbroken round of festivals. The horses are in request, and the light foils are in play. The young athletes, their shoulders glistening with oil, are bathing wearied limbs in baths supplied by the virgin stream. The stage is in full swing, and the audiences are clapping their favourite actors, and the three theatres are echoing instead of the three forums. Oh four times, oh beyond all counting, happy he who may enjoy the city unforbidden ! " It had been the object of Augustus to make the city splendid and attractive, and to keep the citizens comfortable and contented and proud of their home. He had doubtless succeeded ; but it was sometimes at the cost of a lowered standard of public duty and a growing devotion to personal ease and enjoyment.

CHAPTER XIV

THE LAST DAYS

Let the sound of those he fought for,
And the feet of those he wrought for,
Echo round his bones for evermore.

THE public and private troubles mentioned in the last chapter did not break the spirit or paralyse the energies of the aged Emperor, or prevent him from taking a strenuous part in the administration of the Empire. The last eight years of his life were full of stir and movement, though our meagre authorities give us few details. He actively supported the campaigns of Tiberius and Germanicus; he was introducing reforms in Gaul;[1] he was pushing on improvements in the East, and founding a series of colonies in Pisidia as a defence against the predatory mountain tribes; he was directing a census of the whole Empire; he was emending his marriage laws by the farther enactments contained in the *lex Papia Poppæa*, which he supported by energetic speeches; he was elaborating a great financial scheme; he was personally attending to the embankment of the Tiber; he was reforming the city police

The activities of the last years of Augustus, A.D. 8–14.

[1] In A.D. 11 the people of Narbonne founded an altar to him in gratitude for some reform in their constitution which he had either granted or initiated. (Wilmanns, 194.)

and fire brigades; and when the Varian disaster occurred we have seen with what energy he acted, how he enforced the law of military service and despatched reinforcements to the Rhine, while he cleared the city of dangerous elements and provided against possible movements in the provinces. Though now seventy-two years old he shewed no sign of senility in heart; and as it was said that at every stage of his life he had the beauty appropriate to it, so in spirit, courage, and prudence he seems always to have answered to any strain to which he was submitted.

To understand the financial changes of these years it is necessary to recall a few broad facts as to the revenue of the Empire. It arose from (1) Italy, (2) the pro-vinces. In Italy the sources of revenue were the customs (*portoria*), the rent of public land, the *vicesima* or 5 per cent. on the value of manumitted slaves. From the time that it became the habit to pay the soldiers, a *tributum* or property tax had been raised, at first as a temporary measure, or even as a loan, but gradually as a regular thing. Since the Macedonian wars, however, B.C. 167, this *tributum* had not been levied: the additional wealth acquired by the new conquests being sufficient. It does not appear that the *tributum* was abolished by law, and indeed for a short time it was reimposed by the Triumvirs, though only as an extraordinary tax (*temerarium*). After the Social war of B.C. 89 the Italians became full citizens and shared this exemption.

Financial measures of Augustus.

The second and most important source of revenue were the provinces. There were royalties on mines, customs, rent of public land, and other sources of profit to the government; but also every province paid a *stipendium*—a certain sum of money —to the Roman treasury. The manner in which it was paid —whether in money or produce, or a mixture of the two— differed in different provinces, as also did the mode of its assessment and collection; but the broad fact was that each province had to furnish a sum of money, and that owners of property in a province were liable to a *tributum* or tax. [1]

In the time of Augustus there was no great change made in the nature or incidence of this taxation ; but the management of the treasury itself was revolutionised. In the first place, the *ærarium* instead of being under the care of the yearly elected quæstors, who issued money on the order of Senate or magistrates, was put under *præfecti* appointed by the Emperor, and though the Senate still had a nominal control over it, it was really under his power. In the next place, a new *ærarium* was formed, afterwards called the *fiscus*, into which was paid the revenues of the imperial provinces. This was entirely under the Emperor, and the tendency was in time to have every extraordinary revenue, such as confiscations, lapsed legacies (*caduca*), and the like, paid into it. Besides this there was the *patrimonium Cæsarum*, the private property of the Emperor in virtue of his office. To this belonged the whole revenues of Egypt and the Thracian Chersonese, and other large estates. When Augustus talks of his having supplemented the treasury or made distributions to the people, it is often from this fund that he drew, though he had besides large personal property (*res familiaris*), which he employed at times for the same purpose.

Of course from the revenue of the provinces had to be deducted the cost of their administration and defence. Provinces, therefore, which needed large forces and constant defence from surrounding barbarians did not pay. Cicero, indeed, asserts that in his time none of the provinces except Asia paid for their expenses. This probably is an exaggeration, but there is no doubt that the loss on some had to be put against the gain on others, and that the balance of the yearly budget was not always on the right side, as, at a later date, we know that Vespasian said that the treasury wanted four hundred

[1] Asia and Sicily originally did not pay a *stipendium*, but tithes on produce. This system was abolished by Iulius Cæsar.

million sesterces (about £3,000,000 sterling) to be solvent. The outbreak of the German wars in A.D. 4, and the large forces which it had long been necessary to keep upon the Rhine had caused, if not a deficit, at any rate the near prospect of one. It was just such a crisis as in old times would have justified the levying of a *tributum* as a special war tax. There were, however, two reasons against Augustus doing this. In the first place, such a *tributum* would be temporary, and he wanted a permanency ; and, in the second place, the citizens had come to view freedom from the *tributum* as their special privilege, differentiating Italy from the subject provinces, and marking them out as a governing body. True to his policy of avoiding offensive names, while at the same time getting what he wanted, Augustus decided against the *tributum*. What he did was to create a new department, an army-pay treasury (*aes militare*), with two præfects of prætorian rank. The money in this treasury was to be devoted to the pay and pensions of the soldiers. He started it with a gift in his own name and that of Tiberius of 170,000,000 sesterces (about £1,500,000), and arranged that the tax which he had contrived soon after the end of the civil wars, the 1 per cent. on goods sold at auctions or by contract, should be paid into it. But this was not sufficient for the purpose, and he had to look round for other means of raising revenue. He did therefore what a late Chancellor of the Exchequer did for us—he imposed death duties : 5 per cent. on all legacies except those from the nearest relatives. This avoided the offensiveness of depriving the people of Italy of a valued privilege, while it in fact brought them financially almost in a line with the provinces. For those who paid *tributum* did not pay *vicesima*, and *vice versâ*. Still the tax offended a powerful class and met with much resistance. The practice of leaving large legacies to friends, as an acknowledgment of services rendered, was common in Italy, and the tax therefore fell heavily upon the rich. In A.D. 13 a determined move was made in the Senate to obtain its abolition. Augustus sent a written communication to the Senate, pointing out that the money was necessary, but asking them to contrive some other method of raising it. The Senators declined to formulate any plan, and only answered that they were ready to submit to *anything* else. Thereupon Augustus proposed a *tributum* or tax on land and houses. Confronted with this alternative the Senate at once withdrew from opposition. It was a case of financial necessity, and it must not be supposed that Augustus wished to lower the prestige of Italy or the value of the citizenship. That was one of the points in which he reversed the policy of Iulius, who had been lavish in bestowing the citizenship, and seems to have had visions of a uniform Empire united in privilege as in government. Augustus, on the other hand, was even ultra-conservative and ultra-Roman in this respect. He made constant difficulties about granting the citizenship. In answer to Tiberius, who begged it for some favourite Greek, he insisted upon only granting it if the man appeared personally and convinced him of the soundness of his claim. Even Livia met with a refusal in behalf of some Gaul. The Emperor offered to grant the man immunity from tribute, saying that he cared less about a loss to his treasury than for vulgarising the citizenship.

Though Augustus shewed in this transaction all his old tact and statesmanship with no failure either in determination or power of *finesse*, yet he was growing visibly feebler in body. He gave up attending social functions ; and it was too much for him to appear any longer at meetings of the Senate. Accordingly, instead of the half-yearly committee of twenty-five members who used to be appointed to prepare measures for the House, a sort of inner cabinet of twenty members appointed for a year—with any members of his family whom he chose—met at his house and often round the couch on which he was reclining, and their decisions were given the force of a *Senatus-consultum*. His interest, however, in every detail was as keen as ever. For instance, we have a

Declining health and strength.

letter from him to Livia, written at the end of A.D. 11, as to
the advisability of allowing Claudius (the future Emperor) to
appear in Rome during the ceremonies connected with the
consulship of his brother Germanicus. Claudius (now twenty-
one) was reported to be deformed and half-witted, and his
mother Antonia herself described him as scarcely human
(*monstrum hominis*). The letter is worth reading, partly
because it is the only complete one (at any rate, of any
length) which we possess, and partly because it illustrates the
care which Augustus took to keep up the prestige of the
imperial family, to avoid, above all things, incurring popular
ridicule, and his attention to minute details :—

"I have consulted with Tiberius, as you desired me to do,
my dear Livia, as to what is to be done about your grandson
(Claudius) Tiberius. We entirely agree in thinking that we
must settle once for all what line we are to take in regard to
him. For if he is sound and, to use a common expression, has
all his wits about him, what possible reason can there be for our
doubting that he ought to be promoted through the same grades
and steps as his brother ? But if we find that he is deficient,
and so deranged in mind and body as to be unfit for society, we
must not give people accustomed to scoff and sneer at such
things a handle for casting ridicule both on him and on us.
The fact is that we shall always be in a state of agitation if we
stop to consider every detail as it occurs, without having made
up our minds whether to think him capable of holding offices
or not. On the present occasion, however, in regard to the
point on which you consult me, I do not object to his having
charge of the triclinium of the priests at the games of Mars if
he will submit to receive instructions from his relative, the son
of Silanus, to prevent his doing anything to make people stare
or laugh. We agree that he is not to be in the imperial box
at the Circus. For he will be in full view of everybody and
be conspicuous. We agree that he is not to go to the Alban
Mount or to be in Rome on the days of the Latin festival.

For if he is good enough to be in his brother's train to the mountain, why should he not be honorary city prefect? Those are the decisions at which we arrived, my dear Livia, and we wish them to be settled once for all to prevent our wavering between hope and fear. You are at liberty, if you choose, to give Antonia this part of my letter to read."

Perhaps the voice is the voice of Tiberius, but the courtesy and well-bred style are all Augustus's. By this time the influence of Tiberius was well established, and Augustus treats him as a successor who has a right to be consulted on all family matters and important State affairs. Since his return from Rhodes Tiberius had done eminent service to the State both on the Rhine and in Illyricum. In appointing Varus to Germany Augustus had made a mistake which he seldom committed. He had nearly always picked good men, but P. Quintilius Varus had not only been extortionate in his former province, but was neither energetic nor prudent; and his experience among the unwarlike inhabitants of Syria was not a good preparation for dealing with the brave and warlike Germans. Tiberius knew him well, having been his colleague in the consulship of B.C. 13, and would certainly not have appointed him. It was to Tiberius that the Emperor then turned to retrieve the disaster and confront the almost more serious dangers in Illyricum. And if he found him trustworthy in the field, this letter shows how much confidence he felt in him at home. It was a common report that Augustus knew and disliked his character. The lackeys of the palace gave out that he had on one occasion exclaimed, "Unhappy people of Rome who will some day be the victims of those slow grinders!" And in a speech to the Senate some expressions used by him were taken to convey an apology for his reserved and sullen manners, and an acknowledgment, therefore, of his mistrust or dislike. But it is abundantly plain that in these last years he not only trusted his military abilities, but felt a sincere affection for himself. In

Confidence in Tiberius.

earlier times, before the retreat to Rhodes, the short notes written to him (parts of which are preserved by Suetonius [1]) are playful and intimate ; and though he was vexed at his retirement and answered a suggestion of return by a message bidding him "dismiss all concern for his relatives, whom he had abandoned with such excessive eagerness," [2] yet the fragments preserved of the Emperor's letters to him in these later times breathe not only admiration, but warm affection. "Goodbye, Tiberius, most delightful of men ! Success to you in the field, you who serve the Muses as well as me ! Most delightful of men, and, as I hope to be happy, bravest of heroes and steadiest of generals !" And again : "How splendidly managed are your summer quarters ! I am decidedly of opinion that, in the face of so many untoward circumstances and such demoralisation of the troops, no one could have borne himself with greater prudence than you are doing ! The officers now at Rome who have served with you all confess that the verse might have been written for you, 'One man by vigilance restored the State.'" Once more : "Whenever anything occurs that calls for more than usually earnest thought or that stirs my spleen, what I miss most, by heaven, is my dear Tiberius, and that passage of Homer always occurs to me—

> "'If he but follow, e'en from burning fire
> We both shall back return, so wise is he !'"

And in the midst of his laborious campaign the Emperor writes to him anxiously : "When I hear or read that you are worn out by the protracted nature of your labours, heaven confound me if I do not shudder in every limb ; and I beseech you to spare yourself, lest if we hear of your being ill your mother and I should expire and the Roman people run the risk of losing their empire. It doesn't matter a bit whether I am well or not as long as you are not well. I pray the gods

[1] Suet., *August.* 76.   [2] Suet., *Tib.* 11.

to preserve you to us and to suffer you to be well now and always, unless they abhor the Roman people."

These letters seem sufficiently to refute the idle stories of the *gêne* that his presence was to Augustus, of his being a wet blanket to cheerful conversation, and a makeshift with which the Emperor was forced to put up in default of better heirs. Nor did Tiberius fall short in respect and loyal service. After his adoption in A.D. 4, he immediately accepted the position of a son under the *patria potestas*, abstained from manumissions and other acts of a man who was *sui iuris*, and apparently transferred his residence to the palace, and seems really to have taken the burden from shoulders no longer strong enough to bear it.

For now the end was near, portended as the pious or credulous believed by many omens. There was an eclipse of the sun,[1] and various fiery meteors in the sky.

Death of Augustus at Nola, August 19, A.D. 14.

On one of his statues the letter C of Cæsar was melted by lightning, and the augurs prophesied, or afterwards invented the prediction, that he would die within a hundred days and join the gods—*æsar* being good Etruscan for " divinities." He himself seems to have been made somewhat nervous by certain accidents that might be twisted into omens. The early part of A.D. 14 was taken up with the usual legal business, but also with the Census, which he held this year in virtue of his consular power and with Tiberius as his colleague. The organisation of the city into *vici* probably made the actual clerical work easy and rapid, but when that was over came the ceremony of " closing the lustrum " (*condere lustrum*), and the offering of solemn sacrifice and prayer. This took place in the Campus Martius, and large crowds assembled to witness it. But the Emperor, uneasy at something which he thought ominous, or perhaps really feeling unwell, would not read the solemn vows, which

---

[1] Dio, 56, 29. But there does not appear to have been one that year. There was a partial eclipse of the moon on the 4th of April and a total eclipse on the 27th of September.

according to custom had been written out and were now put into his hands. He said that he should not live to fulfil them and handed them over to Tiberius to read. After this ceremony was over, Augustus was anxious to get away from Rome and take his usual yachting tour along the Latin and Campanian coast. On this occasion he had the farther object of accompanying Tiberius as far as Beneventum on the Appian road, on his way to Brundisium and Illyricum, where some difficulties resulting from the recent war required his presence and authority. But various legal causes awaiting decision detained the Emperor in the city. He was restive and impatient at the delay, and petulantly exclaimed that "if they let everything stop them he should never be at Rome again." At length, however, he set out, accompanied by Livia and Tiberius and a numerous court. They reached the coast at Astura, in the delta of a river of the same name, which falls into the sea at the southern point of the bay of Antium. It was a quiet place though there were seaside villas near, and there Cicero had spent the months of his mourning for Tullia, finding consolation in the solitude of the woods which skirt the side of the stream. At Astura the party embarked, but owing to the state of the wind they did so by night. A chill then caught brought on diarrhœa, and laid the foundation of his fatal illness. Nevertheless the voyage along the Campanian coast and the adjacent islands was continued till they reached Capreæ. It was on this voyage that, happening to touch at Puteoli, he was so much delighted and cheered by the thanks offered him by the crew of an Alexandrian corn-ship for his safeguarding of the seas. At Capreæ he seems to have stayed some time, amusing himself by watching the young athletes training for the Greek games at Naples—the only town in Italy except Rhegium which at this time retained any traces of Hellenic customs and life. He gave parties, also, at which he asked his Roman guests to dress in Greek fashion and speak Greek, and the Greeks to use Roman dress and speak Latin. There was the usual distribution of presents, and on one occasion he gave a banquet to the athletes in training, and watched them after dinner pelting each other with apples and other parts of the dessert. It was a custom, more honoured in the breach than in the observance, with which he was familiar. He once entertained a certain Curtius, who prided himself on his taste in cookery, and who thought a fat thrush that had been put before him was ill-done. "May I despatch it ? " he said to the Emperor. " Of course," was the reply ; upon which he threw it out of the window. On this occasion the aged Emperor, feeling, we may suppose, somewhat better and glad to be away from the cares of State, enjoyed this curious horse-play. He was also particularly cheerful during these days at Capreæ, pleasing himself with inventing Greek verses and then defying one of Tiberius' favourite astrologers to name the play from which they came.

Before long, however, he crossed to Naples, with his illness still upon him, but with alternate rallies and relapses. At Naples he had to sit through some long gymnastic contests that were held every fifth year in his honour. Such a function in an August day at Naples would have been trying to the most vigorous and healthy, but for a man in his seventy-sixth year, and suffering from such a complaint, it must have been deadly. He preferred, however, not to disappoint people eager to shew him honour. He then fulfilled his purpose of accompanying Tiberius to Beneventum, and having taken leave of him there turned back towards Naples. But he was never to reach it. At Nola, about eighteen English miles short of that town, his illness became so acute that he was obliged to stop at the villa there in which his father had died seventy-two years before. Messengers were hastily sent to recall Tiberius. With him the dying man had a long private conversation, in which he seems to have imparted to him his wishes and counsels as to the government ; and perhaps it was now that he pointed out the three nobles who were possible candidates for the succession—"Marcus Lepidus, who was fit for it, but would not care to take it ; Asinius Gallus, who would desire it, but was unfit ; and L. Arruntius, who was not unfit for it and would have the courage to seize it if opportunity offered." But this conference over he busied himself with no other affairs of State. He seemed to acquiesce in the fact that he had done with the world, its vexations and problems. On the last day of his life, the 19th of August (his lucky month !) the only question which he continually repeated was whether his situation was causing any commotion out of doors. Then he asked for a mirror and directed his attendants to arrange his hair and close his already relaxing jaws, that he might not shock beholders by the ghastliness of his appearance. Then his friends were admitted to say good-bye. With a pathetic mixture of playfulness and sadness he asked them whether "they thought that he had played life's farce fairly well ?" quoting a common tag at the end of plays :—

> "If aught of good our sport had, clap your hands,
> And send us, gentles all, with joy away."

These being dismissed, he turned to Livia and asked for news of one of her granddaughters who was ill ; but even as he spoke he felt the end was come—"Livia, don't forget our wedded life, goodbye !" And as he tried to kiss her lips he fell back dead.

It was a rapid and painless end, for which he had so often hoped, an *euthanasia* that he used to pray for, for himself and his friends. Up to the last his mind had been clear, with only the slightest occasional wandering. And so after long years of work and struggle, of mixed evil and good, of stern cruelties and beneficent exertion, of desperate dangers and well-earned honours, the great Emperor as he lay dying looked into the eyes which he had loved best in the world.

The body was borne to Rome by the municipal magistrates of the several towns along the road, the *cortège* always moving by night because of the heat, and the bier being deposited in the court-house of each town till it reached Bovillæ, twelve miles from Rome. There a procession of Roman knights took it in charge, having obtained that honour from the consuls, conducted it to Rome, and deposited it in the vestibule of his own house on the Palatine.

With not unnatural or unpardonable emotion some extravagant proposals were made in the Senate as to funeral honours and general mourning. But Tiberius disliked such excesses, and the funeral though stately was simple. The bier was carried on the shoulders of Senators to the Campus. Twice the *cortège* stopped, first at the Rostra, where Drusus, the son of Tiberius, delivered a funeral oration (*laudatio*), and again at the front of the temple of Iulius, where Tiberius himself read a panegyric. Drusus had dwelt chiefly on his private virtues, Tiberius confined himself to his public work. He began with a reference to his youthful services to the state immediately after the death of Cæsar ; his success in putting an end to the civil wars, and his clemency after them. He spoke of the skill with which, while splendidly rewarding his ministers, he yet prevented them from gaining a power detrimental to the state ; of his disinterested and constitutional conduct when, having everything in his hands, he yet shared the power with the people and Senate ; of his unselfishness in the division of the provinces in taking the difficult ones upon himself ; of his equity in leaving Senate and constitution independent ; of his economy and liberality ; of the good order which he kept and the wholesome laws which he carried ; of his sympathy with the tastes and enjoyments of the people ; of his hatred of flattery and tolerance of free speech. The address was read and had been carefully composed. There is not much fervour or eloquence in it, but it skilfully put the points which Augustus would himself have put, and indeed had put in that *apologia pro vita sua* which we know from the inscription at Ancyra.

The speeches over, the *cortège* moved on to the Campus Martius, where the body was burnt on the pyre prepared for it, and the ashes ceremoniously collected by eminent equites, who according to custom wore only their tunics, without the toga, ungirdled, and with bare feet. The urn was then deposited in the Mausoleum which Augustus had himself erected in B.C. 28 on the Campus close to the curving river-bank, which had already received the ashes of his nephew Marcellus, of his sister Octavia, of his two grandsons, and of his great friend and minister Agrippa, but was sternly closed by his will to his erring daughter and granddaughter.

Always careful and businesslike, he left his testamentary dispositions and the accounts of his administration in perfect order. His will, which had been deposited with the Vestal Virgins and was now read aloud by Drusus in the Senate, made Tiberius heir to two-thirds, Livia to one-third of his private property. In case of their predeceasing him it was to be divided between Drusus (son of Tiberius), Germanicus, and his three sons, as "second heirs." There were liberal legacies to citizens and soldiers and to various friends. The property thus disposed of was the *res familiaris*: the *Patrimonium Cæsarum*—Egypt, the Thracian Chersonese, and other estates—went to his successor in the principate. The will contained an apology for the smallness of the amount thus coming to his heirs (150,000,000 sesterces or about £1,200,000) on the plea that he had devoted to the public service nearly all the vast legacies which had fallen to him. By the will Livia was also adopted into the Iulian *gens* and was to take his name. She was thenceforth therefore known as Iulia Augusta, and seems to have assumed that thereby she obtained a certain share in the imperial prerogatives, a claim which led to much friction between herself and her son.

His will, and other documents left by him.

Besides the will, and a roll containing directions as to his funeral, there were two other documents drawn up by Augustus with great care. One was a *breviarium totius imperii*, an exact account of the state of the Empire, the number of soldiers under colours, the amount of money in the treasury or the *fiscus*, the arrears due, and the names of those freedmen who were to be held responsible. As a kind of appendix to this were some maxims of state which he wished to impress upon his successor : such as, not to extend the citizenship too widely, but to maintain the distinction between Roman and subject ; to select able men for administrative duties, but not to allow them to become too powerful or think themselves indispensable ; and not to extend the frontiers of the Empire.

A third roll contained a statement of his own services and achievements (*index rerum a se gestarum*). Meant to be preserved as an inscription, it is in what we might call the telegraphic style, a series of brief statements of facts without note or comment beyond the suggestiveness of a word here and there designedly used. Yet it is essentially a defence of his life and policy—the oldest extant autobiography. He directed it to be engraved on bronze columns and set up outside the Mausoleum. This was no doubt done, but the bronze columns have long ago disappeared.[1] Fortunately, however, copies of the inscription were engraved elsewhere (with a Greek translation) in temples of " Rome and Augustus," as at Apollonia in Pisidia and Ancyra in Galatia. That at Ancyra (*Angora*) exists nearly complete to this day, and some portions at Apollonia. No life of Augustus could be complete without

---

[1] The Mausolem was a huge mound of earth covered with shrubs, upon a substructure or dome cased with white marble and surrounded by walks and plantations, and surmounted by a bronze statue of Augustus. On the still-existing foundation there is now what is called the *Teatro Correa*. Besides this the spot on which his body was burnt was also enclosed and planted. Strab., iv. 53. Middleton, *Remains of Ancient Rome*, vol. ii. p. 288.

this document, which is therefore given in an English dress at the end of this book.

The Senate at once proceeded to decree divine honours to him. A temple was to be built at Rome, which was afterwards consecrated by Livia and Tiberius. Others were erected elsewhere, and the house at Nola in which he died was consecrated. His image on a gilded couch was placed in the temple of Mars, and festivals (*Augustalia*) were established with a college of Augustales to maintain them in all parts of the Empire, as well as an annual festival on the Palatine which continued to be held by succeeding Emperors.

The usual foolish rumours followed his death. Some said that Tiberius did not reach Nola in time to see him alive; that he had died some time before, but that Livia closed the doors and concealed the truth. Others even said that his death had been hastened by Livia by means of a poisoned fig; and professed to explain it by a piece of secret court history. Shortly before his death, they said, Augustus had gone attended only by Fabius Maximus on a secret visit to Agrippa Postumus in the island of Planasia, to which he had been confined since the cancelling of his adoption in A.D. 5; and that Livia fearing that he would relent towards him and name him as successor, determined that he should not live to do so, Fabius Maximus having meanwhile died suddenly and somewhat mysteriously. But the authentic accounts of his last illness and death give the lie to such an unnecessary crime. Unhappily the jealousy of the unfortunate Agrippa Postumus was a fact which helped to spread such stories, but it was a jealousy roused by the knowledge of some secret plots to carry him off and set him up as a rival, and "the first crime of the new reign"—his assassination by his guards —must, we fear, lie at the door of either Tiberius or Livia. Another report was that the soul of Augustus flew up to heaven in the shape of an eagle that rose from his pyre. Nor must the ingenious Senator—Numerius Atticus—be omitted, who

Rumours as to the death of Augustus.

declared on oath that he had seen the soul of the Emperor ascending, and was said to have received a present of 25,000 denarii (about £1,000) from Livia in acknowledgment of this loyal clearness of vision.

The prudent forethought of Augustus in regard to the succession answered its purpose. There was practically no break in the government. Tiberius was possessed

The continuous government. of *tribunicia potestas*, which enabled him to summon and consult the Senate. He also, in virtue of his proconsular imperium, gave the watchword to the prætorian guard, and despatched orders to the legions in service in the provinces. There was, indeed, some question as to whether this imperium legally terminated with the death of the *princeps*, but the matter was settled by all classes taking the oath (*sacramentum*) to him, and all the powers and honours (except the title of *pater patriæ*, which he would not accept) were shortly afterwards voted to him in the Senate and confirmed by a *lex*. His professed reluctance to accept the whole burden only brought out more clearly how the work of Augustus had made the rule of a single man inevitable : " I ask you, sir, which part of the government you wish to have committed to you ? " said Asinius Gallus. No answer was possible. A man could not control the provinces without command of the army. But he could not control the army if another man controlled the exchequer. He could not keep order in Rome and Italy, if another had command of all the legions and fleets abroad, and could at any moment invade the country or starve it out by stopping the corn-ships. And if a man had the full control of the purse and the sword, the rest followed. It was well enough for the officials to have the old titles and perform some of the old work, but if the central authority were once removed there would be chaos. The Senate had attempted to exercise that central authority and failed. It could not secure the loyalty of men who, exercising undisturbed power in distant lands, soon grew impatient of the control of a body of mixed elements and divergent views, which they often conceived to be under the influence of cliques inimical to themselves. The provinces too as they became more Romanised were certain to claim to be put on a more equal status with Italy: they could only be held together by a man who had equal authority everywhere, never by a local town council. Augustus, indeed, did not realise this development, or rather he feared its advent. In his eyes Rome ought still to rule, but could only do so by all its powers being centred in one man, who could consult the interest and attract the reverence of all parts of the Empire alike. The success of this plan depended, of course, on the character of the man, and perhaps, above all, on his abilities as a financier ; but, at any rate, it was impossible to return to a system of divided functions, and constitutional checks, which were shewn to be inoperative the moment a magistrate drew the sword and defied them. So far the work of Augustus stood, and admitted of no reaction. Republican ideals could only be entertained as pious opinions, not more practical than some of the republican virtues, on the belief in which they were founded.

CHAPTER XV

Hic vir hic est, tibi quem
promitti sæpius audis.

WHEN a great piece of work has been done in the world it is not difficult to find fault with it. A man seldom if ever sees the bearing and ultimate results of his own actions, or carries out all that he intended to do. Even when he seems to have done so, time reveals faults, miscalculations, failures. At an age when among us a boy is just leaving school, Augustus found himself the heir of a great policy and a great name amidst the ruins of a constitution and the *disjecta membra* of a great Empire. A comparatively small city state had conquered the greater part of the known world, and proposed to govern it by the machinery which had sufficed when its territory was insignificant, not extending at any rate beyond the shores of Italy. A close corporation, greedy and licentious, had divided amongst its members the vast profits from the gradually extending dominions. The central authority which should have restrained the rulers of distant provinces and the collection of their revenues was composed to a great extent of those most deeply interested in the corruptions which it was their duty to judge and condemn. Loyalty to this central authority grew

The early career and change of character.

weaker and weaker, party spirit grew stronger and less scrupulous. In the desperate struggle for wealth and luxury men stuck at nothing. Bloodshed bred bloodshed, violence provoked violence, till good citizens and honourable men (and there were always such) found themselves helpless; and the constitution which had rested on the loyalty of magistrates and citizens was ready to fall at the first touch of resolute disobedience. Then a great man appeared. Iulius Cæsar had not been free from the vices or corruption of his contemporaries; but party connections at home led him to sympathise with the people, and the ten years of war and government in Gaul, during which his enemies at home were constantly threatening and thwarting him, had convinced him that the existing constitution was doomed. He was resolved to attempt its reconstruction, even at the risk of civil war. But civil war is a sea of unknown extent. Conqueror though he was in all its battles, it left him only a few months to elaborate reforms. In those he did some great things; but his revival of the Sullan Dictatorship was too crude a return to monarchy, while the exigencies of civil war forced him to employ inferior agents. The aristocratic clique saw themselves about to lose their cherished privilege of tyranny and extortion, and they killed him.

When Octavian came home to take up his inheritance, he would naturally have joined Antony, and taken immediate vengeance on the guilty clique. But he found him intent upon the consolidation of his own position, and not inclined to admit his claim to the inheritance or to any share of power. He therefore outwardly joined the leaders of the party which he detested in order to get rid of Antony and forestall his bid for autocracy. The vissicitudes of the struggle which followed ending in the triumvirate and the division of the Roman world, infected him with the poison of civil strife—the cruelty which treats honourable enemies as outlaws, and regards personal triumph as the only end of political exertion. This period in his career and in the development of his character ends with the victory over Sextus Pompeius, in B.C. 36, and the additional security gained by the successes of Agrippa in Gaul during the two preceding years. From that time he began to regard himself as the champion of law and order, as the defender of Italy, and the guarantee of peace in the Western Provinces.

Then came a great danger—the danger of a separation of East and West. Under the influence of his passion for Cleopatra, Antony was building up a new empire of subordinate kings, it is true, but subordinate to Alexandria not Rome : and Alexandria was being adorned with the spoils of Asiatic temples to make it a worthy capital of the Eastern world. How far this was really to involve a diminution of the Roman Empire was probably not clear to Antony himself. The old provinces were not formally separated, but they were pared and diminished to round off the new kingdoms for his and Cleopatra's children. At Rome the danger was looked upon as a real one ; and once more Augustus felt that if he was to have a free hand in the renovation of the Empire which he contemplated, Antony must disappear. No doubt every artifice was employed to discredit his opponent, and to convince the Roman people that their dominion in the East was slipping from them. But, however Machiavellian his tactics, there was a solid basis of fact beneath them ; a real danger of separation had existed. The victory of Actium settled that question ; and when the few severities which followed it were over, we are happily called thenceforth to contemplate the legislator and reformer, the administrator of, on the whole, a peaceful Empire. There were no more civil wars, and no serious conspiracies. With rare exceptions—perhaps only the Arabian expedition—the wars in which Augustus was henceforth engaged were the necessary consequences of a long frontier. War was often prevented by diplomacy, and such wars as were undertaken were always successful, with the exception of those with the Germans, and even in their case immediate danger was averted.

The moral problem presented by the change from ruthless cruelty to wise and persistent clemency has exercised the minds of philosophers and historians ever since. " It was not clemency," says Seneca, " but a surfeit of cruelty." But this explains nothing. If Augustus had ever been cruel for cruelty's sake, the increased opportunities of exercising it would have whetted his appetite for blood as it did in some of his successors. It was circumstances that had changed, not altogether the man. Still, no doubt, success softened (it does not always) Augustus's character. His ministers were humane men and in favour of milder methods ; his wife was a high-minded woman, and always ready to succour distress, as she shewed during the proscriptions, and afterwards in her son's reign. He had among his immediate friends philosophers and men of letters, whose influence, so far as it went, was humanising. And lastly such opposition as still existed was no longer of irreconcilables who had known "liberty " ; a new generation had grown up which on the whole acquiesced in the peace and security of a benevolent despotism. It was a new era, and Augustus became a new man. Full of honours and possessed with irresistible powers, feeling the responsibility heavily, and often in vain desiring rest, he had no farther personal object to gain beyond the credit of having served his country and saved the Empire. The apologia of the *index rerum*, brief and bald as it is, was intended to shew that he had done this.

In estimating the value of his work we are met with this difficulty at the very threshold of the inquiry, that his object was to avoid quick and conspicuous changes. The value of his work. Instead of discussing some heroic measure we have to examine a multitude of details. In every department of political and social life we trace his hand. Working day and night, he was scheming to alter what he thought bad, and to introduce what he thought good. The reconstruction and embellishment of the city, the restoration of religion, the rehabilitation of marriage, measures necessary for the security of Rome and Italy, for the better government and material prosperity of the provinces, for the solvency of the exchequer, and for the protection of commerce—all these continually occupied his time and his thoughts. Of this steady industry this or that result may be open to criticism, but, on the whole, it seems certain that it increased the good order and prosperity of the Empire, and therefore added to the comfort and happiness of innumerable lives.

But of course the upshot of it all was the establishment of a monarchy ; and it still remains to be considered how far its benefits were counterbalanced by evils arising from the loss of freedom. It might be argued that tyrants always appeal to their right use of power however irregularly obtained, but that the plea is beside the question. Freedom is the only guarantee of the *continuance* of good government. The beneficent tyrant may any day be succeeded by a bad one. The policy of Augustus had led the people on step by step to forfeit this freedom, and lose even the taste for it, lulled to sleep by the charms of safety and luxury. When the glamour had faded from some eyes, it was too late. The generation which had known freedom had disappeared ; the experience necessary for working the old machinery no longer existed. The few who still remembered with regret the old constitution, under which they had hoped to take an independent share of political activity, had nothing left to them but sullen submission.

Advantages and disadvantages of the autocracy.

In the provinces, indeed, this consideration did not apply. The despotism there added to the sum of happiness and took nothing away. They had lost their independence long ago. They were already under a master, a master who was changed at short intervals, whom it was very difficult to bring to an account if he were oppressive, in whose selec-

In the provinces.

tion they had had absolutely no share, and whose character they had no means of calculating beforehand. They might one year be enjoying all the benefits of an able and disinterested ruler, the next they might find themselves in the power of a tyrannical extortioner, selfish, cynical, cruel. The old republican names and ideals were nothing to them; or rather they suggested organised oppression and a conspiracy to refuse redress. The change to one master, who had everything to gain by their prosperity, and was at the same time master of their old oppressors, must have seemed in every respect a blessing. If there was any drawback it was that nationality and the desire for self-government were killed by kindness. In all difficulties and disasters they looked to the Emperor for aid and seldom looked in vain. In the East especially this was probably not wholesome; yet the immediate effects in producing prosperity and comfort were marked enough to put aside for the present all such scruples.

But for the governing nation itself, while some of the benefits were no less manifest, the mischievous results were more easy to point out. Material prosperity was much increased. The city was made a pleasant and attractive place of residence. Italy was partially repeopled with an industrious class. Commerce was encouraged and protected, literature and the fine arts were fostered, and the Palace on the whole set a good example of simplicity of living. But, on the other hand, the rule of a single person stifled political life. By the system of *curæ* or special commissions all administrative work was transferred to nominees of the Emperor, who were often his intimate friends, or even his freedmen, bound to him by the closest ties of subordination. The old magistracies became unattractive, not only because they no longer led as a matter of course to profitable employment abroad, but because their holders had little of interest to do. The Senate, though treated with respect and retaining some importance as a high court of justice, was practically no longer a governing body. It was wholly at the beck of the Emperor, and such work of consequence as it still performed was often transacted by small committees, the main body merely assenting. In spite, therefore, of the dignity of the Senator's position, it ceased to attract the best men. The higher classes turned away from a political career, and gave themselves up more and more to luxurious idleness. The rise of the freedman—practically the rule of favourites—was clearly foreshadowed, though owing to the industry of Augustus, and his genius for detail, it did not become prominent in his time. As the upper classes were thus to a certain extent demoralised by the Principate, so the city proletariate was pampered and made still more effete. The city was made only too attractive to them, and they were to be kept in good humour by an endless series of games and shows. There was a good deal of truth in the retort of the player Pylades, when reproved by Augustus for his feud with Bathyllus, that it was for the Emperor's advantage that the people should have their attention fixed on the playhouse rather than on politics. But they soon began not only to regard these amusements as their right : they expected also to be fed at the cost of the government, whether by direct gifts of money, or by the distribution of cheap or even gratuitous corn. Nor can it be said that the amusements provided for them were of an elevating nature. Augustus boasts in the *Index* (c. 20), that he gave seven shows of gladiators in his own name or that of his sons, in which about 10,000 men in all had fought ; [1] and besides other games twenty-six *venationes* of " African beasts," *i.e.*, mostly elephants, in which about 3,500 were killed. The mob of Rome needed little brutalising, but they got it in abundance.

With such drawbacks, however, it still must be owned that the administration of Augustus largely increased the sum of

---

[1] It ought, however, to be said to his credit that he forbade the exhibition of gladiators *sine missione*, *i.e.*, without the right of being allowed to depart safe from the arena when defeated if the people so willed it.

human happiness by the mitigation of oppression in the provinces, and by the suppression of disorder in Rome and Italy. The finances were placed on a sound footing, property was rendered secure, and men felt everywhere that they might pursue their business with every chance of enjoying the fruits of their labours. This was something after a century of revolution more or less acute, and twenty years of downright civil war. It is worth while to attempt to picture to ourselves the man who was the author of these good and bad results.

Augustus was a short man (just under five feet seven inches), but so well proportioned that the defect in height was not noticed unless he was standing by much taller men. He was remarkably handsome at all periods of his life, with an expression of calm dignity, whether silent or speaking, which involuntarily inspired respect. His eyes were grey, and so bright and keen that it was not easy to meet their gaze. If he had a personal vanity it was in regard to them. He liked to think that they dazzled those on whom he looked, and he was pleased at the answer of the Roman eques, who, when asked why he turned away, replied, " Because I could not bear the lightning of your eyes." Vergil gratified this vanity of his patron when in the description of the battle of Actium (*Æn.*, viii. 650) he pictures him,

The personal appearance and character of Augustus.

> *Stans celsa in puppi; geminas cui tempora flammas*
> *Læta vomunt.*

And the Emperor Iulian, in " The Banquet of the Emperors," laughs not unkindly at the same weakness when he introduces him, " changing colour like a chameleon, and wishing that the beams darting from his eyes should be like those of the mighty sun." The busts, statues, and coins of Augustus fully confirm this statement as to his beauty ; and in the triumphal statue found in Livia's villa at Prima Porta, the artist has succeeded in suggesting the brightness and keenness of his eyes. He was usually clean shaven, but from his uncle's death to B.C. 38, according to Dio (48, 34), he grew his beard as a sign of mourning; though coins showed him with a slight whisker till about B.C. 36. These portraits are full of life and character. The clear-cut features, the firm mouth and chin, the steady eyes, the carelessly ordered hair, the lines on forehead and cheeks, suggest a man who had suffered and laboured, who was yet self-controlled, calm, and clear-headed. It is a face not without some tenderness, but capable of firing up into hot indignation and even cruelty. There is an air of suffering but of determined victory over pain; altogether a face of a man who had done a great work and risen to a high place in the world and knew it; who had confidence, lastly, in his star. On taking leave of Gaius Cæsar, it is said, he wished him "the integrity of Pompey, the courage of Alexander, and his own good fortune." On some of his coins beneath the head crowned with the crown of twelve rays, is the Iulian star, first observed at the funeral of Iulius Cæsar, and which he adopted as the sign of his own high fortunes: on others the Sphinx, which he at first adopted as his signet—emblem perhaps of a purpose unbetrayed. Augustus was accomplished in the subjects recognised in the education of his time, though he neither wrote nor spoke Greek with ease. He had studied and practised rhetoric, and had a good and correct taste in style, avoiding the use of far-fetched or obsolete words and expressions, or affected conceits. He ridiculed Antony for his "Asiatic" style of oratory, full of flowers of speech and flamboyant sentences; and writing to his granddaughter, Agrippina, while praising her abilities he warns her against pedantic expressions whether in conversation or writing. Without being an orator, he spoke clearly and to the point, assisted by a pleasant voice, which he took pains to preserve and improve. In the Senate, the camp, and private conferences, he preferred to read his speeches, though he could also speak well on the spur of the moment In domestic life, though somewhat strict, he was generally simple and charming. He lived much with wife and children, associating himself with their employments, and even joining in the games of the latter. He personally superintended the education of his adopted sons, taught them his own method of shorthand, and interested himself in their reading. He had old-fashioned ideas about the proper employment of the women in his family. They were expected to busy themselves in weaving for the use of the household, to visit and receive visits only with his approval, and not to converse on subjects that could not with propriety be entered on the day's journal. Though his daughter and granddaughters were well educated, and had a taste for literature, it may well be that a home thus conducted was so dull as partly to account for their aberrations in the fuller liberty of married life.

His attachments were warm and constant, and he was not illiberal to his friends or disinclined to give them his full confidence. But he was always his own master. No friend or freedman gained control over him or rose to the odious position of "favourite." He allowed and even liked freedom of speech, but it was always without loss of dignity. He was not a man with whom liberties were taken even by the most intimate. He was quick tempered, but knew it, and was ready to admit of caution and advice, as in the well-known story of Mæcenas, watching him in court about to condemn a number of prisoners (probably in the civil war times), and throwing across to him a note with the words, *Surge tandem carnifex !* " Tis time to rise, hangman ! " Or when he received with complaisance the advice of Athenodorus (hero of the covered sedan) that when he was angry he should say over the letters of the alphabet before coming to a decision.

In later times he was always looked back upon by his successors as the true founder of the Empire, and His ultra-Roman views. the best model for their guidance ; yet it is doubtful how far he had wide and far-reaching views. He was a statesman who dealt with facts as he found them and did the best he could. He was deeply impressed with the difficulty of his task. Commenting on the fact of Alexander the Great having accomplished his conquests by the age of 32, and then feeling at a loss what to do for the rest of his life, he remarked that he "was surprised that Alexander did not regard the right ordering of the empire he possessed a heavier task than winning it." But in one important respect at least he was wrong in his idea of what he had done. He never conceived of an empire filled with citizens enjoying equal rights, or in which Rome could possibly occupy a secondary place. He was ultra-Roman in his views; and worked and schemed to maintain the supremacy of the Eternal City. That supremacy may indeed be said to have remained to this day in the region of spiritual affairs. But it was destined to disappear politically, except in name, before many generations had passed away, and as a logical consequence of much that he had himself done. A new Rome and a new Empire—though always resting on the old title and theory— were to arise, in which Italy would be a province like the rest, and old Rome but the shadow of a mighty name.

Among those who exercised a permanent influence on Augustus, the first place must be given to Livia (b.c. 54– a.d. 29). The writers on Augustus comment

The court circle.

on the romantic revolution of her fortunes. After the affair of Perusia she fled with her husband, Nero, and her little son, Tiberius, from Augustus, who was to be her husband, and was to be succeeded by her son. Her divorce and prompt marriage to Augustus, while within a few months of being again a mother, is not only a thing revolting to our ideas, it was strictly against Roman principles and habits, and required all her new husband's commanding influence to be admitted as legal. Yet Suetonius says, and says truly, that he continued "to love and honour her exclusively to the end" (*dilexit et probavit unice et perseveranter*). The same writer gives an account of the Emperor's intrigues with other women. To our ideas the two statements are contradictory, but Suetonius would not have thought so. Conjugal love was not *amor;* the latter was thought even inconsistent with, or at least undesirable in, conjugal affection. He means that throughout his life Augustus continued to regard her with affection, to respect her character, and give weight to her opinion. For my own part, I believe that something more might be said, and that much of what has come down to us as to the conduct of the Emperor may be dismissed as malignant gossip. But however that may be, the influence of Livia over him seems never to have failed, and it was exercised on the side of clemency and generosity. She set an excellent example of pure and dignified conduct to Roman society, and, though abstaining from interference generally in political matters, was ready to give advice when called upon. She seems usually to have accompanied him, when possible, on his foreign progresses or residences away from Rome. When Herod visited Augustus at Aquileia in B.C. 14, she appears to have shared her husband's liking for that strange medley of magnificence and cruelty, and sent him costly gifts for the festivity which accompanied the completion of the new city of Cæsarea Sebaste in B.C. 13. The usual allegation against her is that she worked for the succession of her sons, Tiberius and Drusus, as against the Iulian family, represented by the son of Octavia and the children of Iulia. To secure this object she was accused in popular rumour of compassing the deaths successively of Marcellus, of Gaius and Lucius Cæsar, of Agrippa Postumus, and, finally, of having even hastened the end of Augustus himself. This last is not mentioned by Suetonius, and is only related by Dio as a report, for which he gives no evidence, and which he does not appear to have believed. Tacitus records the criticism of her as a *gravis noverca* to the family of the Cæsars, and seems to accept her guilt in regard to Gaius and Iulius (*Ann.* 4, 71). But he is also constrained to admit that she exercised a humanising influence over Tiberius, that his victims constantly found refuge and protection in her palace, and that she was benevolent and charitable to the poor—maintaining a large number of orphan boys and girls by her bounty. The most suspicious case against her is the execution of Agrippa Postumus immediately after the death of Augustus—"the first crime of the new reign." It will never be known whether the order for that cruel deed issued from her or her crafty son. The death of Marcellus was in no way suspicious, as it occurred in a season of exceptional unhealthiness, when large numbers were dying at Rome of malarial fever. As to the deaths of Gaius and Lucius, no suspicion seems to have occurred to Augustus, and he was keenly anxious for their survival. The poisoned fig supposed to have been given to himself is a familiar feature in the stories of great men's death of every age in Italy. Tacitus in the famous summing up of her character, while acknowledging the purity of her domestic conduct, yet declares that her social manners were more free than was considered becoming among women of an earlier time ; that as a mother she was extravagantly fond, as a wife too complaisant ; and that her character was a combination of her husband's adroitness and her son's insincerity. He by no means intends to draw a pleasing portrait. He seldom does. But what we may take for true is that she was beautiful, loyal to her husband, open-handed and generous to the distressed, merciful and kind to the unfortunate. To those who think such qualities likely to belong to a poisoner and murderess, her condemnation must be left. It is curious that neither Vergil, Horace, nor Propertius mention or allude to Livia ; nor does Ovid do so until after the death of Augustus—for the *consolatio ad Liviam* on the death of Drusus is not his. On some of the inscriptions of a later period in the reign her name appears among the imperial family as wife of the Princeps. That was itself an innovation, and it seems as if the poets abstained from mentioning her under orders. It was improper for a matron of high rank to be made public property in this way. Horace, for instance, only once alludes to the wife of Mæcenas, and then under a feigned name.

Of those who influenced the earlier policy of Augustus, and supported him in the first twenty years of the Principate, the first place must be given to Agrippa and Mæcenas.

M. VIPSANIUS AGRIPPA (B.C. 63–13), differed widely from Mæcenas, but was like him in constant attachment and fidelity to Augustus. He was with him in Apollonia, and on the news of the murder of Iulius advised an appeal to the army. Even before this he had accompanied him to Spain when he went to join his uncle in B.C. 45, and ever afterwards served him with unswerving fidelity and conspicuous success. In the war with Sextus Pompeius, at Perusia, in Gaul, Spain and Illyria, in the organisation of the East, and on the Bosporus, it was his energy and ability that decided the contest in favour of his master, or secured the settlement that he desired. He was the organiser of the Roman navy, and though his great work at the Lucrine lake proved to be only temporary, the squadrons that guarded the seas at Misenum, Ravenna and Forum Iulii were the result of his activity and foresight. His acts of splendid liberality in Rome have been already noticed. He shewed the same magnificence in Gaul and elsewhere, and seems also to have largely assisted in the great survey of the empire instituted by Augustus. Not only did he support all the plans and ideas of his master, he was ready to take any position and make any personal sacrifice to further his views. After his first marriage to Pomponia, by whom he was the father of Vipsania, he was married to Marcella, the Emperor's niece. To support his master's plans for the succession he submitted to divorce her and marry Iulia, after having previously made way for the rise of Marcellus by accepting a command in the East. The Emperor shewed his confidence in him on every occasion. In B.C. 23 when he thought himself dying he placed his seal in his hands, in B.C. 18 he caused him to be admitted to share his tribunician power for five years, which was renewed again in B.C. 13 ; so that though his two sons were adopted by Augustus, the succession would almost certainly have fallen to him had the Emperor died in their minority. This elevation however did not give him rest : the last years of his life were spent in the East, on the Bosporus and in Pannonia, from which last he only returned to die. This faithful service had been rendered in spite of the fact that he had advised against the acceptance of the principate. He had urged the financial difficulties, the irreconcilable nature of the opposition, the impossibility of drawing back, and Octavian's own weak health. But when his master preferred the advice of Mæcenas, he took his part in the undertaking without faltering and with splendid loyalty. Though Augustus owed much of his success to his own cautious statesmanship, he owed even more to the man who failed in nothing that he undertook, and would claim no honour for himself in return. The Emperor delivered the funeral oration over this loyal servant, and deposited his ashes in the Mausoleum which he had built for his own family.

C. CILNIUS MÆCENAS (*circ.* B.C. 65–B.C. 8), was probably a few years older than Augustus, but near enough to his age to have been one of his companions at Apollonia. His influence was maintained till about B.C. 16. It is most conspicuous from the time immediately following the Perusian war. He negotiated the marriage with Scribonia, the peace of Brundisium with Antony (B.C. 40), and the subsequent reconciliation of B.C. 38. In the war against Sextus Pompeius (B.C. 38–36), he was partly with Augustus, but partly at Rome, with full powers to act for him and even to alter his despatches and letters as seemed necessary, having the triumvir's private seal entrusted to him for that purpose. This was possible from the fact of such letters being written by amanuenses and being therefore only recognisable by the seal. Thus Cicero often commissions Atticus to write formal letters to his friends for him. This position—it was no definite office, or perhaps was more like being *legatus* to Octavian than anything else— he seems to have retained till after the battle of Actium, at which he probably was not present, though that has been disputed. He detected the conspiracy of the younger Lepidus, and sent him to Octavian to be judged. In B.C. 29, on Octavian's return from the East, he recommended the establishment of a despotism, as a republic was no longer possible. The speech preserved by Dio (52, 14–40) may very well be genuine, in view of the habit of the day, and of Augustus himself, of reading addresses even in comparatively private conferences on matters of importance.[1] Even if it is not the genuine speech, it correctly represents many of the principles on which Augustus did act, and as to which he doubtless consulted Mæcenas. It counsels him to keep in his hands legislation, foreign affairs, elections, executive appointments and the courts of law, and to hear cases of appeal himself : exactly what Augustus did under various disguises. It argues that it was necessary both for his own safety and that of the state that he should remain in power, the glory being well worth the risk. Other recommendations are a reform of Senate and equites, the maintenance of the old republican magistrates for home service, the establishment of a *præfectus urbi*, the exercise by himself of censorial functions, the subordination of provincial governors to the Emperor, and their payment by a fixed salary, with the appointment of procurators to superintend the finances of the provinces. A system of education for the equites is also suggested, which does not seem to have been carried out ; but many of the financial proposals were adopted, as well as the idea of keeping the people amused by games and shows. The advice to abolish the *comitia* Augustus could not follow consistently with his policy of compromise. They remained and were the causes of more than one trouble and disturbance, but their freedom of election was gradually but surely destroyed,

[1] See note on p. 147.

and one of the first measures of Tiberius was to abolish them as no longer a reality. The reform of the Senate was, as we have seen, carried out. As for the judicia, the Senate became a high court for cases of treason (*maiestas*), before which alone Senators could be tried; the *decuriæ iudicum* were reformed, and Augustus himself performed the functions of a court of appeal in various ways, sometimes by his tribunician power of "interceding" against the sentences of magistrates or Senate, and sometimes by hearing cases from the provinces of citizens who disputed the competence of provincial courts and claimed to be heard at Rome. Mæcenas holding no office never became a Senator; but he represented the Emperor in his absence, unless Agrippa was appointed to do so instead. In this capacity he really exercised a greater power than any definite office would have given him, and the whole business of the Empire passed through his hands.[1]

But it was not only as the ostensible representative of the Emperor that he worked for his support. In the comparative retirement of his palace on the Esquiline he contributed to that object by gathering round him the best intellects and first men of letters of the day, whom he induced to devote their talents not only to glorify the Emperor personally, but to popularise his policy and magnify his service to the state. How far this may have been effectual by making it the fashion to accept and admire the principate may perhaps be questioned, but that he should have secured such writers as Vergil, Horace, and Propertius on his side says much for his insight and literary taste. One of the weaknesses of the position of Iulius had been that he had the literary class mostly against him. The present reputation and future fame of Augustus were to be better safeguarded. Personally Mæcenas was luxurious and effeminate, always a valetudinarian, and in his later years afflicted with almost constant insomnia. This accounts well enough for the retirement from

[1] Horace, *Od.* iii. 8.

public business during the last eight years of his life without those other causes of the Emperor's displeasure which have been already discussed.   His wife was a beauty, much younger than himself, wilful and wayward; and if it is true that she intrigued with Augustus, it seems also true that her husband repaid her in kind.   There were frequent quarrels and reconciliations, so that Seneca says that he married her "a thousand times;" and once at any rate the family trouble found its way into the law courts, where, however, the *bona fides* of the divorce which she was alleged to have made was questioned.[1] In spite of some coldness between them in later years, and the physical infirmities which removed him from public business, Augustus sincerely mourned his loss, as of a counsellor who never betrayed his confidence or spoke idle words.   He had no real successor.   From the time of his death the Emperor seems more and more to have become his own prime minister, or to have looked to his own family for assistance as well as for a successor.   Tacitus (*Ann.* 3, 30) says that his place was taken by Sallustius Crispus, great-nephew of the historian; but Augustus does not seem to have thought highly of his ability, and the part he took in affairs was not prominent enough to have secured mention by either Suetonius or Dio.   Mæcenas wrote himself both in prose and verse, but in an affected and obscure style, which Augustus playfully ridiculed.   The stoic Seneca is particularly severe on a poem in which he declares that he clings to life in spite of all physical sufferings however painful :—

> "Though racked with gout in hand and foot,
> Though cancer deep should strike its root,
> Though palsy shake my feeble thighs,
> Though hideous hump on shoulders rise,
> From flaccid gum teeth drop away ;
> Yet all is well if life but stay.
> Give me but life, and e'en the pain
> Of sharpest cross shall count as gain."

---

[1] Seneca, *Epp.* 114 ; *Digest.* 24, 1, 64.

The chief writers of the Mæcenas circle, who either became intimate with Augustus himself, or were induced by Mæcenas to join in the chorus of praise, were Vergil, Varius, Horace, Propertius. Of the epics of L. Varius Rufus (*circ.* B.C. 64-14) on Iulius Cæsar and Augustus, we have only a few fragments. The historian, Livy, (B.C. 59-A.D. 16) was also on friendly terms with Augustus, and seems to have had some hand in teaching Claudius, son of Drusus, the future emperor. But his great work—from the foundation of Rome to the death of Drusus (B.C. 9) was afterwards regarded as being too republican, and even Augustus used laughingly to call him the Pompeian. It was the poets who made Augustus and his policy the subject of their praises, and who employed their genius to support his views.

Augustus and the poets.

The first to do this was P. Vergilius Maro (B.C. 70-17). The earliest of his writings, the *Eclogues*, composed between B.C. 42-37, do not show any close connection with Augustus. The first indeed celebrates the restoration of his farm after a personal interview with Octavian, on the suggestion of Pollio and Mæcenas, and the poet declares that never will there fade from his heart the gracious look of the young prince. But the chief object of praise in the *Eclogues*, so far as there is one, is Pollio, who had been left in charge of the distribution of lands by the Triumvirs in B.C. 42. In the *Georgics*, however, finished after B.C. 30, we find that he has fallen in with the new *régime*. They are dedicated to the minister Mæcenas, they celebrate Augustus's triple triumph of B.C. 29, and they were composed partly, at any rate, at the wish of Mæcenas, who with Augustus was anxious to make country life and pursuits seem desirable. No doubt the theme itself was congenial to Vergil, who preferred a country life at Nola, or near Tarentum, to the bustle of Rome; but it also happened to chime in with the views of Augustus, who all his life believed in the influence of literature and wished to have the poets on his side. Accordingly, soon after his return from

Vergil.

the East in B.C. 29 he seems to have suggested to Vergil to compose a poem that would inspire men with a feeling of national pride and an enthusiasm for the greatness of Rome's mission. The plan and form were no doubt wholly Vergil's, but the spirit and purpose, like those of Horace's more patriotic odes of about the same time, were those which the Emperor desired. He was not satisfied with mere suggestion, he was eager for the appearance of the poem. While in Gaul and Spain from B.C. 27–24 he frequently wrote to the poet urging the completion of the work. A part of one of Vergil's answers has been preserved :

" As to my Æneas, upon my honour if I had anything written worth your listening to, I would gladly send it. But the subject thus begun is so vast, that I almost think I must have been beside myself when I undertook a work of this magnitude ; especially considering that—as you are aware—I am also devoting part of my time to different and much more important studies."

The *Æneid* was thus undertaken at the solicitation of Augustus. The legend on which it turns—perhaps a late one —of the landing of Æneas in Italy and the foundation of Rome by his descendant, is with great skill interwoven with a fanciful descent of the *gens Iulia* from his son Iulus, to magnify Rome and her divine mission, and at the same time to point to Augustus as the man of destiny, and as representing in his own person and career the majesty of the Roman people. In such a poem detailed allusions cannot be expected as in the occasional odes of Horace. Yet, besides the fine passage in the eighth book describing the victory of Actium and the discomfiture of Cleopatra, and that in the sixth announcing the victorious career of Augustus, we have, more or less, direct references to the restoration of religious worship in the *vici*, to the return of the standards by the Parthians, and the death of the young Marcellus. In form, the *Æneid* follows the model of Homer, the supreme epic. But in substance it is original, in that it does not take for its theme one of the old myths—as the Alexandrine poets always did—but while teeming with all kinds of mythological allusions it finds its chief inspiration in the greatness of Rome, measured by the elemental strife preceding the accomplishment of the divine purpose : *tantæ molis erat Romanam condere gentem*—"So vast the task to found the Roman race," is the key-note of the whole. It is original as the epic of Milton was original who, with details borrowed from every quarter, took for his theme the foundation of a world and the strife in heaven that preceded it. Vergil's epic is Roman history on the highest plane, and has crystallised for ever a view of that history which has done more than arms and laws to commend it to the imagination of mankind. Augustus had a true intuition when he forebade the poet's executors to obey his will and burn the rolls containing this great national epic.

Q. Horatius Flaccus (B.C. 65–B.C. 8) is not perhaps so great a poet as Vergil, but he possessed the charm which keeps such work as his alive. His connection with Augustus

Horace.

is a remarkable phenomenon in literary history. Having fought on the side of his enemies at Philippi, and having shared in the amnesty granted to the bulk of the troops, he returned home to find his paternal property confiscated. Poverty drove him to poetry, poetry gained him the friendship of Varius and Vergil, who introduced him to Mæcenas, who saw his merit, relieved him from the uncongenial employment of a clerk, and eventually introduced him to Augustus. The Emperor, in his turn, was not long in recognising his charm. He writes to Mæcenas :

"In old times I was vigorous enough to write my friends' letters for them. Nowadays being overwhelmed with business and weak in health, I am very anxious to entice Horace away from you. He shall therefore quit your table of parasites and come to my table of kings and assist me in writing letters."

The refusal of Horace—prudent no doubt in view of his

tastes and habits—did not lose him the Emperor's favour. He twice received substantial marks of it, and some extracts of letters to him from Augustus have been preserved which exhibit the latter in his most gracious mood :

"Consider yourself a privileged person in my house, as though an habitual guest at my table. You will be quite within your rights and will always be sure of a welcome ; for it is my wish that our intimacy should be on that footing if your state of health permits it."

And again :

"What a warm recollection I retain ot you, you will be able to learn from Septimius among others, as I happened to be talking about you in his presence the other day. For you need not suppose, because you were so high and mighty as to reject my friendship, that I am on the high horse too to pay you back."

Augustus, in fact, had a great opinion of Horace, and predicted his immortality. He selected him to write the ode for the secular games, pressed him later in life to immortalise the achievements of Tiberius and Drusus, and was desirous of his own name appearing as the recipient of one of his Satires or Epistles.

"I am quite angry, let me tell you, that you don't give me the preference as a person to address in your writings of that kind. Are you afraid that an appearance of intimacy with me will damage your reputation with posterity ?"

Horace made the Emperor a return in full for such condescension. How far the genius of a poet is warmed or chilled by patronage it is not easy to decide. So far as he is tempted away from his natural bent, or confined in the free expression of thought, he suffers : so far as he is saved from sordid cares, he is a gainer. Horace, in early youth, sympathised with the republican party in whose ranks he had served, and probably in later life still felt a theoretical preference for it, and could speak of the *nobile letum* and *atrox animus* of Cato with a true note of admiration. But he was a man of his time. The policy of Octavian had made the supremacy of Augustus inevitable, and it at least secured peace and safety. The patronage and liberality of Mæcenas assuredly helped to turn the scale, but I see no reason to doubt that the poet was convinced, though, perhaps, without enthusiasm, that the new *régime* was one to be supported by reasonable men. The kindness of the Emperor naturally enhanced the effect of his commanding personality, but it would be difficult for a poet so placed to write with greater dignity and less fulsomeness than Horace does in the first epistle of the second book, addressed to Augustus at his own request. But it is in the *Odes* that we must trace the unbroken sympathy with the career and policy of Augustus. If they are closely examined, with an eye to chronological arrangement, the ingenuity with which these imitations of Greek models are framed to support and recommend the purposes or celebrate the successes of the Emperor, will stand revealed in a striking manner. The *Epodes* and the first three books of the *Odes* were apparently written between B.C. 35 and B.C. 25. Dropped in among a number of poems of fancy, or passion, or mere literary *tours de force*, are compositions that follow not only the actual achievements of Augustus, but his ideals, his intentions, and his aspirations, from the years just before Actium to his return from Spain in B.C. 25. We begin with the Second Epode, which refers with regret to the abandoned intention of invading Britain in B.C. 35, and expresses his alarm at the prospect of a renewed civil war. In the Sixteenth Epode this terror has become a reality ; the civil war has begun, and the poet, foreseeing the downfall of the state, turns longing eyes to the peace and calm of the fabled islands of the West. From Italy and all its horrors they must at any rate depart. In the Ninth Epode the relief has come ; the shameful servitude of a Roman imperator and Roman soldiers to a foreign queen is over ; Antony and Cleopatra are in full flight

(B.C. 31). In another year it is known that Antony has fallen by his own hand, and that Cleopatra has saved herself the indignity of the triumphal procession by the adder's aid (*Od.* i. 39). The discharge of the legions follows, and their settlement in Italian and Sicilian lands (2 *Sat.*, 6, 54). In the other odes of the first book the devotion to Augustus proceeds apace. The Iulian star is in the ascendant (1, 2, 20); Augustus is *pater* and *princeps*, anticipating the future titles (1, 2, 20); he is again contemplating the invasion of Britain (1, 35, 29); the Arabian expedition is being planned with all its futile hopes of wealth (1, 29; 1, 35). In the second book of the *Odes*, beginning with reflections on the evils of civil war (2, 1), the poet notices one after the other the triumphs of Augustus or his generals in B.C. 27-24. The Cantabrian war (2, 6, 2; 2, 11, 1); the triumphal arch at Susa (2, 9, 19); the success of his diplomacy in Scythia, Armenia, and Parthia (*ib.*) In the third book the embassy of British chiefs is treated as though the island were annexed (3, 5, 2); the Cantabrians are regarded as conquered after the expedition of Augustus (3, 8, 22; 3, 14). Then succeeds a period of statesmanship and reform. The Emperor's Roman policy, and his determination to keep Rome the centre of government, are warmly supported (3, 3); the moral evils, the extravagance and debauchery of the age must be cured, and Horace proceeds to support the abortive legislation of B.C. 27, and to foreshadow the censorial acts, and the legislation of B.C. 18. There is a protest against the magnificence and extent of country houses (2, 15); against the effeminacy of youth (iii. 2); against the immorality of women and the licentiousness that led to civil strife (3, 24). The *Carmen sæculare* speaks of the legislation as effected, and foretells its success (20); while in the fourth book he asserts that, at any rate while Augustus is with them, that success has been secured (4, 5), and that he has not only given them peace, but a great moral reform (4, 15). The policy of the Emperor in regard to the bugbear of the East, the Parthian power, is also followed step by step. They are the dangerous enemy whose subjection will make Augustus divine (3, 5, 1-4), and whose threatened invasions keep his ministers in constant anxiety (3, 29, 27). This is before B.C. 20; but in B.C. 19 they have made submission and restored the standards and prisoners (*Epist.* i. 18, 56), and this is one of the triumphs of Augustus that requires a master hand to record (*Epist.* ii. 1, 255); it is the glory of the Augustan age (*Od.* 4, 15, 6), and as long as Augustus is safe, no one will fear them more (4, 5, 25). Finally, at the Emperor's request, he celebrated the victories of Drusus and Tiberius over the Vindelici and Rhæti (4, 4 and 14), and especially the defeat of the Sugambri who had routed Lollius (4, 2, 34; 4, 14, 51), with a compliment to Augustus himself for having gone to Gaul to support Tiberius and Drusus with reinforcements and advice (4, 14, 33), and for having at length closed the door of Ianus (4, 15, 9). The lyrical career of Horace, therefore, corresponds remarkably with the activities of Augustus. His genius presented those activities to his fellow citizens (and Horace's verses were soon read in schools) exactly in the light in which the Emperor wished them to be viewed. If we lay aside some expressions of overstrained compliment, which favoured the growing fashion of paying the Emperor divine honours, it cannot be said that the language is fulsome or degrading to the poet. The " parasitic table " of Mæcenas may, as M. Beulé asserts, have been a misfortune to the poets, and attenuated their vein of inspiration : but a man must have something in practical life on which to pin his faith ; and Horace might have done worse than devote his genius to promote loyalty to the great statesman who had saved Roman society and given peace and prosperity to an empire. Just as Vergil, if he had followed his own impulse, might have perhaps produced a fine poem on the Epicurean cosmogony, but not one that lives and breathes with the noble glow of patriotism.

Sextus Propertius (*circ.* B.C. 45–*circ.* B.C. 15) was another of the Mæcenas circle of poets who did something to glorify
Propertius. Augustus. He is not (but that is a personal opinion) on anything like the same level as either Vergil or Horace as an artist. He is said to have died young, perhaps at thirty years of age, and there is no evidence of personal intimacy with Augustus, but there is some indication of his having been on bad terms with Horace. His elegies also are nearly all poems of passion. Politics and emperors are mere episodes, and were introduced in deference to Mæcenas. Still many points in the career of Augustus are referred to in the same spirit as that of Horace. The siege of Perusia— described in tones of horror, which would scarcely have been acceptable—precedes his conversion (1, 21), and the failure of the marriage law of B.C. 27 is only referred to with relief (2, 7, 1). In more complimentary terms he speaks of the victory of Actium (3, 7, 44), and of the downfall of Antony and Cleopatra (4, 8, 56 ; 4, 10, 32, *sqq.* ; 4, 7, 56) ; and the end of the civil wars is attributed to Augustus (*illa qua vicit condidit arma manu*, 3, 8, 41). Then came the intended invasion of Britain (3, 23, 5) ; the Arabian expedition and the Indian envoys (3, 1, 15 ; 4, 3, 1) ; the opening and description of the Palatine Library—the best extant (3, 29) ; the raids of the Sugambri and their suppression (5, 6, 77) ; while he has the Parthians frequently on his lips, though rather as predicting what is to be done with them than as recording the return of the standards.[1] In the fifth book there are signs of a beginning of a *Fasti* like that of Ovid as a record of events in Roman history ; and it is possible that this was in obedience to a wish of Augustus, who, on his death, transferred the task to Ovid. Thus his voice also was secured, in part at least, in support of the imperial *régime.*

Publius Ovidius Naso (B.C. 43–A.D. 18) belongs to the last part of the reign. He had only seen Vergil, and though he

---

[1] 2, 17, 13 ; 3, 1, 13 ; 3, 23, 5 ; 4, 3 ; 4, 4, 48 ; 4, 11, 3 ; 5, 6, 79–84.

had heard Horace recite, he does not profess to have known

Ovid.

him. He was quite young when Augustus was winning his position and reforming the constitution, and there are no signs of his coming forward as a court poet till Mæcenas and his circle had disappeared, and if he had attracted the attention of Augustus at all, it was probably not altogether in a favourable manner. His earliest poems—the *Amores* and *Heroidum Epistulæ*—do not touch on public affairs; they are poems of passion—the former personal, the latter dramatic. In the *Ars Amatoria* (about B.C. 2–A.D. 2) for the first time we detect the court poet from a complimentary allusion to the approaching mission of Gaius Cæsar to Syria and Armenia, with his title of *princeps iuventutis* and that of Augustus as *pater patriæ*, as also to the *naumachia* or representation of the battle of Salamis given by Augustus in the flooded *nemus Cæsarum* in B.C. 2 (*A. A.*, I, 171–2). The *Metamorphoses* had been composed before his exile in A.D. 9, but after the death of Augustus he apparently introduced the Epilogue (xv. 745 *sq.*) containing an eulogy on Tiberius, and on the now finished career of Augustus. It is the *Fasti*—the Calendar of events in Roman history—that probably was undertaken in obedience to a wish of the Emperor, and in which accordingly we find points in his career touched upon. It was dedicated to Germanicus, and contains an allusion to his own exile, and was therefore, partly at least, composed between B.C. 2 and A.D. 10. His allusions to Augustus are not those of an intimate acquaintance, but of an admiring subject—real or feigned. He mentions the battle of Mutina (iv. 627); the bestowal of the title Augustus (i. 589); the recovery of the standards from the Parthians as a triumph of the Emperor (vi. 467). He alludes to Augustus becoming Pontifex Maximus (iii. 415); to the laurels on his palace front (iv. 957); to the demolition of the house of Vedius Pollio as connected with the reforms and the laws of B.C. 18 (vi. 637); to the division of the city into *vici*, and the worship of the Lares Augusti (v. 145); to the Forum Augusti and the temple of Mars dedicated in B.C 2. (v. 551, *sqq.*). Ovid afterwards protested that his books had been read with pleasure by Augustus, and assumed to have some knowledge of the private chambers of the palace (Trist., 1, 5, 2 ; 2, 520), but there is nothing in the allusions to matters which he knew that Augustus wished to have recorded that has the air of close or intimate relations. They are the conventional expressions of the outside, and perhaps humble, panegyrist, not those of a friend and supporter, like Horace. The abject expressions in the Tristia and the letters from Pontus need not be taken into account. They are merely bids for a recall, and they often express in the crudest form the growing fashion of worshipping the Emperor or his genius. Perhaps the most subtle of these appeals is that in which he explains why he had spent his youth in writing frivolous poetry instead of celebrating the glories of the Emperor—he was not a good enough poet, and would have dishonoured a subject above his reach (Tr., ii. 335–340). This was using a weapon forged by the Emperor himself, who had always let it be known that he disliked being the subject of inferior artists. The melancholy and feebleness of these later poems of Ovid seem to bear a sort of analogy with the cloud that descended on the later years of Augustus. Vergil and Horace have the freshness of the morning or the vigour of noon, Ovid the gathering sadness of the evening.

AUGUSTUS'S ACCOUNT OF HIS REIGN (FROM THE INSCRIPTION IN THE TEMPLE OF ROME AND AUGUSTUS AT ANGORA)

1. WHEN I was nineteen I collected an army on my own account and at my own expense, by the help of which I restored the republic to liberty, which had been enslaved by the tyranny of a faction ; for which services the Senate, in complimentary decrees, added my name to the roll of their House in the consulship of Gaius Pansa and Aulus Hirtius [B.C. 43], giving me at the same time consular precedence in voting ; and gave me imperium. It ordered me as pro-prætor " to see along with the consuls that the republic suffered no damage." Moreover, in the same year, both consuls having fallen, the people elected me consul and a triumvir for revising the constitution.

2. Those who killed my father I drove into exile, after a legal trial, in punishment of their crime, and afterwards when these same men rose in arms against the republic I conquered them twice in a pitched battle.

3. I had to undertake wars by land and sea, civil and foreign, all over the world, and when victorious I spared surviving citizens. Those foreign nations, who could safely be pardoned, I preferred to preserve rather than exterminate. About 500,000 Roman citizens took the military oath to me. Of these I settled out in colonies or sent back to their own towns, after their terms of service were over, considerably more than 300,000 ; and to them all I assigned lands purchased by myself or money in lieu of lands. I captured 600 ships, not counting those below the rating of triremes.

4. I twice celebrated an ovation, three times curule triumphs, and was twenty-one times greeted as imperator. Though the Senate afterwards voted me several triumphs I declined them. I frequently also deposited laurels in the Capitol after performing the vows which I had taken in each war. For successful operations performed by myself or by my legates under my auspices by land and sea, the

Senate fifty-three times decreed a supplication to the immortal gods. The number of days during which, in accordance with a decree of the Senate, supplication was offered amounted to 890. In my triumphs there were led before my chariot nine kings or sons of kings. I had been consul thirteen times at the writing of this, and am in the course of the thirty-seventh year of my tribunician power [A.D. 13–14].

5. The Dictatorship offered me in my presence and absence by the Senate and people in the consulship of Marcus Marcellus and Lucius Arruntius [B.C. 22] I declined to accept. I did not refuse at a time of very great scarcity of corn the commissionership of corn supply, which I administered in such a way that within a few days I freed the whole people from fear and danger. The consulship—either yearly or for life—then offered to me I declined to accept.

6. In the consulship of M. Vinicius and Q. Lucretius [B.C. 19], of P. and Cn. Lentulus [B.C. 18], and of Paullus Fabius Maximus and Q. Tubero [B.C. 11], when the Senate and people of Rome unanimously agreed that I should be elected overseer of the laws and morals, with unlimited powers and without a colleague, I refused every office offered me which was contrary to the customs of our ancestors. But what the Senate at that time wished me to manage, I carried out in virtue of my tribunician power, and in this office I five times received at my own request a colleague from the Senate.

7. I was one of the triumvirate for the re-establishment of the constitution for ten consecutive years. I have been *princeps senatus* up to the day on which I write this for forty years. I am Pontifex Maximus, Augur, one of the fifteen commissioners for religion, one of the seven for sacred feasts, an Arval brother, a *sodalis Titius*, a fetial.

8. In my fifth consulship [B.C. 29] I increased the number of the patricians by order of people and Senate. I three times made up the roll of the Senate, and in my sixth consulship [B.C. 28] I took a census of the people with M. Agrippa as my colleague. I performed the *lustrum* after an interval of forty-one years; in which the number of Roman citizens entered on the census roll was 4,063,000. A second time with consular imperium I took the census by myself in the consulship of Gaius Censorinus and Gaius Asinius [B.C. 8], in which the number of Roman citizens entered on the roll was 4,223,000. I took a third census with consular imperium, my son Tiberius Cæsar acting as my colleague, in the consulship of Sextus Pompeius and Sextus Appuleius [A.D. 14], in which the number of Roman citizens entered on the census roll was 4,937,000. By new laws passed I recalled numerous customs of our ancestors that were falling into

desuetude in our time, and myself set precedents in many particulars for the imitation of posterity.

9. The Senate decreed that vows should be offered for my health by consuls and priests every fifth year. In fulfilment of these vows the four chief colleges of priests or the consuls often gave games in my lifetime. Also individually and by townships the people at large always offered sacrifices at all the temples for my health.

10. By a decree of the Senate my name was included in the ritual of the Salii; and it was ordained by a law that my person should be sacred and that I should have the tribunician power for the term of my natural life. I refused to become Pontifex Maximus in succession to my colleague during his life, though the people offered me that sacred office formerly held by my father. Some years later I accepted that sacred office on the death of the man who had availed himself of the civil disturbance to secure it; such a multitude flocking to my election from all parts of Italy as is never recorded to have come to Rome before, in the consulship of P. Sulpicius and C. Valgius [6 March, B.C. 12].

11. The Senate consecrated an altar to Fortuna Redux, near the temple of Honour and Virtue, by the Porta Capena, for my return, on which it ordered the Vestal Virgins to offer a yearly sacrifice on the day on which in the consulship of Q. Lucretius and M. Vinucius [B.C. 19] I returned to the city from Syria, and gave that day the name *Augustalia* from my cognomen [15 Dec.].

12. By a decree of the Senate at the same time part of the prætors and tribunes of the plebs, along with the consul Q. Lucretius and leading nobles, were despatched into Campania to meet me—an honour that up to this time has been decreed to no one else. When I returned to Rome from Spain and Gaul after successful operations in those provinces, in the consulship of Tiberius Nero and Publius Quintilius [B.C. 13], the Senate voted that an altar to Pax Augusta should be consecrated for my return on the Campus Martius, upon which it ordered the magistrates and priests and Vestal Virgins to offer an annual sacrifice [30 Jan.].

13. Whereas the Ianus Quirinus, which our ancestors ordered to be closed when peace throughout the whole dominions of the Roman people by land and sea had been obtained by victories, is recorded to have been only twice shut before my birth since the foundation of the city, the Senate three times voted its closure during my principate.

14. My sons Gaius and Lucius Cæsar, whom fortune snatched from me in their early manhood, in compliment to me, the Senate and Roman people designated consuls in their fifteenth year with a

proviso that they should enter on that office after an interval of five years. From the day of their assuming the *toga virilis* the Senate decreed that they should take part in public business. Moreover, the Roman equites in a body gave each of them the title of *Princeps Iuventutis*, and presented them with silver shields and spears.

15. To the Roman plebs I paid 300 sesterces per head in virtue of my father's will; and in my own name I gave 400 apiece in my fifth consulship [B.C. 29] from the sale of spoils of war; and a second time in my tenth consulship [B.C. 24] out of my own private property I paid a bounty of 400 sesterces per man, and in my eleventh consulship [B.C. 23] I measured out twelve distributions of corn, having purchased the grain from my own resources. In the twelfth year of my tribunician power [B.C. 11], I for the third time gave a bounty of 400 sesterces a head. These largesses of mine affected never less than 50,200 persons. In the eighteenth year of my tribunician power and my twelfth consulship [B.C. 5] I gave 320,000 of the urban plebs sixty denarii a head. In the colonies of my soldiers, in my fifth consulship [B.C. 29] I gave from the sale of spoils of war 1,000 sesterces a head; and among such settlers the number who received that triumphal largess amounted to about 120,000 men. In my thirteenth consulship [B.C. 2] I gave 60 denarii apiece to the plebeians then in receipt of public corn; they amounted to somewhat more than 200,000 persons.

16. The money for the lands, which in my fourth consulship [B.C. 30], and afterwards in the consulship of M. Crassus and Cn. Lentulus the augur [B.C. 14], I assigned to the soldiers, I paid to the municipal towns. The amount was about 600,000,000 sesterces, which I paid for lands in Italy, and about 260,000,000 which I disbursed for lands in the provinces.

I was the first and only one within the memory of my own generation to do this of all who settled colonies in Italy and the provinces. And afterwards in the consulship of Tib. Nero and Cn. Piso [B.C. 7], and again in the consulship of C. Antistius and D. Lælius [B.C. 6], and of C. Calvisius and L. Pasienus [B.C. 4], and of L. Lentulus and M. Messalla [B.C. 3], and of L. Caninius and Q. Fabricius [B.C. 2], to the soldiers, whom after their terms of service I sent back to their own towns, I paid good service allowances in ready money; on which I expended 400,000,000 sesterces as an act of grace.

17. I four times subsidised the *ærarium* from my own money, the sums which I thus paid over to the commissioners of the treasury amounting to 150,000,000 sesterces. And in the consulship of M. Lepidus and L. Arruntius [A.D. 6], to the military treasury, which was established on my initiative for the payment of their good service

allowance, to the soldiers who had served twenty years or more, I contributed from my own patrimony 170,000,000 sesterces.[1]

18. From and after the year of the consulship of Gnaeus and Publius Lentulus [B.C. 18], whenever the payment of the revenues were in arrear, I paid into the treasury from my own patrimony the taxes, whether due in corn or money, sometimes of 100,000 persons, sometimes of more.

19. I built the curia and Chalcidicum adjoining it, and the temples of Apollo on the Palatine with its colonnades, the temple of the divine Iulius, the Lupercal, the colonnade at the Flaminian circus, which I allowed to be called Octavia, from the name of the builder of the earlier one on the same site, the state box at the Circus Maximus, the temples of Jupiter Feretrius and of Jupiter Tonans on the Capitol, the temple of Quirinus, the temples of Minerva and of Juno the Queen, and of Jupiter Liberalis on the Aventine, the temple of the Lares at the head of the *via Sacra*, the temple of the divine Penates in the Velia, the temple of Youth, the temple of the Mater Magna on the Palatine.

20. The Capitolium and the Pompeian theatre—both very costly works—I restored without any inscription of my own name. Water-conduits in many places that were decaying from age I repaired ; and I doubled the aqueduct called the Aqua Marcia, by turning a new spring into its channel.

The Forum Iulium and the basilica, which was between the temple of Castor and the temple of Saturn, works begun and far advanced by my father, I completed ; and when the same basilica was destroyed by fire, I began its reconstruction on an extended plan, to be inscribed with the names of my sons, and in case I do not live to complete it I have ordered it to be completed by my heirs.

In my sixth consulship [B.C. 28], I repaired eighty-two temples of the gods in the city in accordance with a decree of the Senate, none being omitted which at that time stood in need of repair. In my seventh consulship [B.C. 27] I constructed the Flaminian road from the city to Ariminum, and all the bridges except the Mulvian and Minucian.

21. On ground belonging to myself I built a temple to Mars Ultor and the Forum Augustum, with money arising from sale of war spoils. I built a theatre adjoining the temple of Apollo, on ground for the most part purchased from private owners, to be under the name of

---

[1] For purposes of comparison of these sums with our money, 1,000 sesterces may be taken as equivalent to about £8 10s., and a denarius as about 10d.

my son-in-law Marcus Marcellus. Offerings from money raised by sale of war-spoil I consecrated in the temple of Apollo, and in the temple of Vesta, and in the temple of Mars Ultor, which cost me about 100,000,000 sesterces. Thirty-five thousand pounds of gold,[1] crown money contributed by the municipia and colonies of Italy for my triumphs, I refunded in my fifth consulship [B.C. 29], and subsequently, as often as I was greeted Imperator, I refused to receive crown money, though the municipia and colonies had decreed it with as much warmth as before.

22. I three times gave a show of gladiators in my own name, and five times in the name of my sons and grandsons; in which shows about 10,000 men contended. I twice gave the people a show of athletes collected from all parts of the world in my own name, and a third time in the name of my grandson. I gave games in my own name four times, as representing other magistrates twenty-three times. In behalf of the quindecimviri, and as master of the college, with M. Agrippa as colleague, I gave the Secular games in the consulship of C. Furnius and C. Silanus [B.C. 17]. In my thirteenth consulship [B.C. 2], I gave for the first time the games of Mars which, since that time, the consuls have given in successive years. I gave the people wild-beast hunts, of African animals, in my own name and that of my sons and grandsons, in the circus and forum, and the amphitheatres twenty-six times, in which about 3,500 animals were killed.

23. I gave the people the spectacle of a naval battle on the other side of the Tiber, in the spot where now is the grove of the Cæsars, the ground having been hollowed out to a length of 1,800 feet, and a breadth of 1,200 feet, in which thirty beaked ships, triremes or biremes, and a still larger number of smaller vessels contended. In these fleets, besides the rowers, there fought about three thousand men.

24. In the temples of all the states of the province of Asia, I replaced the ornaments after my victory, which he with whom I had fought had taken into his private possession from the spoliation of the temples. There were about eighty silver statues of me, some on foot, some equestrian, some in chariots, in various parts of the city. These I removed, and from the money thus obtained I placed golden offerings in the temple of Apollo in my own name and in that of those who had honoured me by the statues.

25. I cleared the sea of pirates. In that war I captured about 30,000 slaves, who had run away from their masters, and had borne

---

[1] A pound of gold worth about £45.

arms against the republic, and handed them back to their owners to be punished. The whole of Italy took the oath to me spontaneously, and demanded that I should be the leader in the war in which I won the victory off Actium. The provinces of the Gauls, the Spains, Africa, Sicily, Sardinia, took the same oath. Among those who fought under my standards were more than seven hundred Senators, eighty-three of whom had been, or have since been, consuls up to the time of my writing this, 170 members of the sacred colleges.

26. I extended the frontiers of all the provinces of the Roman people, which were bordered by tribes that had not submitted to our Empire. The provinces of the Gauls, and Spains and Germany, bounded by the Ocean from Gades to the mouth of the river Elbe, I reduced to a peaceful state. The Alps, from the district near the Adriatic to the Tuscan sea, I forced to remain peaceful without waging unprovoked war with any tribe. My fleet sailed through the Ocean from the mouth of the Rhine towards the rising sun, up to the territories of the Cimbri, to which point no Roman had penetrated, up to that time, either by land or sea. The Cimbri, and Charydes, and Semnones and other peoples of the Germans, belonging to the same tract of country, sent ambassadors to ask for the friendship of myself and the Roman people. By my command and under my auspices, two armies were marched into Æthiopia and Arabia, called Felix, nearly simultaneously, and large hostile forces of both these nations were cut to pieces in battle, and a large number of towns were captured. Æthiopia was penetrated as far as the town Nabata, next to Meroe. Into Arabia the army advanced into the territories of the Sabæi as far as the town Mariba.

27. I added Egypt to the Empire of the Roman people. When I might have made the Greater Armenia a province after the assassination of its king Artaxes, I preferred, on the precedent of our ancestors, to hand over that kingdom to Tigranes, son of King Artavasdes, grandson of King Tigranes, by the hands of Tiberius Nero, who was then my stepson. The same nation being afterwards in a state of revolt and rebellion, I handed over to the government of King Ariobarzanes, son of Artabazus, king of the Medes, after it had been reduced by my son Gaius ; and after his death to his son Artavasdes, upon whose assassination I sent Tigranes, a member of the royal family of the Armenians, into that kingdom. I recovered all the provinces on the other side of the Adriatic towards the East and Cyrenæ, which were by this time for the most part held by various kings, and before them Sicily and Sardinia which had been overrun by an army of slaves.

28. I settled colonies of soldiers in Africa, Sicily, Macedonia, both the Spains, Achaia, Asia, Syria, Gallia Narbonensis, Pisidia. Italy has twenty-eight colonies established under my auspices, which have in my lifetime become very densely inhabited and places of great resort.

29. A large number of military standards, which had been lost under other commanders, I recovered, after defeating the enemy, from Spain and Gaul and the Dalmatians. I compelled the Parthians to restore the spoils and standards of three Roman armies, and to seek as suppliants the friendship of the Roman people. These standards I laid up in the inner shrine belonging to the temple of Mars Ultor.

30. The tribes of the Pannonii, which before I was *princeps* an army of the Roman people never reached, having been subdued by Tiberius Nero, who was then my stepson and legate [B.C. 11], I added to the Empire of the Roman people, and I extended the frontier of Illyricum to the bank of the river Danube. And when an army of the Daci crossed to the south of that river it was conquered and put to flight under my auspices ; and subsequently my army, being led across the Danube, forced the tribes of the Daci to submit to the orders of the Roman people.

31. To me there were often sent embassies of kings from India, who had never before been seen in the camp of any Roman general. By embassadors the Bastarnæ and the Scythians and the kings of the Sarmatians, who live on both sides of the river Don, and the king of the Albani and of the Hiberi and of the Medes, sought our friendship.

32. Kings of the Parthians—Tiridates, and afterwards Phrates, son of King Phrates—fled to me for refuge ; of the Medes Arta-vasdes ; of the Adiabeni Artaxares ; of the Britons Dumnobellaunus and Tim . . ;[1] of the Marcomanni and Suebi . . . .[1] Phrates, king of the Parthians, son of Orodes, sent all his sons and grandsons to me in Italy, not because he had been overcome in war, but seeking our friendship by means of his own sons as pledges. And a very large number of other nations experienced the good faith of the Roman people while I was *princeps*, with whom before that time there had been no diplomatic or friendly intercourse.

33. The nations of the Parthians and the chief men of the Medes by means of embassies sought and accepted from me kings of those peoples—the Parthians Vonones, son of King Phrates, grandson of

---

[1] These names and some other words are obliterated in the inscription, both Latin and Greek.

King Orodes; the Medes Ariobarzanes, son of King Artavasdes, grandson of King Ariobarzanes.

34. In my sixth and seventh consulships [B.C. 28, 27], when I had extinguished the flames of civil war, having by universal consent become possessed of the sole direction of affairs, I transferred the republic from my power to the will of the Senate and people of Rome. For which good service on my part I was by decree of the Senate called by the name of Augustus, and the door-posts of my house were covered with laurels in the name of the state, and a civic crown was fixed up over my door, and a golden shield was placed in the Curia Iulia, which it was declared by its inscription the Senate and people of Rome gave me in recognition of valour, clemency, justice, piety. After that time I took precedence of all in rank, but of power I had nothing more than those who were my colleagues in the several magistracies.

35. While I was administering my thirteenth consulship [B.C. 2], the Senate and equestrian order and the Roman people with one consent greeted me as FATHER OF MY COUNTRY, and decreed that it should be inscribed in the vestibule of my house, and in the Senate house, and in the Forum Augustum, and under the chariot which was there placed in my honour in accordance with a senatorial decree.

When I wrote this I was in my seventy-sixth year [A.D. 13–14].

INDEX

A

Abydos, 80

Achæan League, the, 27

Achaia, 27, 28 ; colonies in, 133

Acilius, M., 23

Actium, 86, 123–24, 290 ; colony at, 175

Ad capita bubula, 1

Ad gallinas, 205

Ægina separated from Athens, 176

Ælius Gallus, 155, 174

Æmilius Lepidus, M., as prætor (B.C. 49) holds election for dictator, 8 ; appointed to Hispania Citerior, 23 ; visits Sextus Pompeius, 42 ; in Transalpine Gaul, 59 ; joins Antony, 64 ; becomes one of the triumvirate, 70, 71 ; announces the close of the proscriptions, 74 ; suspected of intriguing with Sextus Pompeius, 82, 87 ; his inferior position, 88 ; in Africa, 99 ; comes to Sicily, 104 ; claims to govern Sicily, 105 ; deposed from the triumvirate, 106 ; his office of Pontifex Maximus, 107, 112, 160 ; his death, 160 ; see also 202, 221, 222

Æmilius Lepidus, M. (son of the triumvir), his conspiracy, 123 ; his brother, 258

Æmilius Paullus Lepidus, L., (brother of the triumvir), proscribed, 72

Ærarium, the, 148, 249, 296

Æthiopia, 174, 299

Afranius, 23

Africa, province of, 24–26, 99 ; see also 9, 11, 65, 71, 171 ; colonies in, 133 ; New Africa, 25, 113

Agrippa, *see* "Vipsanius"

Agrippa, Postumus, 167, 168, 277

Agrippina, 167

Ahenobarbus, *see* "Domitius"

Aix, 134

Alaudæ, the, 47

Alba Fucensis, 49, 51, 53

Albis (R. Elbe), 184, 186, 187

Alexandria, 11, 116, 117, 120, 121, 125, 127, 198

Allienus, Aul., 23, 31, 80

Alps, provinces of the, 17, 172

Amanus, Mount, 30

Amatius (the pseudo-Marius), 13

Amisia (R. Ems), 184

Amnesty to the Assassins, 38